DATE DUE		
Apr 25 '72		
Feb 9 '76		
Feb 23 '76		
Mar 29 '76		
Apr 18 '83		
GAYLORD M-2		PRINTED IN U.S.A.

A BRIEF HISTORY OF
MODERN PHILOSOPHY

THE MACMILLAN COMPANY
NEW YORK · BOSTON · CHICAGO
DALLAS · SAN FRANCISCO

MACMILLAN & CO., Limited
LONDON · BOMBAY · CALCUTTA
MELBOURNE

THE MACMILLAN CO. OF CANADA, Ltd.
TORONTO

A BRIEF HISTORY OF MODERN PHILOSOPHY

BY

DR. HAROLD HÖFFDING

PROFESSOR OF PHILOSOPHY AT THE
UNIVERSITY OF COPENHAGEN

AUTHORIZED TRANSLATION BY

CHARLES FINLEY SANDERS

PROFESSOR OF PHILOSOPHY AT PENNSYLVANIA COLLEGE, GETTYSBURG, PA.
AUTHOR OF THE ENGLISH TRANSLATION OF JERUSALEM'S
INTRODUCTION TO PHILOSOPHY

New York
THE MACMILLAN COMPANY
1922

PREFACE

Professor Harold Höffding is already well known to the English-speaking world through the translations of his Psychology, Ethics, Philosophy of Religion, Problems of Philosophy and his History of Modern Philosophy (2 vols.), all published by the Macmillan Company. The fact that his works are rapidly finding their way into English and other languages is the best evidence of the esteem in which his work is held and of his importance as a thinker. Born in 1843, professor of philosophy in Copenhagen since 1883, Doctor Höffding has worked over the whole field of philosophy with great thoroughness. The original (German) edition from which this translation is made appeared in 1905. It is therefore the fruit of his ripest scholarship. The book is clear, compact and comprehensive. The various schools are analyzed and criticized, and the thread of continuous development is constantly kept clearly in view. These features constitute the exceptional merit of the book as a text. The student is constantly aware that a familiar spirit is safely guiding him through the bewildering maze of philosophic problems and tentative solutions.

As a psychologist Doctor Höffding is an empirical introspectionist. He is thoroughly modern in his antipathy towards metaphysical speculation. He discovers a native tendency in man, manifesting itself in the impulse towards well-being, the source or further meaning of which is beyond our knowledge, which furnishes the basis of ethics.

Religion is the reaction of the human mind to the sense of value and represents the highest function of the human mind. As a critical empiricist he possesses a peculiar advantage in the interpretation of the trend of philosophic thought. We offer this book to the English student because of its merit, as an efficient guide to the understanding of modern philosophy.

C. F. SANDERS.

Gettysburg, Pa.
    July 20, 1912.

TABLE OF CONTENTS.

SIXTH BOOK

THE PHILOSOPHY OF ROMANTICISM

SEVENTH BOOK

POSITIVISM

EIGHTH BOOK

NEW THEORIES OF THE PROBLEM OF BEING UPON A REALISTIC BASIS

NINTH BOOK

NEW THEORIES OF THE PROBLEMS OF KNOWLEDGE AND OF VALUE

Test 4

A BRIEF HISTORY OF MODERN PHILOSOPHY

BRIEF HISTORY OF MODERN PHILOSOPHY

INTRODUCTION

THE subject matter of the history of philosophy consists of the efforts which individual thinkers have made to explain or perchance to solve the ultimate problems of knowledge and of being. Modern philosophy—i. e. the philosophy of the last three centuries—has been specially concerned with four great problems. These problems, moreover—as I have shown in my *Philosophic Problems* (Eng. Tr. 1905)—are intimately related to each other, and there likewise exists a most significant analogy between them, in that the antithesis of continuity and discontinuity is of fundamental importance in each of them, except that it manifests itself under different forms.

1. *The psychological problem* originates from the inquiry concerning the essential attributes of psychic life. Is the soul a distinct substance, or does its essential nature consist of a peculiar activity? Is the soul composed of a variety of independent elements, or is it characterized by unity and totality? The discussion of these questions can be of value only as it is based upon a detailed investigation of psychical phenomena and functions. It will likewise appear that the solution of these questions has a very important bearing on the treatment and the solution of the remaining philosophic problems.

Whilst psychological investigation finds its subject matter in the bare facts of psychic life, there are two further problems which are conditioned by the antithesis of fact and value as it appears in psychic life, *the problem of knowledge* and *the problem of evaluation*.

2. *The problem of knowledge* springs from the inquiry into the presuppositions of knowledge and the limits within which our thought processes are valid (thus including the sphere of psychological investigation). The primary origin of thought is spontaneous, a reaction produced by events which are not the result of thought. To what extent are we then justified in ascribing real meaning to the results of thought? Wherein does the truth of knowledge consist?

3. Whilst the problem of knowledge has special reference to the intellect, *the problem of evaluation* grows out of the inquiry into the validity of judgments pertaining to human conduct and social institutions—particularly those that rest on the processes of will and emotion. What constitutes the standard for such a judgment? Upon what foundation does the validity of the concepts of good and bad rest? And is it possible to apply these concepts with logical consistency? The scope of the problem becomes increasingly comprehensive the moment we test the validity of the judgment, not only as pertaining to human conduct and vital forms, but likewise to Being and the universe in general. We then pass from the problem of ethics to that of religion.

4. Finally we may also inquire concerning the nature of Being, of which thinking, feeling and volitional being are but a single part. This gives rise to *the problem of Being*, i. e. the problem of cosmology or metaphysics. Is it possible to elaborate a general world theory according to scientific methods? And what would be the nature of such a theory? If we organize our experiences and

infer the ultimate consequences of our knowledge, what principles will furnish an adequate explanation of the universe?

The nature and method of the treatment of these problems will vary with the instruments of knowledge and the historical conditions of the different periods. And in those problems which lie on the borderland of thought even the personality of the thinker will likewise have its effect. It is for this reason that a comparative treatment of the problems as history presents them is of such great importance. The various statements and solutions of the problem possess more than a purely philosophic interest. They have likewise an important bearing on the history of civilization and on psychology. They are responses in a great discussion which is proceeding through ages. Each response is something more than a mere intellectual structure, it is likewise the sign of a spiritual current. The history of philosophy therefore bears a direct relation to the general history of culture and of mind

FIRST BOOK

THE PHILOSOPHY OF THE RENAISSANCE

A. THE DISCOVERY OF THE NATURAL MAN

BURCKHARDT, in his famous treatise, *Die Kultur der Renaissance in Italien,* characterizes the Italian renaissance as the discovery of man. The historical conditions led to the emancipation of the individual. Man was no longer estimated from the mere viewpoint of his relationship to the Church or to his guild. He now became the subject of specialized interest and study. The discovery of ancient literature and art likewise contributed to this end. Man found a distinct form of culture outside the Church, with laws and ideals of its own. This expansion of the horizon furnished the opportunity for comparative study. In the north Protestantism, with its emphasis on personal experience and its insistence that civil life is independent of the Church, showed a similar tendency. In this way it became possible even here to develop both a theoretical and a practical interest in things which are purely human. Hence, both in the north and in the south, we find a number of interesting movements in the realm of the mental sciences during the period of the Renaissance.

1. *Pietro Pomponazzi's* little book, *De immortalitate animæ* (1516), may be regarded as an introduction to the philosophy of the Renaissance. *Pomponazzi* was born at Mantua in 1462, served with great distinction in the capacity of teacher of philosophy in Padua and Bologna, and died in the latter city in 1525. His friendship with

4

Cardinal *Bembo*, who enjoyed the favor of Pope Leo X,
saved him from persecution; but his book was burnt by
the inquisition. His philosophic significance is due to
his theory that the various forms and gradations of soul-
life constitute a continuous natural series, and that ethics
is self-explanatory. In opposition to the ecclesiastical
Aristotelians he shows that the immortality of the soul
is incapable of philosophic proof. Even in its highest
forms soul-life is dependent on material conditions and
its existence after the dissolution of the body cannot be
demonstrated. There is no occasion moreover to criticize
this conclusion on ethical grounds. On the contrary,
man is obliged as well as capable of doing good without
the hope of immortality; virtue is its own reward. This
is the conclusion of the philosophy which is based on
natural reason. But, according to Pomponazzi, the will
may transcend reason: man can believe things which he
is incapable of proving; faith proceeds from will, from
personal impulse. By means of this separation between
reason and will, between knowledge and faith, Pomponazzi
conformed his theory with the authorized doctrines of
the Church. He resorted to the same expedient in rec-
onciling the reality of the human will with divine omnipotence. The Church rejected this distinction.

Nicolo da Machiavelli introduced the naturalistic
method of investigation into politics and ethics in the
same manner as Pomponazzi had revived the naturalistic
psychology and ethics of genuine Aristotelianism. De-
scended from an old Florentine family (b. 1469), he entered
the diplomatic service of the republican government of
his native city which furnished him a splendid opportunity
for studying men and affairs. After the fall of the Republic (1512) he joined the Medici, which brought him the pro-

found contempt of his fellow citizens, who refused to accept his services after the republican government was again restored. He died in 1527.—Political interest made him a thinker. The misfortunes of Italy and its consequent conditions inspired him with a desire to restore its ancient spirit and power. Why should we imitate the splendid arts of the ancients and neglect their splendid deeds? But the sole possibility of accomplishing anything great requires us to press forward to the realization of great ideals without scruple! There are passages (especially in his *Principe*) in which *Machiavelli* seems to regard the ideal which a man proposes as an indifferent matter, if he only pursues it unscrupulously and energetically. But in the background of his thought there was constantly but a single ideal; the unity and the greatness of Italy. He regarded everything right which would contribute towards the realization of this ideal. Finding the Italians of his age lacking in a proper appreciation of greatness, he attributes it to the softening influence of the Church and of Christianity. In his *Discorsi* (Dissertations on the first ten books of Livy) he draws comparisons between the mind of antiquity and that of his own age, thus laying the foundation for a comparative ethics which was highly unfavorable to the modern period. Honor, magnanimity and physical prowess are not sufficiently appreciated now, and this is due to the fact that Christianity places the ideal of humanity in a transcendent world. To *Machiavelli* it is perfectly clear that these attributes possess more than secondary value, they are intrinsically meritorious. *Machiavelli* reveals the true spirit of the Renaissance both by the purely human ideal which he presents to his fellow countrymen, as well as by his emulation of power for its own sake.

The spirit of the Renaissance was likewise manifest in France. *Michel de Montaigne* (1533-1592), a French nobleman, spent his life in his private castle in the neighborhood of Bordeaux, far removed from the great movements agitating his age, devoting himself to literary pursuits. His interest in a purely naturalistic interpretation of human life, as he knew it from travel, books and above all from introspection, reveals his thoroughly modern spirit. At the beginning of his essays (which appeared 1580-1588) he remarks; *je suis moy-mesme le sujet de mon livre.* Closer study however reveals the fact that it is the way in which nature manifests itself in his own life that really appeals to him. Nature, the great Mother of us all, reveals herself in a distinctively unique manner in every individual. Every human being has his *forme maistresse,* his ruling passion. It is this interest that accounts for *Montaigne's* own personal observations as well as for his thorough study of ancient literature. His enthusiasm for nature and his insight into the multiplicity of individual peculiarities cause him to revolt against all dogmatism, both the rationalistic and the theological. He opposes them both on the ground of the inexhaustible wealth of experience, which neither the faith of reason nor of dogma can satisfy. Our investigations constantly lead to the discovery of a greater number of differences and variations and thus increase the difficulty of reducing them to general laws. And we must remember, furthermore, that our knowledge of the objective world is through sense perception, and that the sense organs as a matter of fact only reveal their own state, not the real nature of objects. And finally, if we attempt to form a conception of Deity, we imagine Him in human form, just as animals would conceive Him in

animal form, and we presume that this whole universe
was created and is preserved for the welfare of man alone.
—But *Montaigne* is not a sceptic.   There are two fundamental ideas, vitally related to each other, to which he
firmly holds, viz. the idea of the variety of individual
peculiarities, and the idea of the eternity of nature re-
vealing itself in every natural event.

Luis Vives (born in Valencia 1492, died in Brügge
1542), a Spanish scholar, whose contributions to philology
and pedagogy have likewise been of great importance,
became the forerunner of modern empirical psychology
through his book *De anima vita* (1538).   He insists that
experience must be the foundation of all knowledge and,
true to this principle, he holds that our chief concern is
not to know what the soul is, but to know how it acts.
He therefore undertakes to emancipate psychology from
metaphysics and theology.   He follows the descriptive
rather than the analytic and explanatory method.   His
description of the various psychical phenomena, especially
of the emotions, still retains its interest.   He regards the
soul and the vital principle as identical, and he constantly
seeks to combine physiology, as he understands it from
the works of *Galen*, with his psychology.   He holds
however that, whilst the souls of plants and of animals
(the principle of organic life and of sensory experience)
evolve from matter, God creates the human soul.   The
proof of the divine origin of the soul consists of the fact
that man is never satisfied with the sensible and finite,
but is forever striving to realize the infinite.

Two years after the appearance of *Vives'* work, *Philip
Melanchthon* (1495-1560), the reformer and "Preceptor of
Germany," published his *Liber de anima,* a book which
made a profound impression upon Protestantism.   He

follows *Aristotle* and theology more closely than *Vives* and his book is therefore of less importance for the history of psychology than that of *Vives*. *Melanchthon's* mild conception of human nature, contrasting sharply with that of *Luther* and the Lutheran zealots, had a wholesome influence however. His theory of the "natural light" shows this clearly: there are a number of ideas implanted in us by God, hence innate (notitiæ nobiscum nascentes), and these form the basis of all thought and of all value-judgments. This "natural light" was darkened by the Fall which necessitated the giving of the law at Sinai. The content of the ten commandments however is the same as the "natural light." It follows therefore that ethics may be founded on human nature (naturalistically). But it is powerless to quicken the life of the spirit and give peace. (Philosophiæ moralis epitome.)

The doctrine of the natural light was taken up enthusiastically by the Reformed provinces and applied most rigorously, especially with reference to the idea of authority and of the state. *John Althaus* (Althusius, 1557-1638), the Burgomaster of Emden, made this theory the basis of his idea of popular sovereignty in his *Politica methodice digesta* (1603). Even before him, *Jean Bodin* (in *La republique*, 1577) had conceived and elaborated the idea that sovereignty is indivisible and can exist in but a single place in the state. *Althaus* now teaches that it always belongs to the people. Rulers come and go, but the people constitute the permanent foundation of the state. They are the source of all authority because it is their welfare that constitutes the cause and purpose of the existence of the state. As a matter of history the sovereignty of the people is revealed in the first place by the fact that in most states there are a number of officers

exercising governmental control by virtue of their appointment by the people, and, in the second place, by the fact
that the people terminate the government of tyrannical
princes by revolution.   From the viewpoint of philosophy,
on the other hand, the theory of popular sovereignty is
demonstrated by the fact that either an expressed or
tacit contract (pactum expressum vel tacitum) underlies
the origin and perpetuity of the state; it is by virtue of
such contract that the people institute organized society
and submit themselves to governmental authority.
Althaus therefore maintains that the purpose of this contract can be nothing else than the welfare of the people.
He seems to construe this contract more in the form of a
directive idea than as an historic fact. The state is
simply the most comprehensive community; its antecedents being the narrower circles of the family, the
neighborhood and the corporation.

The appearance of *Hugo Grotius' De jure belli et pacis*
(1625) marks an epoch in the sphere of jurisprudence and
political theory.   Born at Delft in 1583, his great learning in the field of jurisprudence and of theology attracted
attention early in life.   Politically he belonged to the
aristocratic and liberal theological party of *Obernbarnevelt*.
He was rescued from the imprisonment into which he was
cast after the fall of *Obernbarnevelt* by his wife's cunning.
Thereafter he lived in Paris, and finally received the
appointment of ambassador to Sweden (1645).   *Grotius*
makes war his starting point and inquires how it may be
abolished.   There are four kinds of war between states:
between an individual and the state—between different
individuals—between the state and the individual.
1.   When states declare war they have no right to abrogate
the rights of the individual and the obligations of humanity.

War must be conducted for the sake of peace, and hence not in such a way as to make peace impossible. It is through this principle that *Grotius* became the founder of the modern theory of popular sovereignty. 2. When the individual declares war against the state it is an act of rebellion, and, in evident opposition to *Althaus*, *Grotius* denies the right of the people to revolt. 3. War between individuals, in a well-regulated state, is limited to justifiable self-defense. 4. War of the state against the individual takes the form of punishment. The state's right to punish must not be construed as the right of expiation. Punishment is justified only in case the pain imposed on the individual contains the possibility of greater good both to the individual himself and to the community.—In all of these various contingencies the authority of the law is independent of theological grounds. It proceeds from human nature (ex principiis homini internis). Human beings congregate and are led to organize societies under the influence of a native social impulse (appetitus societatis); but the constitution of society presupposes certain principles of government—above all the inviolability of every promise—and the people therefore pledge themselves to the observance of these rules either by expressed or tacit contract. The obligation to keep promises, according to *Grotius*, rests upon a primitive promise. In direct opposition to *Althaus*, *Grotius* holds that the people—i. e. after they have constituted society on the basis of the primitive contract—can renounce its sovereignty absolutely because it confers it on a prince or corporation. His theory of the relation of the state to religion, on the other hand, is more liberal than that of the strictly confessional *Althaus*: The only requirement which the state can make

of its subjects is the acceptance of general religious ideas
(the unity of Deity, predestination).

3. The general religious ideas which *Grotius* has in
mind, and which even *Melanchthon* accepted, were elaborated by a series of thinkers in more or less direct opposition to the confessional conception. Similar ideas
had already been expressed during the period of the older
Italian Renaissance (especially in the Platonic Academy
at Florence). *Jean Bodin* (a Frenchman learned in
law, d. 1596), previously mentioned, in his remarkable
work called the *Dialogue of Seven Men* (Colloquium
Heptaplomeres) describes a conversation between men
whose religious viewpoints were widely at variance.
Two of the men, defending natural religion—one of them
dogmatically, the other more critically—engage in controversy with a Catholic, a Lutheran, a Calvinist, a Jew,
and a Mohammedan. According to *Bodin*, true religion
consists in the purified soul turning to God, the infinite
essence. This religion can be exercised within any of the
various religions, and the seven men therefore separate
in charity and peace.

Bodin's book was in circulation for a long time in
nothing but manuscript copies. In 1624, however, the
English diplomat, *Herbert of Cherbury*, published his book
De veritate, which remained the text book of natural
religion for a long number of years. *Cherbury* takes
issue with those on the one hand who regard confessional
faith as superior to rational knowledge, and seek to incul-
cate such faith by threats of future punishment, and those
on the other hand who pretend to depend wholly on the
rational understanding, together with those who would
derive everything from sense experience, conceiving the
soul as a blank tablet (tabula Rasa). He holds that there

is an immediate, instinctive sense which guides all men to the acceptance of certain truths (notitiæ communes). This sense is the natural product of the instinct of self-preservation, which is another instance of the operation of divine predestination. The following propositions are instinctive truths of this order: *Two contradictory propositions cannot both be true; There is a first cause of all things; No one should do anything towards another which he would be unwilling to suffer in return.* According to *Cherbury*, even natural religion rests on an instinctive foundation, an inner revelation experienced by every human soul. The evidences of this revelation consist of the fact that we have capacities and impulses which finite objects fail to satisfy. The following five propositions contain the essence of all religion: *There is a Supreme Being; This Being must be worshipped; The truest worship consists of virtuous living and a pious disposition; Atonement for sin must be made by penitence; There are rewards and punishments after the present life.* Questions which go beyond these five propositions need give us no concern.

Jacob Böhme (1575-1624), the Gorlitz cobbler, and the profoundest religious thinker of this period, does not intend to oppose positive religion, as is the case with *Bodin* and *Cherbury*. He means to be a good Lutheran. He simply wishes to furnish a philosophy which will harmonize with Protestantism. Although a mere artisan, the influence of mysticism and natural science gave rise to grave doubts in *Böhme's* mind. He accepted the Copernican astronomy. He could no longer regard the earth as the center of the universe. But must it not follow therefore that man is but a negligible quantity in the universe, and is it not true that the great world processes must take their course regardless of the fate of man? Notwithstanding all this, if we should still presume to maintain our faith in God as the author of the universe, what shall we say in explanation of the evil, strife and suffering which everywhere abounds? After profound spiritual struggles *Böhme* discovered answers to these questions which he published in his *Morgenröte im Aufgang* (1612). His thought moves in majestic symbols drawn from the Bible and the chemistry or alchemy of his time. He is however fully aware that these symbols can express the pure thought relations but very imperfectly. He was also well aware of the fact that his ideas went beyond the theology of the church. But he stoutly denied the charge that his ideas were heathen. *"I write like a philosopher, not like a heathen!"* He meets the first doubt with the idea of the presence of God's power and nature in everything—in the human body as well as in the stellar spheres, and the latter must therefore be possessed of a kind of life—in human souls and throughout infinite space. As a matter of fact our bodies reveal the same elements as are found in the other objects of nature. In objective nature the divine activity is veiled; but in the mind of man it is clearly conscious. It follows therefore that we possess what is highest within ourselves and there is no need that we should seek it beyond the stars. He solves the second doubt with the idea that man must assume an original multiplicity within the divine unity, on the ground that multiplicity cannot be derived from unity, and moreover because opposition and difference are necessary conditions of consciousness: "A being incapable of experiencing contrasts could never become conscious of its own existence." But multiplicity and contrast furnish the possibility of disharmony, of strife and evil. The origin of evil is explained by the fact that a single element of Deity strives to become the whole Deity. This accounts for the profound conflict and the intense suffering in the world through which man and nature are to fight their way through to peace. In this conflict God is not far off: it is indeed his own inner conflict. "*Everyone whose heart is filled with love and who leads a compassionate and sweet tempered life, fighting against evil and pressing through the wrath of God into the light, lives with God and is of one mind with God. God requires no other service.*"

4. The effort to attain a natural, purely humanistic conception likewise affected the logic of the Renaissance, as well as the psychology, ethics and philosophy of religion. The scholastic logic, by which is meant the logic of the middle ages, was primarily the servant of theology and of jurisprudence; it was adapted to the single purpose of drawing valid conclusions from the presuppositions established by authority. But an effort was now being made to discover the relation which exists between logical rules and natural, spontaneous, informal thought. It was with this end in view that *Pierre de la Ramee* (Petrus Ramus) attacked the Aristotelian logic (*Institutiones Logiciæ*, 1554, French Ed. 1555). He was the son of a charcoal burner (born in northern France 1515), and it was by sheer dint of his thirst for knowledge and his indefatigable energy that he forged to the front and enjoyed a most successful career as a teacher in the College of France. Being a Protestant, he fell a victim to the massacre of St. Bartholomew's night (1572). *Ramus* called attention to the fact that the earliest philosophers had no formal logic, and that the spontaneous functions of thought are not confined to these men, but that they

can be studied in the mathematicians, the statesmen, the orators, and the poets as well. These observations however still failed to lead *Ramus* to the founding of a psychology of thought. As a Humanist, he rejoices in the fact that the classical authors could be of service to logic. His own treatment however does not get much beyond the theory of inference, in which he differs but little from *Aristotle*. A controversy between the Ramists and the Scholastics arose at this time—enlisting France, England, Germany and the North—which contributed greatly to the development of freedom of thought.

Franz Sanchez (1562-1632), a Spaniard, professor of medicine and philosophy at Montpelier and Toulouse, felt the need of substituting a new method for the scholastic logic. He expresses his dissatisfaction with the existing state of knowledge in his book *Quod nihil scitur* (1581). The further he presses his investigations the greater are the number of difficulties which he finds. Owing to the mutual interdependence of all things, and the infinitude of the universe, he has but little hope of attaining certainty in knowledge. He insists on observation and experiment however, and takes as his motto; *Go to the facts themselves. But the ultimate ground of certainty is nevertheless within the human mind itself: no external knowledge can equal the certainty which I have of my own states and actions.* On the other hand however this immediate certainty of inner experience is far inferior to the knowledge of external objects in point of clearness and precision.

Bacon's enthusiastic optimism concerning the future prospects of science presents a sharp contrast to the pessimism of *Sanchez*. He hoped for great things and devised magnificent plans. He anticipated great advancement in culture which was to be brought about by the mastery of the forces of nature through the aid of natural science, a study which ancient and mediæval thinkers had contemned. The aim and purpose of science is the enrichment of human life by means of new discoveries. *Bacon* nevertheless bestows high praise on the love of contemplation (contemplatio rerum): the vision of light is far more glorious than all the various uses of light. These sublime hopes furnish an insight into *Bacon's* personal character and his method of doing things. He justified the use of every available means in acquiring the conditions without which he thought his scientific plans impossible, on the plea of their necessity to the realization of his great purposes.

Francis Bacon of Verulam was born of an excellent family in 1561. In order to acquire the influence and the wealth which he regarded as necessary to his purposes, he threw himself into politics and gradually rose to prominent positions; finally attaining to the office of Lord Chancellor. But he gained this promotion by dishonorable compromises with the despotic caprice of Elizabeth and James the First. Under the charge of bribery and the violation of the law, parliament deposed him in 1621. His last years were spent in retirement engaged in scientific pursuits. He died in 1626. His political activities had not prevented him from continuing his studies and the production of important works. The tragedy of his life consisted in the fact that ulterior demands claimed his attention to so great an extent that not only his real purpose but even his personal character had to suffer under it.

Bacon describes himself as a herald (buccinator) who announces the approach of the new era without participating in it himself. He insists on quitting fruitless speculation and introducing the method of experience, induction, in every department of knowledge,—in the mental sciences as well as in the natural sciences. In the *Novum Organon* (1620) he examines the reasons why the sciences are inadequate and describes the inductive method. In the *De Dignitate et Augmentis Scientiarum* (1623) he presents a sketch of the actual state of the sciences and proceeds to show, frequently in a most brilliant manner, the gaps which still remain to be filled.

If a man would understand nature correctly, he must first of all reduce himself to a blank tablet. No one can enter the kingdom of nature except as a little child. But we are all hindered to a greater or less degree by various illusions, both native and acquired (Idola mentis). These may be divided into four classes. The first class, having its origin in human nature, is common to all mankind (Idola tribus). This is why we are constantly disposed to regard things from the viewpoint of their relation and their similarity to ourselves, rather than from the viewpoint of their true place in the general order of the universe—*ex analogia hominis* instead of *ex analogia universi.* We assume a greater degree of order and simplicity in things than the facts justify. We discover teleologic causes in nature because our own actions reveal such causes. The second class rests on individual peculiarity (Idola specus; every one interprets nature from the viewpoint of his own cave). This accounts for the fact that some minds are more impressed by the differences of things, whilst others are disposed to emphasize their resemblances. Some are constantly striving to analyze and reduce things to their elements; others are engrossed with totalities. The third class is due to the influence of language upon thought (Idola fori). The formulation of words is governed by the needs of practical life, but exact thought frequently requires distinctions and combinations which differ widely from those of common speech. In certain cases there is a superabundance of words, in others there are too few. The fourth class (Idola theatri) is ascribed to the influence of traditional theories.

We must get rid of all these illusions. *Bacon* makes no attempt to show how this may be accomplished. The conception of the idola tribus contains a profound problem which *Bacon* failed to see, a problem however which acquired vast importance at a later period; we are obliged in every case to interpret reality from the human standpoint (ex analogia hominis); but in that case the question arises as to how our knowledge of the world can possess objective validity.

Bacon takes exception to the prevalent method of induction on the ground of its being limited to positive cases (as an induction per enumerationem simplicem). He insists that we must likewise take note of results in cases where the phenomenon under consideration is absent. He demands furthermore that we investigate the modifications of phenomena under varying conditions. After sufficient material has been gathered by these methods—and in order to avoid being overwhelmed by the confused mass of facts (for, citius emergit veritas ex errore quam ex confusione)—it is necessary to formulate a tentative hypothesis and examine the cases which seem to establish or refute the hypothesis. *Bacon's* method is therefore not a pure induction. He has a presentiment of the profound mutual dependence of induction and deduction.

His depreciation of the quantitative method however prevents him from attaining the true method of natural science as we find it in his contemporaries, *Kepler* and *Galileo*.

According to *Bacon*, the method of induction gives us an insight into the "Forms" of things. The Baconian "Forms," from one point of view, bear a close resemblance to the Platonic ideas, and from another they are analogous to the laws of natural science. The latter conception he frequently emphasizes very strongly. He says, e. g. "If the Forms are not regarded as principles of activity, they are nothing more than fictions of the human mind." Generally speaking, *Bacon* occupies a unique position in the transition from the ancient and scholastic world view to that of the modern period. This is clearly manifest in his effort to acquire a mechanical theory of nature. We never understand an object until we are in position to explain its origin, and the genetic processes of nature are brought about by means of minute variations (per minima) which elude our senses. But science uncovers the secret process (latens processus) and thus reveals the inherent relation and continuity of events. We do not discover, e. g. that the "Form" of heat is motion through sense perception; nor do the senses reveal the fact that the sum total of matter remains constant throughout all the changes of nature.

Bacon makes a sharp distinction between science and religion. The former rests upon sense perception, the latter upon supernatural inspiration. In philosophy the first principles must be submitted to the test of induction; in religion, on the other hand, the first principles are established by authority. Reverence towards God increases in direct proportion to the absurdity and in-

credibility of the divine mysteries accepted. *Bacon* however believes in the possibility of a purely natural theology.
The very uniformity of natural causation reveals the
existence of deity.

In ethics *Bacon* makes a distinction between the theory
of the moral idea (de exemplari) and the theory of the
development of the will (de cultura anima). The former
he finds thoroughly elaborated by the ancients; but the
latter has received but very little attention hitherto.

B. THE NEW CONCEPTION OF THE WORLD

THE middle ages developed its theory of nature as
well as that of the spiritual life on the foundation of
Greek antiquity—except where its ideas were derived
from the Bible and Christian tradition.—They received
their theory of medicine from *Galen,* their astronomy
from *Ptolemy,* their philosophy from *Aristotle.* Their
world view was a combination of the theories of *Aristotle* and *Ptolemy* with the Biblical doctrines: the earth
is stationary and forms the center of the universe;
the sun, moon, planets and the fixed stars, attached to
firm but transparent spheres, revolve around it. The
sub-lunar world, i. e. the earth and the space intervening
between the earth and the moon, is the realm of change
and death. Here the four elements (Earth, Water, Air,
Fire) are in a state of constant motion. Each seeks its
"natural place." Weight consists of the natural tendency
to descend, lightness consists of the tendency to ascend.
Beyond this moon-sphere is the realm of ether, consisting
of matter which has no "natural place," which is therefore
capable of continuing its motion eternally with absolute
regularity. The motions of the heavenly bodies—due
to this absolute regularity—are a direct copy of the nature

of Deity. They move in circles because the circle is the most perfect figure; it invariably returns into itself! The universe is bounded by the sphere of the fixed stars which is moved by the Deity himself, whilst the lower spheres are moved by various ethereal spirits.

This world theory seemed to be in harmony with the authorities of the age, *Aristotle* and the Bible, and at the same time to be in accord with the direct evidence of sense perception. This is why it required such a severe struggle to supplant it. It not only required the repudiation of venerable authorities, but even the most familiar sensory impressions. It was this profound revolution that constituted the stupendous task of the great *Copernicus*. The epistemological foundations of the ancient world view were unsettled by two men who had no acquaintance with its doctrine.

1. *Nicholas Cusanus* (1401-1464), a profound thinker with Neoplatonic and mystical tendencies, had even in the fifteenth century gone beyond the traditional view of a limited and stationary universe. Born in Cues (near Trier), he was educated by the "Brothers of the Common Life." He afterwards continued his studies in Italy. He attained to high ecclesiastical positions and his philosophy has its starting point in theological speculations. In his doctrine of the Trinity he regards the Spirit as the uniting principle which combines the oppositions implied in the characters of Father and Son; *spiritus sanctus est nexus infinitus*. He afterwards discovers analogous principles in human knowledge and in nature generally.— *Falckenberg's Grungzüge der Philosophie des Nicholas Cusanus* (Breslau, 1880) and *M. Jacobi's Das Weltegebaude des Kardinals Nicholas von Cues* (1904) are splendid memoirs of this remarkable man.

All knowledge consists of a process of combination and assimilation. Even sense perception combines various impressions into unitary wholes and these are in turn reduced to ideas and the ideas finally to concepts. In this way the intellect (intelligentia) is forever striving for unity—but it invariably requires an antithesis, something "other than" (alteritas) itself to effect its development. Finally, in order to transcend the antitheses, thought undertakes to conceive them as the extremes of a continuous series. In this way maximum and minimum are united by a continuous series of magnitudes. But we are unable to reconcile all antitheses: thought culminates in antitheses, i. e. there always remains an unassimilated increment beyond itself. It is as impossible for our thought to comprehend the Absolute as it is to describe a circle of pure polygons, even though we may constantly approach it more closely. Although we are incapable of conceiving the Absolute, Deity, we nevertheless understand (such is the nature of the intellect) our incapacity, and the ignorance in which our thought culminates, as a matter of fact, is a scientific ignorance (docta ignorantia). (One of the most interesting of the works of Cusanus is entitled *De docta ignorantia*.)

This fundamental peculiarity of our knowledge is likewise of importance in the study of nature. We are constantly striving to form continuous series from given points, but without being able to arrive anywhere. Thus, e. g. we can divide our idea of matter to infinity, in experience we must always be satisfied with a finite division, and the atom concept therefore always remains relative. It is the same with the idea of motion: an everlasting, perpetual motion were only possible in case there were no resistance. Here *Cusanus* anticipates the principle of

inertia. And the same thing applies even to the deter-
minations of locality: we always regard the objects of
the universe from a given place which is, for the time
being, the center of the universe for us; the universe as
such, however, can have neither center nor circumference,
and all motion is relative. The theory that the earth is
at the center of the universe is therefore false. However
if it is not at the center of the universe, it cannot be at
rest; it must be in motion even though we do not perceive
it. There is no ground therefore for the assumption that
the processes of origin and decay should be confined to
the sublunar sphere; we must rather assume that all
world bodies are subject to similar conditions to those
of the earth. According to *Cusanus*, therefore, the same
principle which precludes our knowledge of Deity likewise demonstrates that the world can neither be limited
nor stationary as was hitherto believed.

2. It was characteristic of the ancient, æsthetic conception of nature to emphasize the opposition of Form
and Matter. The "Forms" of natural phenomena likewise contained their explanation. *Bernardino Telesius*
(1508-1588) introduces the concept of Force (principium
agens) instead of Form (in his work *De rerum natura*,
1565-1587), as the opposite of Matter. He believes that
this conforms more closely with the facts of experience.
The "Forms" were mere qualities, which explain nothing.
He rejected the traditional theory of the "natural places"
and the qualitative distinction of the elements. There
are as a matter of fact but two fundamental forces; the
one expands (heat), the other contracts (cold), and the
various "Forms" which Matter, in itself unchanging
and quantitatively constant, assumes must find their
explanation by reference to the interaction of these two

forces. There are no "natural places," for space is everywhere the same. Different places in space do not of themselves involve any qualitative differences.

Telesius was born at Cosenza in the vicinity of Naples. His circumstances were sufficiently comfortable to provide him the opportunity to devote himself to science. He taught in the University of Naples and founded an Academy in his native city. He had planned to substitute a new theory, based on experience, for Aristotelian Scholasticism. But his critical equipment was inadequate to the accomplishment of this ideal. His general principles however mark an important advance. The details of his natural philosophy are no longer of interest. But his ideas on the psychology of knowledge still continue to be of considerable importance. He tries to bring thought and sensation into the closest possible relation. Should an object which has once been perceived in the totality of its parts and attributes recur at some later time with certain of its parts and attributes lacking, we can supply the parts which are lacking and imagine the object as a totality notwithstanding the fact that we perceive it but in part. We can imagine fire, e. g. with all its attributes, even though we only see its light, without perceiving its heat and its consuming energy. Intellection (intellegere) is the process of construing our fragmentary experience into such a totality. Even the highest and most perfect knowledge simply consists of the ability to discover the unknown attributes and conditions of phenomena by means of their similarity to other cases known as a totality. Inference simply means the recognition of the absent attributes by this method. The simplest sensory impressions are therefore related through a large number of intervening degrees to the highest product of scientific thought, and there is no ground for attempting to deduce our knowledge from two different sources or faculties.   The problem as to whether similarity is a sensory quality like color and tone remains unsolved, as even *Patrizzi,* a contemporary of *Telesius,* charged against him.

Telesius is inclined to ascribe sensitivity to all matter, just as, on the other hand, he regards the soul as material (with this exception, he postulated a supernatural part in the soul on theological grounds which he regarded as a forma superaddita).   Every human soul, like everything else, possesses a native impulse towards self-preservation, which constitutes the foundation of ethics.   Human virtues represent the various attributes which are favorable to the preservation of the individual.   Wisdom is an indispensable condition which must therefore co-operate with all the other virtues (as virtus universalis). The social virtues, which are comprehended under the concept humanitas, are of great importance, because intimate association with others is a necessary condition of self-preservation.   The climax of all virtue however is magnanimity (sublimitas), which finds its sufficient satisfaction in its own personal integrity and diligence. *Telesius* conceived his ethics in the spirit of the Renaissance, and it produced a lasting impression.   His natural philosophy and his psychology were likewise very influential, especially over *Bacon* and *Bruno.*

3.   *Nicholas Copernicus* (Coppernick), the founder of the modern theory of the universe, was born at Thorn (1473), studied at Cracow and at various Italian Universities and was prebendary at Frauenburg, partly as Administrator, devoting part of his time to his studies. He took no part in the great controversies agitating his

age. But he seems to have had a measure of sympathy with the religious movement, and he fell into discredit during his latter years on account of his liberal, humanistic tendency. He began the elaboration of his astronomical theory already in 1506, but he was hesitant about its publication, and the first printed copy of his work *De revolutionibus orbium cœlestium* only appeared shortly before his death (1543). The matter which specially concerns us is the epistemological presuppositions which form the basis of this work. Two of its presuppositions must claim our attention.

Nature always takes the simplest course. The theory of the whole universe revolving around so small a body as the earth is inconsistent with this principle. And the case is similar with the theory that the planetary orbits should not be simple circles but a very complicated system of epicycles. On the other hand, if we regard the sun as the center of the universe, and the earth and the planets as revolving around it, we have a very simple theory of the universe.

The second presupposition is *the principle of the relativity of motion* previously suggested by *Cusanus*. The perception of motion is not adequately explained by the mere reference to the fact that a perceived object has really changed its position in space. It may likewise be due to the fact that the perceiving subject has moved. If we therefore assume that the earth, from which we observe the motion of the heavenly bodies, is itself in motion (around its axis and around the sun), we will be in position to explain the phenomenon quite as well (only more simply) as the traditional theory.

Copernicus still adhered to the idea of a finite universe and regarded the firmament of the fixed stars, the boundary of the universe, as motionless. He believed the planets to be enclosed in a series of concentric permanent spheres. But notwithstanding this he prepared the way for a radical change in the theory of the universe. Facts which apparently rested on the direct evidence of sense perception and were supported by the most famous authorities must now be regarded as discredited! We must awaken to the fact that the system of things which constitutes the universe admits of a different interpretation from the apparent demands of sense perception.

4. *Giordano Bruno* (1548-1600) is at once the most profound and the most courageous thinker of the renaissance period. Strongly influenced by the philosophy of antiquity and accepting the theories discovered by *Cusanus* and *Telesius*, he found a real foundation for his theory of the universe in the new astronomy, as elaborated by *Copernicus* and later by *Tycho Brahe*.

Born at Nola in southern Italy, *Bruno* entered the Dominican order in his early youth. He was soon charged with heresy. His active mind and restive spirit could not endure the rigid monastic discipline. He fled the cloister, discarded the monastic garb and began a wandering career of study and travel, which took him to Switzerland, France, England and Germany. He appears in the capacity of teacher in Toulouse, Paris, Oxford and Wittenburg; but nowhere did he find a permanent position. This was due in part to the opposition of the traditional schools, and in part to his restless disposition. But despite his wanderings he found time to write his ingenious works, among which the Italian dialogues, published in London 1584, deserve special mention. He never regarded reconciliation with the Catholic church

as impossible, and even cherished the hope of returning
to Italy and, without re-entering the cloister, continuing
his literary activities. He felt that his career north of
the Alps was a failure and Protestantism, with its many
little popes, was more reprehensible to him than the
ancient church with its single Pope. He finally returned
therefore, but was arrested by the Inquisition at Venice
(1592) and, after a long imprisonment, burnt as a heretic
at Rome in 1600. He died like a hero.

Bruno held *Copernicus* in high esteem because of his
lofty mind. It was he who had lifted him above the
illusory testimony of the senses to which the vast majority
remained enchained. But notwithstanding his unstinted
admiration for the man, he nevertheless regarded the
Copernican theory as inadequate because of its conception
of the universe as bounded by the sphere of the fixed
stars. The basis of *Bruno's* opposition to this theory
was two-fold, its failure to accord with his theory of
knowledge together with his religio-philosophical views.

a. The sensory evidence of an absolute world-center
and an absolute world-boundary is merely apparent. The
moment we change our viewpoint we attain a new center
and a new boundary. Every point in the universe can
therefore be regarded at once as both central and periph-
eral. Abstract thought and sentiency agree in this;
namely, that we may add number to number, idea to
idea, ad infinitum, without ever approaching an absolute
boundary. The possibilities of progress in knowledge
are therefore unlimited, and it is from this characteristic
of knowledge (la conditione del modo nostro de intendere)
that *Bruno* conceives the character of the universe: absolute boundaries are as inconceivable of the universe as
of knowledge.

It follows therefore that there are no absolute positions. Every position is determined by its relation to other positions. One and the same point may be either center, pole, zenith or nadir—depending entirely on the point from which it is observed (respectu diversorum). There can therefore be no absolute motion and no absolute time. The ancients based their theory of absolute time on the absolute regularity of the motions of the fixed stars; but since the motions observed from any particular star differ from that of another star there are as many times as there are stars. And, finally, the traditional theory of absolute heaviness and lightness is likewise an error; its tenability was based on the presupposition of an absolute center of the universe. Heaviness and lightness must therefore be understood with reference to the various world-bodies. Sun particles are heavy in relation to the sun, earth particles in relation to the earth. According to *Bruno*, heaviness is the expression of a natural impulse within the parts to return to the greater whole to which they belong.

The principle of relativity is closely connected with the theory that nature is everywhere essentially the same. We can infer the conditions in other parts of the universe from the conditions about us here on the earth. We observe e. g. that ships, when seen at a distance, appear to be motionless, whilst as a matter of fact they are moving very rapidly, and thus by analogy we may assume that the fixed stars appear to be motionless by reason of their great distance from us. There is no justification for maintaining the fixity of the firmament dogmatically as the ancients and even *Copernicus* had done.

Bruno therefore challenged the dogmatic principles which *Copernicus* had still accepted. He saw very clearly however that the matter cannot be definitely determined by mere speculative generalizations; genuine proof can only come from the discovery of new facts of experience. And he believes furthermore, and rightly so, that no one can investigate the matter without prejudice who adheres dogmatically to the traditional hypothesis.—At one important point he was able to appeal to well-defined facts. He rejected the theory, still accepted by *Copernicus*, that the stars are enclosed in permanent spheres: *If the earth can move freely in space, why should it be impossible for the stars to do the same?* And he found his conclusion verified by *Tycho Brahe's* investigation of comets, which as a matter of fact pass diagonally through the "Spheres" whose crystal masses were supposed to separate the various parts of the universe! It follows therefore that the contrast of heaven and earth, of permanent and changeable parts of the universe, is untenable.

b.   In his philosophy of religion *Bruno* starts with the infinitude of the Deity. But if the cause or principle of the universe is infinite it must follow that the universe itself is likewise infinite! We are unable to believe that the divine fullness could find expression in a finite universe; nothing short of an infinite number of creatures and worlds would be an adequate display of such fullness.

Bruno elaborated his theory of the infinity of the universe in two dialogues, the *Cena de la ceneri* and *Del' infinito universo e mondi* (1584), and in the Latin didactic poem *De immenso* (1591). These works are of epochal importance in the history of the human mind. Just as this wide expanse inspired in *Bruno* a feeling akin to deliverance from the confines of a narrow cell, so the human mind is now presented with a boundless prospect forever promising new experiences and new problems.

c. *Bruno* elaborated his general philosophical principles, which were naturally closely related to the new world theory, in the dialogue *De la causa, principio e uno* (1584).

Inasmuch as the new world theory annulled the opposition between heaven and earth, *Bruno* undertakes the task of annulling all oppositions by means of a profounder speculation. Sharp antitheses originate in the human mind and there is no ground for ascribing them to nature. *Plato* and *Aristotle* e. g. had no warrant in objective fact for assuming a distinction between Form and Matter. There is no absolute Matter, just as there is no absolute position and no absolute time. Absolute Matter must necessarily be absolutely passive, in which case it could acquire form and development only through some external agency. But in the natural world Forms are not introduced into Matter from without, after the manner of a human artist; they originate from within by an evolution of nature's own inherent energy. Matter is no less divine than Form and it persists in constant change even as the ancient Atomists had observed. Nature reveals a constant cycle—from inorganic matter through the organic processes and back again to the inorganic. According to *Bruno's* own statement, he was so profoundly impressed with this idea for a while that he was inclined to regard Forms and the spiritual factor in the universe as unessential and ephemeral. Later on however he perceived that Form and Spirit, no less than Matter, must have their ground in the infinite Principle. He admitted that everything must contain a spiritual principle, at least potentially (secondo la sostanza), even if not always actually (secondo l'atto). The ultimate source of all things consists of a Being which transcends the antitheses of Matter and Form, potentiality and reality, body and mind. In so far as this ultimate source is conceived as something distinct from the universe it is called "Cause," in so far as it is conceived as actively present in natural phenomena it is called "Principle." The Deity is not a far distant being; it reveals its presence in the impulse towards self-preservation and it is more intimately related to us than we are to ourselves. It is the soul of our soul, just as it is the soul of nature in general, which accounts for the all-pervasive interaction throughout universal space.

The culmination of thought likewise marks its limit, because we are incapable of thinking without antitheses. Every conceptual definition imposes certain limitations; the infinite Principle is therefore incapable of definition. Theology must forever remain a negative science, i. e. a science which eliminates the limitations and antitheses from the concept of Deity. The only significance which positive theology can have, i. e. a theology which under-takes to express the infinite Principle by definite pred-icates, is practical, didactic and pedagogic. It must address itself to those who are incapable of rising to a theoretical contemplation of the universe. God is indeed more highly honored by silence than by speech.

d. The ideas described above are characteristic of the most important period of *Bruno's* philosophical develop-ment. It is possible however (with *Felice Tocco*, in his valuable treatise *Opera latine de G. Bruno*, 1889) to distinguish an earlier and a later period in his development. During the first period *Bruno's* philosophy had somewhat of a Platonic character, in that he regarded general ideas as the highest object of knowledge and the universe as an emanation from Deity (*De umbris idearum*, 1582). But his ideas apparently mean something different from the universal concepts (as in Plato). He seems rather to regard them as laws which describe an actual relationship (e. g. between the different parts of the body).—The last period, as is evident from the *De triplici minimo* (1591), is noteworthy for its emphasis on the individual elements of being between which this actual relationship obtains. Sensory objects consist of parts notwithstanding the apparent continuity perceived through sense perception. *Bruno* calls the ultimate, irreducible (or first) parts atoms, minima or monads. There are various classes of monads, and he even calls the universe and God monads, when speaking of them as units.

The distinctions between *Bruno's* three points of view—the theory of Ideas, the theory of Substance, and the theory of Monads—however are simply matters of degree.

e. *Bruno's* ethics conforms with his general theory of the universe.   His *Spaccio de la bestia trionfanta* (1584) evaluates human virtues according to a new standard. Its dominant characteristic is the prominence given to the desire for truth and to honest toil.   Every correct evaluation presupposes truth, and toil is the natural consequence of the task imposed upon man, not merely to follow nature, but to bring forth a new, higher order of nature, that he may become lord of the earth.   In the *Degli eroici furori* (1585) *Bruno* describes the heroic man as one who is aware that the highest good can only be realized through strife and suffering, but who never despairs, because pain and danger are evils only from the viewpoint of the world of sense, not from the viewpoint of eternity (ne l'occhio del eternitade).   The possibilities

of pain increase with the height of the aim. But the
heroic man finds his joy in the fact that a noble fire has
been kindled in his breast—even though the goal should
be impossible of realization and his soul should be con-
sumed by its profound yearning. This courageous wisdom typifies *Bruno's* character as it appears in his life
and in his heroic death at the stake.

C. THE NEW SCIENCE

WITHOUT any disparagement of the tremendous importance of the free investigations in the sphere of mental
science, or even the radical change in the general theory
of the universe, the fact nevertheless remains that the
founding of modern natural science had a far profounder
influence upon human life. The contributions of antiquity are likewise in evidence here, particularly the study
of the writings of *Archimedes*. The real cause however
must be traced to the increasing interest in the industries,
mechanics and engineering operations, especially in the
Italian cities. *Galileo* makes mention of this fact at the
opening of his chief work. It was but natural therefore
that this should give rise to a desire to understand the
laws and principles by which to promote these operations.
Then followed a transition from the achievements of man
to the majestic products of nature, because man depends,
more or less consciously, on the analogy between human
mechanics and the efficiency of nature.

Modern natural science created a new method. It
substituted observation and experiment together with
analysis and computation for speculation and dogmatic
construction on the one hand and the mere collection of
facts on the other. The human mind evolved new functions, whose nature and value necessarily suggested new

problems in the philosophy of knowledge. Owing to the fact that the new method was applied almost exclusively to the realm of matter, the concept of matter naturally came to the foreground. And as a matter of fact it was not until then that the problem of the relation of mind and matter could be sharply and definitely stated. Ethics and the philosophy of religion likewise received their complement of new data. The self-sufficiency of man was magnified. New forms of social life were evolved, especially through the progressive division of labor made possible and necessary through the mechanical inventions. The growing conviction of the prevalence of fixed natural laws required a restatement and a more precise definition of the problem of religion. Man's general attitude to the universe, both in its theoretical and its practical aspects, underwent a most remarkable change.

We shall mention three men as the real founders of modern science.

1.   *Leonardo da Vinci* (1452–1519), the famous artist, whose varied talents made him one of the most remarkable characters of the Renaissance period, is known to us through several fragments in natural science and philosophy which are of great importance. His manuscripts became scattered and none were published until late in the nineteenth century. (*H. P. Richter* has published a good collection. London, 1883. A German translation of the most important fragments was published by *M. Herzfeld*, Leipzig, 1904.)

Experience is the common mother of all knowledge. But we cannot stop on the plane of mere observation. We must find the internal bond of nature (freno e regula interna) which explains the vital relation of things and events. And the only possible method of doing this is by the aid of mathematics. Mathematical deduction is the only method of discovering the unknown from the given facts of nature. We thus find even here a clear expression of all the characteristics of modern method, viz. the proper coordination of induction and deduction.—Certain statements of *Leonardo's* indicate a sturdy naturalism. The only thing we can know about the soul is the nature of its functions and its activity as an organic principle; whoever cares to know more must inquire of the Monks! Nature consists of a majestic cycle between the inorganic and the organic, and between the animate and the inanimate. Nature always takes the simplest course. There is reason therefore to hope for a great future with respect to the knowledge of nature.—*Leonardo* suggested a number of interesting anticipations of the principle of inertia and of energy. He stands solitary and alone in his own age. It was not until a century later that any advancements were made along the lines which he indicated.

b. *John Kepler* (1571–1630), the famous astronomer, is an interesting example of the evolution of an exact scientific conception of nature from a mystic-contemplative starting-point. His first treatise (*Mysterium cosmographicum*, 1597) is based on theological and Pythagorean principles. The universe is the manifestation of God. The paths and motions of the heavenly bodies must therefore reveal certain harmonious and simple geometrical relations. The Holy Ghost is revealed in the harmonious ratio of magnitudes of stellar phenomena, and *Kepler* thinks it possible to construe this magnitudinal ratio. Later on however he simply maintained the general belief that certain quantitative ratios must exist between the motions of the planets and formulated the results deduced from

Tycho Brahe's observations in the laws which bear his name. He afterwards demonstrated the quantitative ratios on the basis of the facts of experience. Here his method involved the combination of the experimental with the mathematical method. Just as he had at first established the principle that nature conforms to mathematical laws by the theological method, so he further believes that the planets are guided in their course by separate planetary souls, even as the entire world-system is directed by the world-soul which dwells in the sun. His explanation of nature therefore was thoroughly animistic or mythological. Later on in life he held that science must make no assumptions except such as can be actually deduced from experience. He calls such causes *vera causa*. He also rejected the idea of planetary souls which as a matter of fact are never actually given in experience. In his *Astronomia nova s. physica cœlestis* (1609) he makes the transition from theology and animism to pure natural science. He defends his belief in the importance and truth of the quantitative method psychologically and empirically as well as theologically. Mathematical knowledge is the clearest and the most certain knowledge which we possess and it becomes us therefore to apply it as widely as possible. The processes of nature are qualitatively modified by our subjective states (pro habitudine subjecti). Perfect certainty and objectivity can only be attained by the quantitative method. And, finally, experience reveals the fact that all material phenomena have quantitative, especially geometrical, attributes; "the method of measurement can be applied wherever there is matter" (ubi materia, ibi geometria). As a matter of fact the universe participates in quantity (mundus participat quantitate).

Kepler elaborates his general conception of scientific

method in his *Apologia Tychonis*. All science is based on hypotheses. But hypotheses are by no means to be regarded as arbitrary notions. They must vindicate their title by the harmony of their logical consequences with the given facts and the consistency of their implications. Science begins with the observation of facts, uses these data for the formulation of hypotheses and finally seeks to discover the causes which account for the uniformity of events.

c. *Galileo Galilei* (1564–1642) is the real founder of modern science, because he shows the clearest understanding of modern methods—the method of induction and deduction as mutually complementary.

If induction demanded the examination of every possible case, inductive inference would be impossible. But it is possible to examine a number of characteristic cases, and formulate a hypothetical principle by an analysis of these cases, and finally prove that the consequences deduced from this principle are in accord with experience. In order to make this deduction and show its agreement with the facts correctly we must be in position to state our facts in quantitative terms. We are therefore under necessity of measuring phenomena exactly. *Galileo* raised the watchword; *Measure everything which is measurable and reduce the things which will not admit of direct measurement to indirect measurement.*

Kepler had previously shown that matter cannot of itself pass from rest to motion. *Galileo* advances a step farther. According to the principle of simplicity,—which, like *Copernicus*, *Bruno* and *Kepler*, he regarded as a universal law—he maintained that a body tends to remain in its given state so long as it is unaffected by external influences. A body can therefore of itself neither change its motion nor pass from motion to rest. In the absence of all external influences a moving body would continue its motion indefinitely at the speed originally given. This as a matter of course represents an ideal case, since absolutely empty space is unrealizable, but *Galileo* showed by the experiment of rolling a ball in a parchment groove that the length of time the ball continued in its course was in direct proportion to its own smoothness and the smoothness of the parchment. In this way he proved the principle of inertia. But *Galileo* likewise thought that circular motion, which he also regarded as simple and natural, as well as motion in a straight line, would be continuous if all external obstacles could be eliminated. In his investigations of the motion of falling bodies he likewise starts with the principle of simplicity, with a view to showing later that it is verified by observation and experiment. "*If a stone, falling from a given position at considerable height, accelerates its speed, why should I not regard the acceleration as due to its simplest explanation? And there is no simpler explanation of acceleration than that of a continuously uniform increase.*"—It follows further from the principle of inertia and the law of falling bodies that we must take account of the energy or the impetus of motion (energia, momento, impetu) present at each moment as well as the actual sensible motion.

Galileo elaborated the modern theory of motion, which forms the basis of physics, in his *Discorsi della nouve scienze* (1638).—His *Dialogo sopra i due massimi sistemi del mondo* (1632) draws a comparison between the Ptolemaic and Copernican world-systems, without, as he thought, taking sides, but in such a way as to leave no doubt as to his real opinion. This brought on the catastrophe of his life. He had even previously (after the discovery of the moons of

Jupiter and of sun-spots) expressed himself publicly as
favoring the Copernican system. When the College of
the Inquisition, therefore, in the year 1616, placed *Copernicus'* book on the Index, he is said to have promised *Cardinal Bellarmin* that he would neither defend nor dissem-
inate the Copernican theory. He denied that the *Dialogo*
was a violation of this promise on the ground that he had
expressed himself hypothetically. But the book was forbidden, and the old man of seventy was required—under
threat of torture—to solemnly abjure "the false doctrine,"
that the earth is not the center of the universe and that it
moves. The Inquisition held him under suspicion for the
rest of his life and he was forced to have his works published in foreign countries.

It has already been observed that the Copernican theory
beautifully illustrates the unwisdom of accepting our
ideas as the expression of reality without further question.
Galileo emphasized this phase of the new theory very
strongly; *"Think of the earth as having vanished, and there
will be neither sun-rise nor sun-set, no horizon even and
no meridian, no day and no night!"* Later on he expanded
this idea so as to include the whole of physical nature. In
the Dialogue he takes occasion to observe that he had
never been able to understand the possibility of the
transubstantiation of substances. When a body really
acquires attributes which were previously lacking, it
must be explained by such a rearrangement of its parts as
would neither destroy nor originate anything. This
clearly asserts the principle that qualitative changes can
only be understood when referred to quantitative changes.
Galileo had already stated this view even more strongly in
one of his earlier works (*Il saggiatore*, 1632). Form, magnitude, motion and rest constitute all that can be said of

things; they are the primary and real attributes of things (primi e reali accidenti). Our disposition to regard taste, smell, color, heat, etc., as the absolute attributes of things, on the other hand, is due to sense-prejudice. We give these names to things when they furnish the occasion of certain sensations, but these sensations take place within our bodies. They do not inhere in things. They would vanish if the corpo sensitivo were to vanish.—This doctrine, which contains the principle of the mechanical conception of nature, acquired vast importance in the investigations into the theory of knowledge in the following period.

SECOND BOOK

THE GREAT SYSTEMS

THE new interests, viewpoints, and discoveries of the Renaissance naturally gave rise to a desire to elaborate a new world-theory, one which would be inherently consistent and at the same time conform to the new thought. It was but natural that men should be anxious to follow the new ideas to their ultimate consequences. The human mind always shows a certain tendency, more or less pronounced, towards the systematization of knowledge into a unitary theory, and the more peaceful period which followed the turmoil and strife of the Renaissance furnished a splendid opportunity for the development of this tendency. It assumed the task of combining the new world-view and the new science with the philosophy of mind or spirit. Here *Bruno* had prepared the way. He had not however completely grasped the new scientific method. He was unable to apply the mechanical conception— by means of which a multitude of problems can be stated with far greater precision—to the statement of his problem.

Of the four fundamental problems of philosophy, the problem of Being now takes first rank. Compared with this, other problems, despite the fact of their frequent and perplexing obtrusiveness, fall into the background. The constructive method was courageously applied to the solution of the profoundest problems of human thought. *Descartes*, the first of the group of the great systematizers, both in his preliminary essays as well as in the later more positive statement of his theory, still reveals a distinct effort to pave the way for speculative construction by means of exhaustive analysis. But with *Hobbes* and *Spinoza* the constructive element is predominant. The only way we can discover the facts and analyses by which these thinkers established their definitions and axioms is by a less direct method. In *Leibnitz,* the fourth and last of the group, the analytic method becomes more prominent again. He marks the transition to the eighteenth century, in which the problems of knowledge and of values acquire an exceptionally prominent place.

The increasing favor of the constructive method of this period is closely paralleled by the dogmatic character of these intellectual efforts. The principles of the mechanical theory of nature were regarded as absolute, objective truths. *Leibniz* likewise shows some divergence from his predecessors on this point, by the fact that he subjects even these "primary and real" attributes of things, which were regarded as absolute data in the mechanical theory of nature, to a critical analysis.

a. *René Descartes* (1596–1650) may be called the real founder of modern philosophy. He was the first to inquire after the ultimate presuppositions of knowledge, and his theory was the first to take explicit account of the mechanical explanation of nature in the statement of the problem. He applies the analytic method in searching for ultimate principles, but he quickly abandons it for the constructive method, because he believes it possible to demonstrate the necessity and rationality of the principles of the mechanical theory of nature. He regards the idea of God, the validity of which he demonstrates by the speculative method, as an absolute terminus of reflective thought. *Descartes* thus presents a peculiar combination of keen analysis and dogmatic assertion.

Descartes was the son of a French nobleman, and his economic independence furnished him the opportunity of devoting himself wholly to meditation and scientific research. His *Discours de la methode* (1637) is an interesting philosophical autobiography. He received his education at a Jesuit College, but, notwithstanding the fact that he had among his tutors the best teachers of his age, he was very much dissatisfied with his acquirements when he had finished his studies. He knew many things, but a consistent system and clear fundamental principles were lacking. He was particularly fond of mathematics but it seemed to be nothing more than a fiction of the human brain. He finally plunged into public life, trying one thing after another, but was invariably driven back to his solitude by his insatiable thirst for knowledge. He finally resolved to make a first hand study of practical life in the army and the courts of the nobility. But at every venture he returned again to quiet meditation. During the winter of 1619, while in camp with the army of the Elector of Bavaria, he experienced a scientific awakening. In a moment of intellectual enthusiasm a plain way of escape from his doubt appeared to him. If we begin with the simplest and clearest ideas and pass step by step to the more complex problems, the confusing multiplicity of our ideas will vanish. We can then arrange our thoughts in such an orderly manner that the successive steps can always be deduced from their antecedents. He followed this principle both in his mathematical and in his philosophical investigations. After several years of study in Paris he returned to Holland, where he believed he could pursue his investigations with less danger of disturbance. There is no doubt however that the severe injunctions against antischolastic theory formed part of his motive for leaving France. But even in Holland he became involved in controversies, because both Protestant and Roman Catholic theologians regarded his philosophy with suspicion. At the invitation of Queen Christina he spent his last years in Sweden.

1. *Descartes*, who was a great mathematician himself (founder of Analytical Geometry), attributed the distinction between geometry and philosophy to the fact that the former is based upon principles concerning which there could be no room for doubt, whilst the controversies in philosophy pertain to these very principles. The discovery and establishment of first principles require the use of the analytic method, i. e. we must proceed from the given or the provisionally established to its presuppositions. Analysis finally leads to simple intuitions, and these in turn originate directly through experience. The subjective movements of intellect are of this sort, e. g. that a triangle is bounded by three lines—that a thing cannot both be and not be at the same time,—that everything has a cause, —that the effect cannot be greater than its cause,—that I must exist if I think (*Régles pour la direction de l'esprit*, evidently written 1628–1629). He called these processes simple intuitions, and afterwards made the last one mentioned the basis of his theory (in the *Discours* and in the *Meditationes* which appeared in 1641). It is possible to doubt every idea or object of knowledge; all our perceptions or postulates might be illusory. But doubt has a definite limit. Even the most radical doubt presupposes thought. Thought is a reality even though all of its conclusions should be illusory. *Descartes* takes the word thought in its broadest sense: thought is everything which goes on in consciousness. When, in the language of his famous proposition, he says: *Je pense, donc je suis!*

(*Cogito, ergo sum!*) he might as well have said: *Je sens, je veux, donc je suis!*—The word "therefore" (*donc, ergo*) is inexact; for *Descartes* does not regard the proposition as a logical deduction, but as an immediate intuition, a simple intellectual step, through which we become conscious that we are conscious.—The clearness and distinctness of this intuition, according to *Descartes*, furnish the criterion by which to test other propositions. There are two more intuitions however which he thinks are just as clear and self-evident as this first one, namely the proposition that everything has a cause, and that the effect cannot be greater than the cause.

If we examine our different ideas, we find that some of them can be attributed to external and finite causes, and that others are produced by ourselves, but that there is one idea which presupposes an infinite cause—namely the idea of God. I am myself (which is proved by the fact that I can doubt) a finite, imperfect being, and I cannot therefore have formed the idea of an infinite, perfect being. This idea must have its origin in an infinite being. This is the only possible explanation of the fact that my intellect, as soon as it has attained mature development, forms this idea. It is "innate," not indeed as if it were consciously present at the very beginning of life, but in the sense that there is a disposition to form it in the very nature of the intellect.—*Descartes* however has another proof of the existence of God: God, the perfect Being, must exist; for existence is perfection, hence the denial of the existence of God would be self-contradictory. This is the so-called ontological proof, which finds the warrant for the existence of God in the concept.

It is only after *Descartes* has established the validity of the idea of God (assuming the principle of causality as a matter of course) that he has a secure foundation for the validity of knowledge in general: for a perfect being cannot deceive.

Descartes bases the knowledge of reality on the idea of God, just as *Kepler* had explained the conformity of nature to mathematical principles on theological grounds. But, in that case, God is merely an explanation of the sublime uniformity of natural phenomena, rather than a specifically religious concept. Thus, e. g. in the sixth meditation, he says, "*By nature in general (natura generaliter spectata) I simply mean God himself or the order and disposition instituted (coordinatio) by Him in created things.*" Everything which is to be accepted as true must fit into this great system. The criterion by which we are able to distinguish between dream and wakeful consciousness consists in the fact that the various experiences of wakeful life can be coordinated with our total experiences and recollections without a break in the system.—*Descartes* had not observed that this criterion was already contained in the causal principle, so that he might have spared himself the indirect route through the idea of God. The establishment of this criterion furnished the basis of a new conception of truth, according to which truth consists of the internal relation of perceptions and ideas, instead of their harmony with something unperceived.

Descartes is fully aware that the idea of God, which he makes the foundation of all science, is not the popular one. He says that when God is conceived as a finite being, receiving honor from men, it is not strange that His existence should be denied. God is however the absolute Substance, i. e. a being, which exists through itself (*per se*), requires no other being, in order to exist. It is true, *Descartes* likewise employs the concept of substance in reference to finite things (e. g. matter and the soul); he says however that the concept cannot be used univocally (*univoce*) of infinite and finite being, because finite beings are always dependent and the term substance is therefore applied to them inexactly. According to the broader, inexact linguistic usage, "Substance" means the same as *thing* or *being*, the subject or matter or substrate of given attributes.

2. The idea of God not only guarantees the reality of things, but it is likewise the source of the fundamental principles of natural science. (*Principia Philosophiæ*, 1644.)

Our sense impressions serve the purpose of guiding us in practical activities. In order to do this they need not be like the things themselves, if only they correspond to them. When we come to think of the real nature of things apart from our sensations, there are only three attributes which are incontrovertible: extension, divisibility and mobility. We cannot even in imagination think these attributes away. And these three attributes furnish the basis of the simplest and clearest understanding of everything that takes place in the material universe, whilst qualities merely furnish illusory explanations. All the attributes of nature may therefore be referred to extension, divisibility and motion. Qualities however are simply to be ascribed to the perceiving subject.—*Descartes* thus deliberately systematizes the mechanical conception of nature. He seems to have been led to this conclusion by his studies in natural science during the years 1620–1629, independent of *Galileo*, although perhaps influenced by *Kepler*.

He derives the first principles of the mechanical conception of nature from the concept of God. As perfect being God must be immutable. The idea of anything

which He has created being capable of changing its state
without some external cause contradicts this immutability.
Material things cannot therefore on their own account
(*sua sponte*) without external interference (of another
material thing) pass from motion to rest or vice versa.
(*Descartes* nevertheless makes a reservation in the interest
of his spiritualistic psychology, namely that it is perhaps
possible for souls or angels to act on matter.) Besides
inertia, *Descartes* likewise deduces the constancy of motion (an imperfect antecedent to the persistence of motion)
from the unchangeableness of Deity. Conservation
(which, according to *Descartes*, consists of an incessant
continuance of creative activity) implies that the sum
total of motion implanted in matter at creation must remain unchanged. The distribution of motion among the
various parts of the universe may vary, but no motion can
be lost and no absolutely new motion arise.

Descartes regards the teleological explanation of nature,
which accounts for natural phenomena from the viewpoint
of ends, as inapplicable. He bases his rejection of final
causes on theological grounds. Since God is an infinite
being, he must have purposes beyond our power to con-
jecture, and it were therefore presumption on our part to
suppose it possible to discover the purposes of natural
phenomena. There are likewise many things in the
finite universe which do not affect us in the least,—what
sense could we therefore ascribe to their having been
created on our account!—The teleological explanation is
therefore rejected, because it is too narrow.

Descartes undertakes a detailed explanation of nature
on the basis of the principles thus established. He differs
from *Bacon* at this point in the importance which he attaches to deduction, and from *Galileo* (whose importance

he decidedly underestimates) in his inability to combine deduction and induction in the investigation of the facts of experience. He regards experience as nothing more than occasional, because he thinks that science can only give the possible, not the real, explanation of phenomena. He aims to restrict himself to hypotheses, and he does not even attempt to verify these hypotheses. His natural philosophy thus assumes an abstract and arbitrary character. His importance rests on the ideal of natural science which he proposed: namely, to deduce phenomena from their causes with mathematical necessity. He therefore took no account of anything but the geometrical attributes of things, and he treated the concepts of matter and extension as identical. He substituted this ideal of knowledge for the prevalent scholastic method of explanation, based on qualities and hidden causes.

Descartes attempted to explain the existing state of the Universe by mechanical processes of development. He assumes a primitive condition in which the particles of matter exist in whirling eddies (vortices) with fixed centers. The smaller particles, resulting from the mutual friction of the larger particles, were compelled to congregate around these centers, and thus formed the various world-bodies. Some of these bodies, like the earth, have lost their independence, because they are carried along by the more powerful cycles in which the great world-bodies are found. Weight consists of the pressure due to the rotary motion, which drives the smaller particles into close proximity to the larger bodies.—In suggesting this theory, imperfect as it is, *Descartes* anticipated *Kant* and *LaPlace*.

Organisms, as well as the World-all, are to be regarded as machines. If physiology is to become a science, it must be mechanics. The organism must be subject to the general law of matter. *Harvey's* discovery of the circulation of the blood (1628) strengthened *Descartes'* conviction. *Descartes* did much to suppress the fruitless theory of vitalism which explained organic phenomena by the assumption of a specific vital energy. In the department of nerve physiology, like *Harvey* in the doctrine of the circulation of the blood, he is a pioneer because he was the first to describe what is now called reflex action, i. e. muscular activity resulting directly from an objective stimulus without the intervention of any attendant consciousness. *Descartes* ascribed consciousness to man alone; he regarded animals as mere machines.

The human soul interacts with the brain, or, to be more exact, with a distinct part of the brain (the pineal gland, glandula pinealis), which, in *Descartes'* opinion, was centrally located, and it does not consist of pairs, like the other parts of the brain. The "vital spirits" (the delicate fluid, which, according to the physiology of the age, inherited from antiquity, pours through the nerves) strike this pineal gland and the impact translates it to the soul, thus giving rise to sensations. If the soul on the other hand strikes the pineal gland it can produce changes in the tendencies of the "vital spirits" and thus give rise to muscular activity.—Here *Descartes* contradicts his own doctrine of the persistence of motion; for if the pineal gland strikes the soul, a loss of motion must result, and, conversely, if the soul excites motion in the pineal gland, new motion must arise. He of course limits the action of the soul to the mere matter of producing a change of tendency; but this requires him to postulate an arbitrary exception to the principle of inertia.

Descartes places great stress on the distinction in defining the soul as thinking being, and matter as extended being. Their fundamental attributes are so different that they must be called two different substances, and moreover in the full sense of the word, since it must be possible for the one to exist without the other. But, in that case, their interaction becomes an impossibility; for Substance, strictly speaking, cannot be acted on from without.

In his special psychology (particularly in his interesting treatise on the emotions, published 'n his *Traité des passions*, 1649) he endeavors—in harmony with his dualistic theory—to furnish a separate definition for the mental phenomena which have a psycho-physical basis from those which are purely psychical. Hence he makes a distinction between sensation and judgment, sensory and mental recollection, imagination and intellection, desire and will, affections (passions) and emotions (*émotions intéreures*). His precision at this point is rarely equalled even by spiritualists.

Descartes' ethics bears an interesting relation to his world theory. He elaborated the details of this phase of his theory in his correspondence with Princess *Elizabeth Christina* of Sweden, and *Chanut* the French ambassador to Sweden.—He emphasizes the cultivation of the subjective emotions, rather than the "passions" which depend on external influences. But improvement in knowledge is likewise of great value: we discover that everything depends on a Perfect Being; we find that we are but infinitesimal parts of an infinite world, which cannot have been created on our account. We finally come to regard ourselves as parts of a human society (Family, State), whose interests take precedence over our private interests. It is important above all else to distinguish between what is within our power and what is not. The highest virtues are magnanimity (*generosite*) and intellectual love towards God (*amor intellectualis dei*). The latter is capable of governing our whole life, even though in the eyes of the theologians it should perhaps be regarded as insufficient for salvation.

Cartesianism was the first form in which the thought of the new age became accessible to wider circles. Notwithstanding his hypotheses, which were frequently unfortunate, his rigid insistence on a mechanical explanation of nature marks a distinct advance, and his labors inspired a vigorous movement in the department of natural science. His spiritualism and his attempt to combine theology and science developed a sympathetic attitude towards religion, notwithstanding the fact that many theologians, to whom a criticism of scholasticism was identical with a challenge of faith, were fanatically opposed to him. The clearness with which he expressed his views admitted of easy popularization, and, after the first opposition subsided, he acquired a large following in France, Holland and Germany.

Descartes however bequeathed profound problems to his successors. How can the existence of an absolute Substance be reconciled with the independent existence of particular things (souls and bodies)? And how shall we conceive the interaction of spirit and matter if both are to be regarded as independent beings (Substance), and this moreover if the principle of the persistence of motion is likewise to be maintained!

Occasionalism, so called, which had a tendency to refer all true causality to the absolute essence, so that the states of finite beings merely furnished the "Occasions" for God to interpose, was the logical result of these problems. This principle was at first only applied to the relation of spirit and matter: what takes place in the body furnishes God the occasion to permit a change to take place in the soul, and vice versa. It soon became evident however that, if there is an absolute substance, it is impossible for a finite being to be a cause at all. How can anything produce an effect beyond its own being in some other thing? Not only the interaction between spirit and matter but all interaction between finite beings is impossible, and divine causality alone remains possible. In this way first the psycho-physical problem and then the problem of causality conceived as a whole came to be regarded as insoluble and philosophy resolved itself into theology.

After a number of Cartesians had prepared the way for this conception, it was clearly and definitely elaborated by *Arnold Geulincx* (1623–1669) and *Nicholas Malebranche* (1648–1715).

Geulincx, originally a Catholic (he was born at Louvain), but later a convert to Protestantism, experienced a vigorous opposition both from Protestant as well as from Catholic scholasticism on account of his Cartesianism. During his latter years he occupied the chair of philosophy at the university of Leyden. His most characteristic work is his ethics (1665, complete 1675). In order to do right, man must learn to understand his position in the world; self-examination (*inspectio sui*) is therefore the foundation of ethics. It reveals the fact that intellect and will are all that really belongs to my Self. My body on the other hand is a part of the material universe where I can accomplish nothing. For I am only responsible for the things of which I can know the origin, and this knowledge is limited to my intellect and will. My activity cannot transcend my essential nature (i. e. my intellect and will). It is utterly impossible for a thing to produce changes be-

yond itself and its own states.   If the changes of one being
(e. g. the soul) correspond to the changes in another being
(e. g. the body), it can only be explained by the fact that
their common author forever adapts them to each
other—like two clocks which a clockmaker is constantly regulating in successive order (a figure used
already by the Cartesian *Cordemoy*).—The ethical
system which *Geulincx* elaborates on this foundation
consistently assumes the character of resignation, and
its chief virtue is humility.   For, where I am unable to
do anything, it is sheer folly that I should desire (*ubi
nihil vales, nihil velis!*).

Malebranche, a member of the Oratory, gives the mystic
phase of occasionalism still greater prominence.   His
philosophic inspiration came from one of *Descartes'* books,
and it permeated his entire life, which was spent in the
cloister.   The senses—as appears in his *Recherche de la
verité* (1674ff)—are given us for practical purposes and they
are unable to discover the real nature of things.   The
senses deceive us every time we are misled into ascribing
sensible qualities to things themselves.   Whence therefore do we get knowledge of things?   The understanding
is quite as incapable as sensibility to teach us anything
about things which exist independently of us.   Neither
we ourselves nor things can produce knowledge, for no
finite being can create anything new.   Causation is a
divine thing, and it is pagan to ascribe causality to finite
beings.   Finite beings forever remain simply *causes oc-
casionelles*.   We can neither regard the motions of matter
nor the thoughts of men as causes.   God could not even
give a finite being the power to be a cause, for God cannot
create gods.   Our knowledge is entirely the work of God;
we see everything in Him.   It is only through his inter-

position that we get ideas of material things.   Each idea
is really a limitation of the idea of God.

Joseph Glanvil (1636–1680), of England, had even prior
to this defined the problem of causality in his *Scepsis
Scientifica* (1665), a book which was influenced by the
philosophy and the natural science of *Descartes*.   The
greater the difference between cause and effect the less
do we understand their connection.   Causality cannot
as a matter of fact be conceived at all (causality itself is
insensible).   Our perception is invariably limited to the
fact that two things succeed each other.

Glanvil and the *Occasionalists* are the antecedents of
Hume.   There are two additional thinkers who are
strongly influenced by *Descartes*, who however, each in his
own way, are radically opposed to him, and in fact challenge every attempt to solve ultimate problems with the
aid of reason.

Blaise Pascal (1623–1662) is closely related to *Descartes*
in his conception of scientific method, and he likewise accepts his concise distinction between mind and matter.
He makes frequent reference to these ideas in his *Pensées*.
But philosophy could not wholly satisfy him.   His heart
longed for a living God, finally even for a God of flesh and
blood, despite the fact that faith in such a God was repulsive to the understanding.   He required such a faith as
this to subdue the fear which the thought of the eternity
of the world had kindled within him.   The ideas of *Bruno*
and *Böhme* failed to give him peace.   Knowledge is un-
certain, and the learned are at variance.   Reason refutes
the dogmatic philosophers, nature the sceptical philosophers.   As a matter of fact in the last analysis the scep-
tics are right; otherwise were revelation unnecessary.   In
reply to those who find it difficult to subordinate reason

to faith, *Pascal* applies the Cartesian psychology and says: *We are machines as well as mind; begin with the machine, accustom yourself to the ceremonies, and your mind will also finally yield.*

Pierre Bayle (1647–1706) was rather a man of letters than a philosopher. His interest consisted in explaining and interpreting literary productions and speculative opinions in their manifold variety. But his desire for clearness impelled him to distinguish sharply between the various standpoints and to emphasize the crux of the problems rather than any illusory solution. (*Dictionnaire historique et critique*, 1695 ff.) He was particularly opposed to all efforts to reconcile faith and knowledge, theology and philosophy. He regarded the problem of evil as the great rock of offense. If we resolutely follow reason, it is impossible to reconcile the reality of evil with the omnipotence and goodness of God, and the only consistent solution that remains is the Manichæan assumption of two world principles, one evil, the other good. We are obliged to choose between reason and faith. (*Dictionnaire Art. Manicheisme.—Response aux questions d'un provincial.*) He nevertheless believes in a natural basis for ethics, and, furthermore, because the actions of men are determined more by their nature than by their religious opinions, he was in position to defend toleration and religious freedom with great zeal. (*Pensées diverses a l'occasion de la comète.*)

2. *Thomas Hobbes* (1588–1679) made the first independent attempt to treat the new mechanical theory of nature as the only science, to maintain its viewpoints as the only ones from which reality is to be conceived. Energetic as a thinker and controversialist, mild and timid in his mode of life, *Hobbes*, like *Descartes*, was dissatisfied with his scholastic training, and hence devoted himself to literary

pursuits,—e. g. he published a translation of Thucydides.
The unsettled conditions in England aroused his interest in
political and ethical questions, which soon led, especially
after he became acquainted with the new viewpoints of
natural science, to general philosophical investigations.
For a while he was private tutor and afterwards an intimate friend of the noble family *Cavendish*.   While travel-
ling in Italy he made the acquaintance of *Galileo*, and in
France he became a friend of *Pierre Gassendi* (1592–1655),
likewise an admirer of *Galileo*, who, having resigned his
clerical position, was then living in Paris as professor
of mathematics.   In his philosophical thought *Gassendi*
reveals a philosophical tendency similar to that of *Hobbes*
(*Opera Omnia*, Lugd., 1658). His revival of the Epicurean
atomic theory became a matter of signal importance, for
it was from the writings of *Gassendi* that *Newton* became
acquainted with this doctrine, and *Dalton*, the chemist,
afterwards received it from the writings of *Newton* and
adapted it to chemistry.   *Gassendi* insisted that all the
changes in nature must be explained by the motions of
atoms.   Following *Galileo*, *Gassendi* teaches (what *Descartes* had overlooked) that energy (*impetus*) is not dis-
sipated by actual motion.

Nevertheless, *Hobbes* seems to have arrived at the conclusion that all change is motion independently.   It was
during a discussion with several friends of what constitutes sensation that the thought occurred to him that
if everything in nature were motionless or in uniform motion there would be no sensation.   A change of motion
(*diversitas motuum*) is therefore the condition of sensation.
For sensing unceasingly one and the same thing and
sensing nothing at all amounts to the same thing.   This
principle, which *Hobbes* makes the basis of his psychology,

occurred to him early in life, and the conviction that all change consists of motion, and that sense-qualities are purely subjective, probably occurred about the same time (ca. 1630), at any rate before his acquaintance with *Galileo* and *Gassendi*.

At the outbreak of the revolution *Hobbes* left England and spent a number of years in France, where for a time he was tutor to the fugitive king *Charles II*. He returned under *Cromwell*, devoting himself privately to literary pursuits, occupied with studies and polemics until his death at the venerable age of ninety-one years. The series of articles and the splendid volume in Fromann's *Philosopische Klassiker* by *Ferdinand Tonnies* have contributed much towards a clear understanding of *Hobbes'* development and his philosophical significance.

Hobbes' chief works are: *Elements of Law* (1640), *De cive* (1642), *Leviathan* (1651), *De corpore* (1655), *De homine* (1658).

a. *Hobbes'* first concern in the systematic presentation of his theory given in the *De corpore* is to establish the fundamental principles of investigation. He is certain that these principles must be discovered by a process of analytical regression from the given to that which explains it (*a sensum ad inventionem principiorum*), just as he had previously in fact arrived at the doctrine of motion by a similar regression from sensation. But, on the other hand, he strongly emphasized the fact that the assumption of principles is purely an arbitrary matter, and must necessarily consist of a choice. He does not therefore regard such an analysis as a demonstration; deduction is the only method of demonstration, and this is impossible in the case of first principles.—*Hobbes* described the arbitrary act with which science begins more precisely as an act of naming. But this act is subject to certain conditions even from its very beginning; it is not permissible therefore to give two contradictory names to one and the same thing.

That all change consists of motion (*mutationem in motu consistere*) is therefore the most general principle of science. *Hobbes* thinks that, if we should only rid ourselves of all prejudices, the proof of this principle is wholly superfluous. He assumes several other, purely dogmatic, principles, without inquiring more closely into their respective conditions; the law of causation, the principle of inertia, the principle that only motion can be the cause of motion, and that only motion can be the result, and the principle of the persistence of matter.

If these principles are to explain all existence, then everything must be motion. The classifications of the system are therefore based on a classification of motion. First in order comes the theory concerning the *Corpus* (body in general); here he treats of the geometrical, mechanical and physical laws of motion. The second part contains the theory of the *Homo*, i. e. the motions which take place in Man; here the physiological and psychological motions are treated. The third part is the doctrine of the *Cives*, i. e. of the motions in men which condition their mutual relations and their association.

Hobbes was unable to complete his system by purely deductive processes. He was forced to concede the necessity of introducing new presuppositions at a number of points. Thus, e. g. when we pass from geometry to mechanics: *Hobbes* grants, that a pure geometrical explanation rests on an abstraction, and that we must assume the concept of energy (*conatus, impetus*) at the beginning of mechanics. The same is true when we pass from mechanics to physics: the sensible attributes of body (color, tone, etc.) are discovered only by means of sense perception, which involves a new inductive beginning at this point. And the last two main divisions of the system, the theories of the Homo and the Cives, we can establish by direct (psychological and historical) experience, without going through the first main division. *Hobbes* also wrote his psychological and political works (*Elements of Law, De cive, Leviathan*) before he had completed his theory of the Corpus.

If everything is motion, all reality must be corporeal. An incorporeal thing is a chimera (Unding). It follows therefore that science can only investigate finite things, since only finite things can be in motion. It is impossible to have any knowledge of the universe as a complete whole. All questions concerning the universe as a totality lead into the inconceivable and can only be determined by faith, not by knowledge. Science can tell us nothing concerning either the origin, extent or destiny of the universe. The highest science, the firstlings of wisdom (*primitia sapientiæ*), *Hobbes* remarks ironically, are reserved to the theologians, just as in Israel the firstlings of the harvest were sacrificed to the priests.

b. *Hobbes* started with sensation; from it he derived the principle of change, and thence the principle of motion. If everything is motion, therefore, sensation must likewise be motion. "Sensation is *nothing more* than a motion among the particles of the sensing body." And this applies to consciousness in general. In his criticism of *Descartes' Meditations Hobbes* says "Consciousness (*mens*) is *nothing more* than a motion in certain parts of an organic body." Motion is the reality, consciousness is only the form under which it becomes apparent (apparition). The feeling of pleasure, e. g., is really only a motion in the heart, thought only a motion in the head. The psychology of *Hobbes* is therefore merely a part of his general theory of motion. His materialistic tendency which is apparent at this point is modified by his clear insight into the subjective conditions of knowledge. In a remarkable passage (*De corpore*, xxv, 1) he says: "The very fact that anything can become a phenomenon (*id ipsum*) (το φαινεσφαι) is indeed the most wonderful of all phenomena." The fact that motion can be conceived, sensed, known, is therefore more wonderful than that it exists. The conception, the "apparition," then cannot itself be motion, but must be an evidence that there is still something else in the universe besides motion.

Sensation, memory and comparison are intimately related to each other. If the sensory stimulus vanishes, instantly, there is in fact no sensation (*sensio*), but only a vague impression (*phantasma*). Real sensation presupposes a distinction and comparison of such impressions. The sensory stimuli must therefore vary, in order to make sensation possible.—Memories follow certain laws: they reappear in the same order of sequence as the original sensations, unless disarranged by the feelings and impulses. All order and every definite relation governing our ideas (except our temporal order of sequence) are conditioned by the fact that we are actuated by a purpose and seek the means for the realization of that purpose. The constant fixation of our purpose (*frequens ad finem respectio*) brings system into our thoughts. The capriciousness of dream-ideas is explained by the absence of a constant purpose during sleep.

He derives all individual feelings and volitional experiences from the impulse of self-preservation. Pleasure and pain arise according as our organic life is fostered or suppressed. Every movement and every idea which is favorable to the persistence and advancement of life is conserved; detrimental motions and ideas are suppressed. Here again we are confronted with the idea of change as a condition of soul-life. There can be no feeling and no will without distinctions in experience. An absolute goal, attainable once for all, is unthinkable. If it were attained, the possibility of a wish or of effort would no longer exist and feeling would likewise be impossible. The greatest good can consist only in an unhindered progress towards ever higher goals.

The various forms of feeling and of desire appear as expressions of a feeling of power or of weakness. That is to say whether I feel pleasure or pain depends upon whether I am conscious of having the means of continued existence, development and satisfaction, and, as a matter of fact, it is through a consciousness of this sort that the feeling of power is conditioned by its opposite, the feeling of weakness (which can also be a dependence upon receiving help from friends or from God). Here the comparison with other men plays an important part, for my self-preservation is quite frequently favored as well as hindered by others (and their impulse to self-preservation). Life is a great race. Whenever we surpass others we rejoice, but we feel humbled when we fall behind; while we are making the best progress we are filled with hope, but doubt as we grow weary; we become angry when we see an unexpected obstacle, but we are proud when we have surmounted a serious difficulty; we laugh when we see another fall, but weep when we fall ourselves; we have a sense of sympathy when some one whom we wish well falls behind, indignation when some one whom we wish ill succeeds; love when we can assist another in the race, happiness when we are constantly overtaking those ahead of us, unhappiness when we are constantly falling behind. And the race ends only in death.

c. The human impulses of self-preservation are not primarily in mutual harmony: this is clearly manifested in the experiences of the great world-struggle. Strife will arise, and encroachments are always to be feared. The state of nature, i. e. the state of human life as it would be without state control, is a war of all against all (*bellum omnium contra omnes*). The sole governing principle at this stage is the unrestrained impulse and power of the individual, and fear, hatred, and the restless human passions are supreme. But in calmer moments (*sedato animo*) men perceive that greater advantage can be attained by cooperation and association than by strife. This gives rise to the moral principle: Strive for peace, but if peace is impossible, warfare must be organized! This principle gives rise to the special virtues and duties; fidelity, gratitude, complaisance, forbearance, justice and self-control are necessary if peace and society are to be possible. Hence the general rule, that *one must not do to others what he would not suffer from them*, likewise follows from this principle. But *Hobbes* likewise suggests that to be just towards others and to be able to give them aid (*animi magni opus proprium est auxiliari*) is a sign of strength and magnanimity.

But the efficient execution and maintenance of these laws and rules require a strong political organization. The freedom of the state of nature must be surrendered. This is accomplished either by an expressed or tacit contract, by which each individual at once renounces the right of his unconditioned impulse to self-preservation and pledges unqualified obedience to an established authority (a prince or a convention).—Whilst *Althusius* and *Grotius* made a distinction between the contract through which society originates and that upon which the authority of the state is founded, with *Hobbes* both coincide. He believes that, if the war of all against all is to be brought under control, the opposition between the governing power and the individual must be absolute, and he cannot therefore imagine that a people could exist without government. The governing power must therefore originally proceed from a decision of the people. *Hobbes* is the naturalistic exponent of absolute sovereignty. Every limitation (by class, parliament or church) would involve a division of power, and consequent retrogression to the state of nature. The will of the sovereign executes the will of the people and he alone (to whom indeed the natural rights of every individual are transferred in the original contract).

The sovereign must decide all questions touching religion and morality. He shall above all determine the manner in which God shall be worshipped: otherwise the worship of one would be blasphemy to another, resulting in a source of constant strife and disintegration. For the same reason, the ultimate definitions of good and evil must be fixed by the decree of the sovereign. The first principles of ethics and politics rest upon arbitrary enactment (in this case by the authority of the state).

Theoretically *Hobbes* anticipates the rationalistic despotism of the eighteenth century. He opposes hierarchy and class government and bases the hope of an enlightened political authority, through which the will of the intelligent public will receive recognition, on the prospect of a progressive educational development of the people (*paulatim eruditur vulgis!*).

3. *Baruch Spinoza's* (1632–1677) chief work (*Ethica ordine geometrico demonstrata*, 1677) represents the most profound effort of this period to elaborate the fundamental principles of the new conception of nature into a general world theory. This work, despite its abstract form, is by no means impersonal and purely theoretical. With *Spinoza*, thought and life are identical. Clear thinking was for him the way to spiritual freedom, the highest form of personal life. He aims to regard all the various aspects and forms of existence from the viewpoint of internal harmony. The majesty of his thought consists, first of all, in the resolute consistency with which he elaborates the various intellectual processes, each of which, in itself, expresses an essential characteristic of reality; every essential viewpoint must receive due recognition, without prejudice and without compromise; and, secondly, in the proof that every system of thought which is inherently self-consistent and complete nevertheless signifies nothing more than a single aspect or form of infinite Being. In this way he seeks to maintain unity and multiplicity, mind and matter, eternity and time, value and reality in their inner identity. Each of these fundamental concepts is in itself an expression of the total reality and can therefore be carried out absolutely.

In his chief work, mentioned above, he elaborates this theory deductively or synthetically. Beginning with definitions and axioms we advance through a series of doctrinal propositions. Owing to this method of treatment *Spinoza* failed to give his own ideas their true force. Their content is not adapted to this mode of treatment, and his proofs are therefore frequently untenable. Nor does the method pursued in his treatment correspond with the method by which he discovered his theory. The unfinished treatise *De emendatione intellectus* is the chief source of information concerning this method. Here he begins autobiographically after the manner of *Descartes* in his *Discours*. Experience has taught him that neither enjoyment, nor wealth, nor honor can be the highest good. He finds it, on the contrary, in the knowledge of the relation existing between our mind and nature as a whole. The pleasures of knowledge became his highest and strongest ambition, his ruling passion, and the glory conferred on existence through the possibility of participating in this joy is what made life worth living to him. It is for this very reason however that he institutes the inquiry as to the possibility of realizing this end, and he then indicates how he arrived at the definitions and axioms with which the "Ethics" begins.

Spinoza, the son of a Jewish merchant of Amsterdam, began his career as a Jewish theologian, inspiring great hopes among his brethren in the faith. He however gradually became increasingly critical of the ancestral ideas of faith and was finally ceremonially excommunicated from the synagogue. Thereafter he lived in the country for a while, moving thence to Rhynsberg, in the vicinity of Leyden, and finally to The Hague, occupied with study and the writing of his books. He provided a scanty living by grinding lenses. He enjoyed the active intellectual fellowship of a circle of young friends who studied his ethics, even while it only existed in manuscript. His life is a splendid example of happy resignation and inner devotion to intellectual labor.

The essay, *Von Gott, Menschen und dessen Glück*, written in his youth, is *Spinoza's* first attempt to bring what he regarded as essential in religious ideas into inner harmony with the scientific conception of nature. Later on he wrote an exposition of the Cartesian philosophy for one of his pupils; although strongly influenced by the writings of *Descartes* (together with Jewish theology and the works of scholasticism, and perhaps also by the works of *Bruno*) he was never a Cartesian. He likewise studied and used the works of *Bacon* and *Hobbes*.—In his *Tractatus theologico-politicus* (1670) he advocates religious liberty and makes some interesting contributions to the historical criticism of the various books of the Bible.

a. Our knowledge originates in incidental experience (*experientia vaga*). On this plane we arrange phenomena according to laws which are apparently mechanical, and we are satisfied so long as there is no exception. Science (*ratio*) however institutes exact comparisons of the given phenomena. It begins with experience, and then seeks to discover what belongs to nature as a whole as well as to its various parts—the universal laws, which prevail everywhere. *Spinoza* illustrates this by reference to the laws of motion in the realm of matter and the laws of the association of ideas in the realm of mind. It is only in these laws that our thought processes culminate, whilst the series of particular phenomena continue to infinity, because that which is cause in one relation is effect in another relation and vice versa. The only absolute which can satisfy intellect is the law which governs the causal series, not its supposed beginning or end. *Spinoza* calls this absolute Substance; *that which exists in itself and is to be understood through itself, so that its concept presupposes no other concepts.* *Spinoza's* Substance, the terminus of all thought, is therefore the principle of the uniformity of Nature.

Spinoza's discussion of the validity of knowledge is somewhat vacillating. At times he seems to hold the popular and scholastic definition of truth as the agreement of thought with its object. But when he examines the problem more closely he concludes that the perfection of knowledge consists of complete elaboration and internal consistency. He always regards error as negative, as due to the limitation of our experience and thought. Error is resolved by observing strict logical consistency; we eventually discover that we were regarding a part for the whole. Thus error finds its explanation in the truth: *veritas est norma sui et falsi.* Hence the norm of truth lies in the very nature of our thought, not in its relation to something external.

Knowledge of the laws of nature is however not the highest kind of knowledge. *Spinoza* places intuition above *experientia vaga* and reason. The former apprehends particular events and the latter discovers general principles, but in intuitive knowledge (*scientia intuitiva*) the particular phenomenon is immediately apprehended as a characteristic member of the whole system of nature, the particular being in its relation to the whole of Substance. This higher intuition is only acquired after we have passed through the stages of experience and science. *Spinoza* even says that he himself understood but very little in this highest manner. It appears to be more like an artificial intuition than a pure scientific conception.

We regard things from the standpoint of eternity (*sub specie æterni*) in the second as well as in the third form of knowledge; i. e. not in their isolation and contingency, but as members of a more comprehensive system.

b. Following *Descartes* and *Hobbes*, *Spinoza* bases his entire philosophy on the principle of causality, the validity of which, for him as for them, is self-evident. In his exposition of the law of causation he takes special pains to emphasize that cause and effect cannot be things which differ in kind. He says, e. g., that "If two things have nothing in common, the one cannot be the cause of the other; for then there would be nothing in the effect, which had also been in the cause, and everything in the effect would then have originated from nothing." According to *Spinoza* the fact that two things are related as cause and effect signifies that the concept of the one admits of a purely logical derivation from that of the other. He does not distinguish between cause and ground. He identifies the relation of cause and effect with the relation of premises and conclusion. The fact that cause precedes effect *in time*, as well as in thought, finds no place in his theory. "From the standpoint of eternity" time disappears.

The cause of an event may therefore exist in the event itself or in something else. That which has its cause within itself is *Substance*. Substance is that which exists in itself and is understood through itself, so that its concept does not presuppose any other concept. We have already observed that *Spinoza*'s fundamental principle is revealed in the uniformity of nature. It is therefore the fundamental presupposition of all existence and efficiency. It follows from his definition, that it exists necessarily: it contains its cause within itself, and hence nothing can prevent its existence! Only one Substance is possible: for, if there were several, they would limit each other, in which case neither one could be understood from itself. It is likewise self-evident that Substance can neither have beginning nor come to an end, neither be divided nor limited.

This concept, which is *Spinoza's* inner terminus of all thought, is at once identical with the concept of God and the concept of Nature. These concepts must then how-ever be conceived of in a different manner than usual. Nature is the inherent energy which is active in every-thing which exists (*natura naturans*), not the mere sum of all existence (*natura naturata*). "*I have an opinion about God and Nature*," says *Spinoza*, "*which is different from that commonly held by modern Christians. I hold that God is the internal, not the external, cause of all things. That is, I hold, with St. Paul, that all things live and move in God.*" Another divergence from the ordinary concept of God is contained in the fact that *Spinoza* does not think that hu-man attributes, such as understanding and will, can be ascribed to the Deity; for understanding presupposes given experiences which shall be understood, and will presup-poses that there are ideals which are as yet unrealized, each of which would contradict the absolute perfection of God.

Spinoza calls the things which do not contain their cause within themselves *Modi* (phenomena, individual things). The *Modus* is caused by something other than itself, through which alone it can be understood. The real cause of the Modi is contained in Substance, of which they are the particular manifestations. Externally they stand in a causal relation to each other, but the total aggregate of the Modi, the total series of causes and effects given in experience (the total natura naturata), is a revelation of Substance, which constitutes the vital relation of the whole series of phenomena.

c. According to *Spinoza* real existence can only be ascribed to Substance. Phenomena are its particular Forms. Everything which exists (Substance and its Modi), therefore, comes into experience under two *attri-butes* (fundamental characters or fundamental forms): thought and extension (mind and matter). As an infinite and perfect being Substance must have an infinite number of Attributes; but we know only two, because experience reveals no more to us. An attribute is what thought conceives of Substance as constituting its essence (*essentiam substantiæ constituens*). This definition implies that the whole nature of Substance must be present in every Attribute, in every fundamental form; each individual attribute must therefore, like Substance itself, be understood through itself, and its concept cannot be derived from any other concept. Everything which pertains to a given Attribute must be explained by means of this attribute alone, without reference to any other Attributes; thoughts must therefore be explained only by means of thoughts, material phenomena only by means of material phenomena. Not only Substance as such, but each of its phenomena, each Modus, e. g. man, can be regarded and explained completely under each Attribute. The nature of reality is revealed in the realm of matter as well as in the realm of mind, and the one form of manifestation cannot be derived from the other. Mind and matter (soul and body) are one and the same, only viewed from different sides.—*Spinoza* holds, in opposition to *Descartes*, that two irreducible attributes do not necessarily require two different natures, but that they can very easily pertain to one and the same nature. He differs from *Hobbes* in that he does not regard mind as a mere effect or form of matter, but sees in it an aspect of being quite as distinctive and primary as matter.—*Descartes*, *Hobbes* and *Spinoza* represent the three leading hypotheses concerning the relation of mind and matter.

Spinoza elaborates his theory of mind and matter (which in recent times has frequently been described by the unfortunate term parallelism, or the identity hypothesis) according to the deductive method, because he derives it from his definitions of Substance, Attribute and Modi. We have however already called attention to the fact that he discovered his definitions by means of the analysis of experience and of knowledge. The definition of Attribute presupposes the fundamental principle of the identity of cause and effect, previously mentioned; from this presupposition the relation between the Attributes follows in the same manner as the relation between Substance and Modi. That everything which pertains to a given Attribute must be explained by reference to that attribute is really nothing more than a metaphysical paraphrase of the principle that material phenomena can only be explained by means of material phenomena. *Kepler's vera causa* makes the same demand. That this is really what *Spinoza* meant becomes quite apparent from the following expression: "If any one should say that this or that bodily activity proceeds from the soul, he knows not what he is talking about, and really grants that we do not know the cause of such activity."—He nevertheless likewise calls attention to the fact that the development of the soul advances proportionately with the development of the body, and that we have no right to set arbitrary limits to the material uniformity of nature.

Spinoza does not regard the hypothesis of identity as a mere psychophysical theory. He likewise gives it an epistemological significance in that he speaks of an identity of thought with its object. Here he confuses the relation of subject and object with the relation of soul and body. This is the more remarkable, since he holds that the validity of knowledge depends on its logical consistency rather than on the agreement with its objects. But he is also somewhat vacillating on this last point, which is an after-effect of the scholastic studies of his youth.

Criticism of this most rationalistic of all systems of philosophy must first of all be directed against the central proposition of the homogeneity (or really identity) of cause and effect. Should this proposition prove untenable or even be incapable of consistent elaboration, it must follow that, in the last analysis, Being is not, as *Spinoza* believed, absolutely rational. We shall find this problem discussed by the English empiricists and by the critical philosophers.

d. *Spinoza* teaches, in harmony with this theory of error, that every idea is regarded as true, so long as it is not supplanted by another. Our theory of reality is developed through the rivalry of ideas. The most comprehensive and most consistent theory is the truest.

Spinoza's elaboration of the psychology of the emotions as given in his "Ethics" is unsurpassed in its excellence. Like *Hobbes* he starts from the impulse of self-preservation. But he bases it on the consistency of his system. The infinite Substance is actively present in every individual being (*modus*); the effort towards self-preservation of each individual being is therefore a part of the divine activity. Hence whenever effort is successful, it produces pleasure, and conversely pain. But this only occurs in case of a transition to a more perfect or less perfect state; an absolutely changeless state would neither give rise to pleasure nor pain.—The various emotional qualities result from the association of ideas. We love what produces pleasure, and hate what produces pain. We love whatever contributes to our love, and hate what constrains it. When a being similar to ourselves ex-

periences pleasure or pain, the same emotion involuntarily arises in us. But this moreover not only gives
rise to sympathetic joy and sorrow, but it may also
inspire envy and pleasure at the misfortune of others,
i. e. if we ourselves wish to enjoy another's pleasures,
or if we are previously filled with hatred towards the
unfortunate.—Just as pleasure becomes love by means of
the idea of its cause, so mere appetite (*appetitus, conatus*) becomes desire (*cupiditas*), when joined with the
idea of its object.

In *Spinoza's* description of emotional and volitional
life we discover a degree of vacillation between a purely
intellectualistic and a more realistic (or voluntaristic)
theory. In several passages he describes the emotions
as confused and inadequate ideas (*ideæ confusæ et
inadequatæ*), which vanish as soon as the idea becomes
perfectly clear. But there are other passages in which
the emotions are regarded as real, positive states, which
can only be displaced by other real states. The same
thing occurs with the concept of the will. In several
passages volition is treated as one with the activity of
thought; will and understanding are identical. But
in other passages the will is identical with the impulse
of self-preservation, and all ideas of value and value-
judgments are dependent on it; "We seek, choose,
desire and wish for a thing, not because we think it is
good, but, inversely, we think a thing is good, because
we seek, choose, desire and wish for it." In this case
therefore he asserts the priority of the will.—This vacillation is evidently (in agreement with *F. Tonnies* in
Vierteljahrsschrift für wissenschaftliche Philosophie, VII)
to be explained from the fact that, during the preparation of the *Ethics*, *Spinoza's* older, intellectualistic con-

ception was supplanted by a more realistic conception under the influence of *Hobbes* without a thoroughgoing application of the logical consequences of the new conception.

e. *Spinoza* bases his ethics on the instinct of self-preservation.—Man is conditioned by the fact of being one among many individual beings, and obstacles constantly thwart his instincts. As a member of the total series of causes and effects man does not contain his cause within himself, he is not active, but passive, not free, but necessitated. The sense of dependence enables man to strive for freedom and independence. He then imagines an ideal of human life (*idea hominis, tanquam naturæ humanæ examplar*), as it would be under conditions of perfect freedom and independence. This furnishes a standard of judgment: *whatever contributes towards the realization of that ideal is good; whatever prevents it is evil*. The predicates *"good"* and *"evil"* which are meaningless when applied to absolute Being, Substance, become significant from the viewpoint of temporal experience and finite development. *Sub specie æterni* there is no ethics; all antitheses and differences, and moreover all valuation, disappear when so considered.

A desire can be subdued only by another desire, and hence, if the ideal is to govern our life, it must either give rise to or become a desire. Duty then becomes a matter of making this desire as strong as possible. Social life is a means to this end. Men can make better provision for self-preservation by uniting their energies. Spiritual goods, especially knowledge, which furnishes the only possible means to perfect freedom and activity, can only be acquired under conditions which guarantee the external means of subsistence and this is more readily obtained in organized society than otherwise. Spiritual, unlike material, goods, which only one or a few can possess, are not the occasion of strife; they are rather the common possession of everyone, and here the individual can assist others without sustaining any loss to himself. The courageous instinct of self-preservation (*fortitudo*), which constitutes virtue, appears therefore not only in the form of vital energy (*animositas*), i. e. as power to impress the influence of one's personality, but also in generosity (*generositas*), i. e. power to lend spiritual and material assistance to others.—But the acme of spiritual freedom can nevertheless only be attained through a perfect understanding of ourselves, in our real identity with that which is most essential and highest in Being, because we conceive our own energy as a part of infinite energy and we are filled with an intellectual love for Deity brought about by the joy of knowledge (*amor intellectualis dei*). We then see ourselves *sub specie æternitatis*.

——In his theory of the state, contained partly in the *Tractatus theologico-politicus*, partly in the unfinished *Tractatus Politicus*, *Spinoza*, like *Hobbes*, draws a sharp distinction between the state of nature and life within the state ; but he likewise holds that it is the duty of the state to secure a greater degree of freedom and independence than would be possible in a state of nature. The individual does not surrender his liberty when he becomes a member of the state. The state is not supposed to reduce men to animals or machines, but to provide the conditions for the development of man's spiritual and bodily functions. It would therefore contradict its office if it failed to maintain liberty of thought and speech and to guarantee complete religious liberty.

4. *Gottfried Wilhelm Leibnitz* (1646–1716), like his three predecessors, *Descartes*, *Hobbes* and *Spinoza*, is convinced of the importance of the mechanical explanation of nature. His three predecessors regarded the mechanical principles as self-evident and as given once for all, and assumed the task of interpreting the various elements of reality in harmony with the principle of mechanical causality. *Leibnitz* however subjects the principle of causality to a profounder analysis by inquiring into its presuppositions and seeking to refer it back to something still more fundamental. It is only after he has succeeded in this that he proceeds to the definition of the relation between matter and mind. The motive for this investigation was in part purely theoretical, due to the fact that *Leibnitz* discovered gaps and inconsistencies in his predecessors, in part practical, due to his desire to bring the modern explanation of nature into more perfect harmony with his religious presuppositions. He attempted to accomplish both at a single stroke, by means of a single idea, the idea of *continuity*.

Even as a boy, in the library of his father, who was a professor in Leipzig, *Leibnitz* had become familiar with the writings of Scholasticism. When he afterwards became acquainted with the natural science and philosophy of his own day he felt as if "transported into another world." He saw that the new ideas could not be refuted, but neither could he surrender the conviction that nature is ultimately regulated by prescience, that is to say, that the mechanism must be grounded in teleology. His mathematical ideas were influenced profoundly by the physicist *Huygens* during a visit in Paris, and he afterwards likewise drew personally close to *Spinoza*. From 1676 onwards he lived at Hannover as councillor and librarian, occupied with philosophy, mathematics, history and jurisprudence. His broadly comprehensive mind was capable of engaging productively in a wide range of subjects to their material advancement. He was everywhere affected by the controlling idea of continuity, which can only be rigorously carried through by the continual discovery of more numerous and finer distinctions and nuances of thought.

a. *Leibnitz* discovered a difficulty in *Descartes'* and *Spinoza's* theory that the sum total of motion in the universe always remains constant, namely, that it fails to explain how to account for motion and rest respectively in the various parts of the universe: They exist as antithetical states! Continuity can be established only through the concept of Force (or tendency, *conatus*). If motion has ceased at a given point in the universe, the Force still remains and can be revived again. Motion and rest are only relatively opposed to each other. Instead of the persistence of motion we should speak of the persistence of Force. Force is the factor in any given circumstance which contains the possibility of future change. We first discover a uniform relation between two states and we afterwards call the factor in the first state which makes the second state possible Force. The concept of Force therefore rests on the concept of law, the ultimate presupposition of which is the uniform consistency of changing states. *Leibnitz* calls this presupposition *the principle of sufficient reason*.

But how shall we account for the persistence of energy? According to *Leibnitz* this question can be answered only teleologically. If the energy of a cause were not preserved in the effect, nature would retrograde, which contradicts divine wisdom. *Leibnitz* thus finds a basis for his faith in prescience in the corrected basal principle of mechanical natural science. In explaining particular facts he would apply the strict mechanical method, but the principle of mechanism itself requires the principle of teleology for its explanation.

b. *Leibnitz* carries his analysis further than his predecessors at still another point. They had regarded extension as a fundamental attribute of Being. *Leibnitz* challenges this assumption. Extended things are always manifold and complex, and the true realities are the elements which constitute things. If there were no absolute units (which cannot be extended), there would be no real existence. It is only these ultimate units that can be regarded as Substance (in its strict significance). Inasmuch therefore as Force persists, it follows that this persistent Substance must likewise be Force; it would be utterly impossible for activity to originate from Substances in a state of absolute rest. *Leibnitz* calls these substantial units, whose objective manifestation constitutes matter, Monads. Each Monad is a little universe; its nature is revealed in the laws which govern its inner successive changes.

What then, as a matter of fact, are these Monads? *Leibnitz* answers: Our souls alone furnish us with an immediate example of a unitary being, whose inner states follow a uniform law. We must think of all Monads after this analogy, because we presuppose something in all of them analogous to our sensations and activities. Since, according to the principle of continuity, we permit no leaps in nature, we must postulate innumerable grades and degrees of soul life in the universe. And this enables us to understand the origin of human consciousness. Here the Cartesians, just as in the case of the transition from rest to motion, were confronted by a riddle; for consciousness like motion cannot come into being all at once. The relation of the unconscious to consciousness is analogous to the relation of rest and motion. In order to vindicate the continuity of soul-life, *Leibnitz* directs attention to the fine nuances and changes of consciousness which are frequently overlooked. We are likewise obliged to postulate such minimal elements (petites perceptions) in the unconscious.

Leibnitz first elaborated this, his so-called theory of Monads, in a short essay in 1685 (*Petit discours de metaphysique*) and in his correspondence with *Arnauld* during the following year, but not until he had prepared the way for it by a number of earlier essays. He afterwards published several expositions of the theory especially in the *Système nouveau* (1695) and in the *Monadologie* (1714).—*Leibnitz* approaches his system first by the method of analysis, and then by the method of analogy. He seeks the ultimate presuppositions of science and then explains these presuppositions by means of analogy. Here he made a very important discovery, in showing that analogy is the only method by which to construct a positive metaphysics. Every mythology, religion and metaphysical system had used this method; but *Leibnitz* is the first to understand the principle which forms its basis. His system, the first attempt at a metaphysical idealism (i. e. the theory that the fundamental principle of reality is spiritual) since *Plato* and the pattern of all later idealistic attempts, has, to say nothing of its content, a permanent interest just because of this clear consciousness of its source. However if we should ask him why he uses the principle of analogy with so much assurance, he would answer: Because its help offers the only possibility of comprehending reality and because reality—on the basis of the principle of sufficient reason —must be comprehensible.

c. It was *Leibnitz'* intention that his doctrine of Monads should form the complete antithesis to Spinozism. Whilst *Spinoza* recognized only one Substance, *Leibnitz* postulated an infinite number, each of which forms a universe of its own, or, to invert the expression, constitutes a separate view of the universe. Each Monad develops by virtue of an inner necessity, just like *Spinoza's* Substance. *Leibnitz'* theory thus appears to be an absolute pluralism in contrast with an equally absolute monism. *Leibnitz'* only explanation of the ultimate correspondence and harmony of the Monads however, without which they could not constitute a universe, involves the reference to their common origin in God. The Monads issue or radiate from God, in a manner similar to the way in which Substance, according to *Spinoza*, impelled by the instinct of self-preservation, produced the Modes. But at this point—the conception of unity and multiplicity— *Leibnitz* encounters a difficulty which is even greater than that of *Spinoza*, since even God—just as every reality— must likewise be a Monad together with the other Monads, whilst *Spinoza's* Substance maintains vital relation with the Modes.

Leibnitz also approaches very close to *Spinoza* in his conception of the relation of mind and matter. He insists on the continuity of all material processes and can therefore neither accept any transition from matter to mind nor any influence of mind upon matter. Extension is only the external sensible form of psychical states: that which takes place in the soul finds its material expression in the body and vice versa. *Leibnitz* therefore defends the hypothesis of identity just as *Spinoza* had done. He however gives it an idealistic cast, since he regarded the absolute reality as psychical, and denied the Spinozistic coordination of the two attributes.

d.   A perfect continuity pervades the separate Monads, i. e. the individual life of the soul, just as the Monads among themselves form a complete continuous series. Every conceivable degree of soul-life exists, unconscious as well as conscious. *Leibnitz* developed his views on psychology and the theory of knowledge, as a polemic directed against *Locke*, in his *Nouveaux Essais* (which only appeared long after his death). He criticizes the assertion that the soul is originally a blank tablet. The obscure impulses of the soul must not be ignored. Just in proportion as the distinction and contrast between our sensations are small, the less a single element is distinguishable from the remaining content of the soul, or, more briefly, the more obscure the psychical states are, so much the more readily is their existence denied. But there are no absolute divisions, but rather every possible degree of variation between obscurity and clearness. *Leibnitz* calls the obscure changes within ourselves, which do not really rise to consciousness, perceptions; they correspond to the phantasmata of *Hobbes*. The lowest forms of being, the Monads of the lowest degree, never rise above such perceptions. We approach a higher level when perceptions are combined with memory and consequently possess more than mere momentary significance; consciousness is then present (sentiment, cf. *Hobbes'* sensio). The highest degree is characterized by attention to its own states; here *Leibnitz* uses the terms apperception and conscience; conscience is connaissance reflexive de l'etat interieur, i. e. self-consciousness, not consciousness in general. The fact that the Cartesians attributed psychical life to human beings alone was due, according to *Leibnitz*, to their failure to observe the innumerable gradations of psychical life. Here, even as in material nature, the clear and sensibly apparent is a resultant, an integration of small magnitudes. The apparent evanescence of psychical life is merely a transmutation into more obscure, more elementary forms. The minute distinctions escape observation, and yet we are never wholly indifferent to them (just as in material nature there is no such thing as absolute rest). It is only when the distinctions become great and sharp that we are clearly aware of ourselves and feel the contrast between the self and the rest of the universe.

Leibnitz applies the principle of continuity consistently throughout, both in psychology and in the philosophy of nature, on the basis of the concept of minute differentia. As a mathematician the same thought process led him to the discovery of the integral calculus. His "differentials" are infinitely small magnitudes (or changes of magnitude), but they eventually constitute a finite magnitude through summation (integration). His great mind was occupied with problems in widely different fields of knowledge, but the general type of his thought was everywhere the same.

In referring all the distinctions of mental life to distinctions of obscurity and clearness, he is a forerunner of the century of enlightenment. But we must not overlook the fact that the obscure states have an infinite content, for each Monad is a mirror of the whole universe, even though it is conscious of only a part of it. A finite being is therefore incapable of complete and perfect enlightenment; its sole prospect consists of continuous effort. *Leibnitz* likewise discovers a tendency (appetit-tendance) in the soul, to pass from the single "perceptions" to new perceptions. This is an element which presupposes other distinctions than obscurity and clearness. Both *Spinoza* and *Leibnitz* contain suggestions of a profounder theory of will, which is suppressed by their intellectualistic tendency.

e. Although *Leibnitz,* in opposition to *Locke,* maintains the involuntary and unconscious foundation of knowledge, and objected to the idea of a tabula rasa, he is still in agreement with *Locke's* criticism of "innate ideas" in requiring a proof for all truths, even the "innate," that are not identical propositions. To prove a proposition means to trace it back to an identical proposition. According to him logic culminates in the principle of identity whilst the Aristotelians and Scholastics base their theory on the principle of contradiction. He had sketched an outline of logic in which each judgment is stated in the form of an identical proposition. But this sketch was unknown until 1840 (in *J. E. Erdmann's Opera philosophica Leibnitii*), and the logical investigations of *Boole* and *Jevons,* which reveal a similar tendency, were the first to direct attention to them.

Just as the principle of identity is the criterion of truth in the realm of pure thought, so is the principle of sufficient reason in the realm of experience. *Leibnitz* however, even as *Spinoza,* never made a clear distinction between ground and cause (ratio and causa). He regarded this principle not only as a principle of scientific investigation, but as a universal law.—The difference between truths of experience ("contingent" truths) and truths of pure thought ("necessary" truths) is only a matter of degree: the former can be reduced to identical propositions by a finite, the latter by an infinite analysis. The relation is similar to that which obtains between rational and irrational numbers.

f. The whole of the Leibnizian philosophy is characterized by a harmonizing and conciliatory tendency. He is especially anxious to combine mechanism with teleology, but without compromising the integrity of either. Teleology is simply to be another way of construing mechanism. He says that "everything in nature can be explained by final causes (causæ finales) quite as well as by efficient causes (causæ efficientes)."

But he is not satisfied to stop with this purely philosophical theory, notwithstanding the fact that its empirical verification contained an abundance of problems. He was also anxious to effect a reconciliation between ecclesiastical theology and philosophy. He wrote the *Theodicée* in refutation of *Bayle,* just as he had written the *Nouveaux Essais* in refutation of *Locke.* Here he employs the distinction between *"necessary"* and *"contingent"* truths: nothing can contradict the former; but since "contingent" truths can never be reduced to a final analysis, such as the principle of sufficient reason requires, we are compelled to go beyond the series of actual causes (extra seriem) and postulate a first cause, which is self-caused. The universe, actually created by this first cause, was not the only one possible; —according to the principle of sufficient reason—it must have been given the preference only because it was the best possible. Before the creation of the world the various possibilities presented a conflict in the Divine mind. This world was given the preference because it offered the greatest harmony together with the greatest multiplicity. But even such a world cannot be entirely free from fault. It is impossible for the Divine Nature to reveal itself in finite nature without encountering numerous obstacles and limitations. . Suffering ("physical evil") and sin ("moral evil") are consequences of these obstacles ("metaphysical evil").—This reminds us of the mythology of *Jacob Böhme*. *Leibnitz* must concede to *Bayle* that the world is governed by two principles, with this modification, namely, that he ascribes the one to the divine will, which reduces evil to a minimum, the other to the divine understanding, which determines the various possible world forms.

But these are not the only arguments which *Leibnitz* adduces. He cites the infinitude of the universe, as admitting the possibility that the evil which we experience in our part of the universe (which is perhaps the worst part!) may be insignificant as compared with the world as a whole. This argument is new. It had only become possible through the new world-theory of *Copernicus* and *Bruno*. On the other hand, *Leibnitz* employs an old argument when he says that evil and sin were necessary in order that the good and the beautiful might be rendered conspicuous by contrast. This view occurs already in *Plotinus* and *Augustine*. It is rather æsthetic than moral. And moreover the sacrifice of single parts of the universe, i. e. single Monads, for the good of others, conflicts with *Leibnitz'* own theory.

Leibnitz bases his ethical ideas on the longing for perfection, i. e. for a higher degree of energy and greater spiritual harmony. The sense of pleasure is correlated with an abundance and harmony of energies. The individual is spontaneously impelled to strive not only for his own happiness, but likewise for the happiness of others. In the controversy between *Bossuet* and

Fenelon on the question of "disinterested love," *Leibnitz* agrees with *Fenelon*, affirming the reality and the value of such love ; he however emphasizes the fact that the happiness of others likewise affects us by way of reaction. He regards justice, conceived as the harmony of love and wisdom (caritas sapientis), as the highest virtue. Love is the end, and wisdom discovers the means.—*Leibnitz'* theory, which he elaborated in two small dissertations, *Von der Glückseligkeit* and *De nutionibus juris et justitiæ*, is closely related to that of *Shaftesbury*, with which we shall become acquainted in the next division. Even *Leibnitz* himself referred to their similarity.

THIRD BOOK.

ENGLISH EMPIRICAL PHILOSOPHY.

The great system builders did indeed begin with analysis, but the foundations upon which they built were concepts and presuppositions just the same, and these were not carefully investigated. This is specially true of the principle of causation and several of the principles of natural science, which were regarded as self-evident. The method of using presuppositions without inquiring into their validity has, since the time of *Kant*, been called dogmatism. It is the great merit of English philosophy that it instituted an investigation of the presuppositions of knowledge. It investigates the psychological processes which give rise to these presuppositions, as well as the methods of demonstrating their validity. The problem of psychology and the theory of knowledge thus come into the foreground, and the problem of being gradually recedes into the background.

The consequences of this transposition of problems were of great importance in other departments as well as in the specific domain of philosophy. People began to demand a definite account, not only of scientific presuppositions, but also of the principles which were regarded as fundamental in politics, religion and education. Authorities, which had hitherto been accepted without hesitation, must now give an account of their origin and their trustworthiness. Stated in philosophical terms this means that the problem of evaluation now became more prominent than formerly. This is a matter that can neither be solved by an appeal to authority nor by a mere deduction from theoretical principles, but requires a method of treatment peculiarly its own. The foundation of ethics likewise receives independent treatment more frequently than hitherto.

1. *John Locke* (1632–1704) devotes his chief work, the *Essay Concerning the Human Understanding* (1690), to the investigation of the nature and validity of human knowledge. The first draft of this pioneer work was brought about by a discussion of moral and religious subjects. When it became evident how difficult it is to arrive at definite conclusions, the thought occurred to *Locke* that they must first of all examine the faculty of knowledge, in order to see what subjects it is capable of treating, and moreover what things are beyond its powers. In the first book *Locke* criticizes the doctrine of innate ideas, especially in the form in which it was held by *Herbert of Cherbury;* in the second book he shows that all ideas come from experience, and reduces compound ideas to their simple elements; in the third book he investigates the influence of language on thought; and in the fourth he examines the different kinds of knowledge and defines its limits.

John Locke received a splendid education from his father. He pays a beautiful tribute to his father in his splendid essay *On Education* (1692). But the formal grammatical discipline and the scholastic instruction received at school and the university were repulsive to him. His philosophical development was influenced chiefly by the study of *Descartes, Gassendi* and *Hobbes.* Being unable to subscribe to the 39 Articles, he had to relinquish his original plan of becoming a clergyman. He afterwards studied medicine, but soon entered the service of the *Earl of Shaftesbury*, with whose family he remained connected for two generations, as tutor, secretary and friend. At the fall of the Earl, *Locke* went to Holland, where he composed his most important works and likewise participated in the preparations for the revolution. He returned to England with *William of Orange*, and helped to formulate the policies of the new administration. He spent his last years in rural solitude.

a. In *Locke's* terminology idea represents everything with which we are occupied when engaged in thought. Some have supposed that certain ideas, especially the idea of God and the logical and moral principles, are innate, but experience shows that children, primitive races and the illiterate possess nothing more than particular and sensible ideas. There are men who have no idea of God and no real ideas of morality. Some of our ideas are natural, i. e. such as have been acquired through experience by means of our native faculty; but even these are not innate. *Locke* attributes the doctrine of innate ideas to human indolence, which shrinks from the labor involved in exploring the origin of ideas.

All ideas, all the elements of consciousness originate from two sources: external experience (sensation) and internal experience (reflection). In external experience a physical impression produces a sensation (perception) in the soul; in internal experience we observe the activity of our own mind in elaborating the sensations received from without.

In the acquisition of simple ideas consciousness is for the most part passive. Simple external ideas are of two kinds: ideas of primary and of secondary qualities. The primary qualities can be attributed to the external objects themselves ; such are solidity, extension, figure, mobility. Secondary qualities belong only to our ideas, they are not attributes of the things themselves; they are the results of the influences of primary qualities on us. Such secondary ideas are light, sound, smell, taste, &c.—We have previously met with this distinction in *Galileo*, *Descartes* and *Hobbes*. *Locke* adopted it from *Boyle*, the noted chemist, who is the author of the terms "primary and secondary qualities."

Whilst we are largely passive in acquiring simple ideas, we are active in forming from them, first, complex ideas, second, ideas of relations, third and finally, abstract ideas. Hence there are three forms of activity: composition, association and abstraction. We combine simple ideas into a single idea whenever we form ideas of attributes (modes), such as space and time, energy and motion. The ideas of such attributes as sensation, memory and attention are formed in inner experience. We form our ideas of things or substances by combining ideas of modes. But here a mystery confronts us. We know the single modes by themselves, but we are unable to tell what substance, which presumably supports the modes, really is.—We may likewise place two ideas in juxtaposition, without forming a compound idea. We do this in all cases of ideas of relation, such as cause and effect, time and space relations, identity and difference.— Finally we are active also when we *abstract or isolate* an idea from its original connection. This happens when we form an idea of a color in general, or the idea of space without reference to its content.

b. Touching the matter of validity, *Locke* holds that there can be no question in the case of simple ideas because they are the direct effect of external objects. Even secondary qualities, which do not represent objects, are nevertheless the direct results of objective impressions.

The matter stands quite differently however when we come to consider the validity of the ideas which we ourselves produce (in the three ways noted above)! They cannot of course be copies or impressions! We use them however as archetypes, or patterns, with which to make comparisons. In this case, therefore, we estimate objects from the viewpoint of their agreement or disagreement with the patterns of our own construction. But compound, relative and abstract ideas furnish no information whatever as to the real nature of things. It is in this sense that we use figures in mathematics, and moral ideals in ethics. The proofs of mathematics and moral philosophy are wholly independent of the existence of the things to which they refer. But such is not the case with the idea of substance, which is expressly intended to indicate an external object. The validity of ideas of this kind can only be established therefore on the basis of a complex of attributes given in experience, or if, as in the case of the idea of God, we are in position to offer a separate proof for its validity.

In agreement with *Descartes*, *Locke* distinguishes between *intuition* and *demonstration*. Intuition merely furnishes us knowledge of self and of the simplest relations between our ideas. The combination of a series of intuitions results in demonstration. These two kinds of knowledge alone are fully certain; sense experience is always only probable.—*Locke* proves the existence of God by appealing to the principle of causality: The world must have a cause, and, since matter cannot produce spirit, the cause of the universe must be a spiritual being. He regards our knowledge of the causal principle itself as an intuition, i. e. as self-evident. At this point he agrees with the dogmatic systematizers. Hence he likewise employs this principle complaisantly both in his proof of the validity of simple ideas and of the existence of God. But the causal idea on the other hand belongs to the class of relative ideas, which is therefore a subjective construction albeit on the basis of sense-perception. *Locke* is rather ambiguous at this point (as also on the idea of substance). The profound problems involved in these ideas were not discovered until *Locke's* successors (*Berkeley* and *Hume*) came upon them.

c. In the philosophy of law, *Locke* (in the *Essay on Government*, 1689) makes a sharp distinction between political and patriarchal authority. Political authority consists in the authority to prescribe laws, to enforce the laws which are prescribed, and to protect society against foreign enemies. Such authority can be established only by unconstrained agreement, which may however be tacitly concluded. It is the duty of the state to secure liberty, which, in a state of nature, is constantly in danger of being lost. If the government proves unfaithful to its trust, the people have the right to overthrow it.

In his philosophy of religion (*The Reasonableness of Christianity as Delivered in the Scriptures*, 1695) *Locke* conceives revealed religion as a more developed form of natural religion. Whether or not anything is revelation must be decided by reason. Revelation is necessary, however, on account of the fact that man has not used his reason properly and has consequently fallen into superstition. An elaborate system of doctrine is unnecessary. The illiterate and the poor, whose lives are spent in bitter toil, readily understand the example and teachings of *Christ.*—The English Free-thinkers (the so-called Deists) developed *Locke's* philosophy of religion more fully in the direction of a more pronounced rationalism.

The most important representative of this tendency was *John Toland* (1670-1720), who says, in his *Christianity Not Mysterious* (1696), that there is nothing in the Gospel which either transcends or conflicts with reason; but that priests and philosophers had transformed Christianity into a mystery. In his *Pantheisticon* (1720) he describes pantheism as the private theory of a society of enlightened gentlemen, who conceive God as the efficient energy of the universe. His most important book is the *Letters to Serena* (1704), in which he says, against the Cartesian and Spinozistic conception of nature, that motion is an attribute of matter which is equally primary with extension. Motion persists everywhere in nature, and all rest is only apparent.

2. Neither *Locke* nor the great systematizers of the seventeenth century had fully accepted the sublime ideal of knowledge proposed by *Kepler* and *Galileo*. They still regarded experience and reason as mutually exclusive. It was all the more significant therefore that *Sir Isaac Newton* (1642-1727), in his *Principia Philosophiæ Naturalis Mathematica* (1684), should furnish the most famous product of exact empirical science by means of a combination of induction and deduction. This work had a decisive influence on the further development of philosophy. But this is not the only ground for making reference to *Newton* in the history of philosophy. He is likewise the author of certain characteristic philosophic ideas.

Starting from the fact that weight is greater in the valley than on the mountain tops, and that all bodies which are tossed upward drop to the earth, *Newton* formulated the hypothesis that the heavenly bodies are also heavy and that they deviate from the direction implied by the law of inertia according to a ratio which corresponds to the law of falling bodies at the earth's surface. He then deduces the mathematical consequences of this idea and finally shows that the results of this deduction agree with the facts as actually observed. From this he concludes that the motion of the heavenly bodies is governed by the same law as falling bodies. He calls the energy which manifests itself in this law attraction (attractio). He does not introduce any mystical energy. By attraction he means only an energy which acts according to the well-known law of falling bodies—which likewise constitutes the energy.—As a matter of fact he was later inclined, and his disciples even more so, to regard attraction as an original energy proceeding directly from God.

The expositions of *Newton's* masterpiece likewise involve presuppositions and speculative ideas which are of philosophical importance.—He makes a distinction between "absolute, true, and mathematical space" and sensible spaces. Absolute motion occurs in the former alone, because it contains absolute places (loca primaria), places which are at once places for themselves (sine relatione ad externum quodvis) as well as for other things. Following *Copernicus* and *Kepler*, *Newton* defends the ancient theory of absolute space. He does not simply regard the mathematical method of interpretation as a way of looking at things, which may be regarded as mathematically fundamental, but rather as the true method of interpretation in contrast with the popular or common-sense method. And he even connects this with religious ideas: Space is the sensorium dei, the instrument of the divine omnipresence.

Newton proves the existence of God from the purposeful and harmonious arrangement of the universe, which is peculiarly revealed in the simple and uniform arrangement of the solar system. He asserts most emphatically that the wonderful structure (elegantissima compages) of the solar system—the orbital motions of the planets around the sun, which are concentric with the orbit of the sun and lie almost in the same plane—is inexplicable on the basis of natural law. The orbital motion can only be explained by reference to supernatural energies. Left to themselves, the planets would fall into the sun! —The remarkable structure, the organs and the instincts of animals furnish additional evidence of the supernatural! (Besides the Scholium generale contained in the *Principia* Newton expressed himself on these matters in his *Optics*, Queries 28–29, and in his letters to *Bentley*.) —But *Newton* did not think that the mechanism of the universe was finished once for all. God must interpose as an active regulator from time to time. This problem was the occasion of a very interesting discussion between *Leibnitz* and *Clarke*, one of *Newton's* disciples.

3. *George Berkeley* (1685–1753) occupies a place in empirical philosophy similar to that of *Leibnitz* in the group of systematizers. He represents a reaction against *Locke* and *Newton* similar to that of *Leibnitz* against *Descartes*, *Hobbes* and *Spinoza*, and, like *Leibnitz*, *Berkeley* not only represents a reaction, but an advance and further development. He aimed to refute the conclusions of the new science which were hostile to religion, and he hoped to accomplish this by a criticism of the abstract concepts and by a return to immediate experience and intuition. Childlike piety and acute critical analysis have rarely been so intimately united as in this clear mind. At the University of Dublin he occupied himself with the study of *Locke*, *Boyle* and *Newton*, and his chief works were

composed while he was yet but a young man. He afterwards entered the Anglican church and participated in the controversy against the Free-thinkers. His missionary zeal inspired an interest in America, and he conceived a plan of founding a college in America. The sublime ambition to which he devoted the best years of his life comprehended not only the conversion of the Indians, but likewise the regeneration of science and art in the western hemisphere. He was forced to give up his plan however after a three years' sojourn in America. He afterwards served as Bishop of Cloyne in Ireland, equally zealous as pastor, philanthropist and patriot.

In his chief work, *The Principles of Human Knowledge* (1710), *Berkeley* shows that, strictly speaking, we cannot form any general ideas. His criticism is directed particularly against *Locke's* theory of "abstract" ideas. We can form an idea of part of an object without its remaining parts, but we are unable to form new separate ideas which are supposed to contain that which is common to several qualities, e. g. an idea of color in general, which should contain that which is common to red, green, yellow, &c. If I wish to have an idea which may be applied to a whole series of things which are qualitatively different, I must either use a sign, e. g. a word, or, what amounts to the same thing, regard a simple member of the series as representative or typical.

The idea of matter conceived as a general idea is fallacious. Matter is supposed to be the basis of sensible attributes. Suppose we grant that secondary attributes have only subjective significance: it must follow that matter can only be described by means of its primary attributes. But how can we have an idea whose content is nothing more than extension, mobility, divisibility and solidity? The objects which are really given in experience, and which we are able to perceive, always appear under secondary attributes, they can be seen, heard, touched, &c. The primary attributes are never given independent of the secondary attributes. And moreover an investigation of our conception of space, which *Berkeley* made in his *Theory of Vision* (1709), reveals the fact that we form our ideas of space in part by means of the sense of vision, and in part by means of the sense of touch (with which *Berkeley* also includes the so-called sense of motion). Our idea of space, particularly of distance and magnitude, is formed by a fixed combination of ideas of vision and touch, because the visual image invariably suggests a certain idea of touch. We discover that we can also touch the things which we see, on the single condition that we perform the necessary movements. Hence we suppose that we sense distance and size immediately. Space as such cannot be perceived any more than color as such. Which of the two spaces which we actually know—visual or touch space—shall we regard as "absolute" space? We are unable to form an idea of anything which is common to these two spaces.— And matter, being chiefly characterized by the attribute of extension, must therefore share the same fate as space.

By this radical method *Berkeley* annihilates materialism. But he denies most emphatically that this abolishes the distinction between illusion and reality or destroys the possibility of natural science. Our knowledge of reality depends on distinguishing sensation from imagination, and the criteria for this distinction are very definite; sensations are generally more intense and more distinct than images. They take place in an invariable and uniform order, whilst images are fitful and irregular; and we are conscious of not having produced the sensations ourselves. The problem of natural science therefore consists in discovering the exact uniform relation which obtains between our sensations, so that the presence of a sensation shall indicate to us what other sensation we may expect. The interpretation of nature therefore simply means the discovery of the laws which govern the relations of our sensations. With matter in general, that indefinite something which is supposed to underlie all sensations, science has nothing whatever to do.

Berkeley nevertheless thinks that sensations necessarily require a cause which is distinct from ourselves. In attempting to formulate an idea of this cause, he starts from an analogy with our own activity. Our own faculty of producing and changing ideas is the only activity of which we have knowledge. *Berkeley* calls this faculty the will and regards the will as the essence of the soul: the soul is the will (*Commonplace Book*). He also conceives the causes of our sensations after the analogy of this will: these are produced immediately by God. Thus *Berkeley's* philosophy passes over into theology. This immediate relationship with God satisfies his religious feelings. He regards the idea that God should first have created matter and then ordained that it should influence our minds as unnecessarily circuitous. —The divine will is not only evident in the separate sensations, but likewise in their uniform sequence, and the teleology of phenomena reveals the divine prescience.

Berkeley elaborates his philosophical ideas in popular form and in polemical controversy against the Freethinkers in two beautiful and ingenious dialogues (*Dialogues between Hylas and Philonous*, 1712, and *Alciphron*, 1732).

4. *Anthony Ashley Shaftesbury* (1671-1713) introduced a new tendency in the moral philosophy of the modern period. During the period of reaction against the Middle Ages the custom of basing ethics on individualism —the emphasis of the rights of the individual—was almost universal. Magnanimity and sublimity of thought were regarded as the highest attributes of character. Such was the case with *Telesius, Bruno, Descartes, Hobbes* and *Spinoza. Shaftesbury*, on the contrary, emphasized spontaneous emotion, the instinctive impulse to complete devotion.—He was a grandson of the famous statesman of the same name, the patron of *Locke*, and *Locke* had been his tutor. But he had also been introduced to the classical languages and literature at an early age, and he was profoundly affected by the ancient ideas of harmony, especially as developed in later stoicism. Both from taste and on account of feeble health he lived quietly, devoting himself to his literary pursuits, or to travel.

According to *Shaftesbury* there is no absolute opposition between nature and culture or between self-assertion and devotion or loyalty. An involuntary impulse unites the individual with the whole race, just as naturally as the instincts lead to the propagation of the species and care for the young.—But thought, deliberate reflection, however is not superfluous on this account. It is through reflection that we become conscious of a spontaneous impulse and as a matter of fact this is the only way in which affections, such as the admiration of nobility of character and contempt for the ignoble, can possibly arise—affections which bear a close relation to the appreciation of beauty except that they bear more of an active character. But such an affection (reflex affection, moral sense) is nevertheless natural because it is evolved from natural instincts. The conditions of human life are such that we are working for our own interests whenever we are concerned for the common welfare, and the happiness which we procure for others returns upon ourselves. The problem that remains is the further development of this harmony between self-assertion and devotion. Whatever is conducive to social harmony likewise produces harmony in the soul of the individual and this subjective beauty has an inherent value which renders egoistic awards and theological sanctions superfluous. A splendid harmony likewise pervades the universe in general, but due to our limited vision we sometimes fail to discern it. *Shaftesbury* collected his most important writings under the title *Characteristics of Men, Manners, Opinions and Times* (1711). Rand has recently (1900) published one of *Shaftesbury's* essays, *Philosophical Regimen*, which was hitherto unknown. The background of his ethical ideas, formed by his faith in the harmony of the universe, receives even greater emphasis in this than in his other writings.

The ideas advanced by *Shaftesbury* received a more systematic treatment at the hands of *Francis Hutcheson* (1694–1747). *Hutcheson* was professor of moral philosophy at the University of Glasgow and his ideas were thus introduced into the Scottish Universities. He too places the chief emphasis upon immediate feeling. Reason is a faculty whose function it is to discover the means for the realization of our purposes. Indispensable though it is to the moral feelings, if these are not to act blindly, it is nevertheless not the final court of appeal in matters pertaining to morality. Experience is likewise a necessary condition for the successful operation of moral feeling; this can only take place on the basis of clear observations.   Nevertheless moral feeling does not therefore proceed entirely from experience.   But under the guidance of reason and experience it ascribes the highest value to such actions as produce the highest degree of happiness to the greatest number of men.   (The importance of the personages may however supplant the number.)   Thus *Hutcheson* was the first to propound (in his *Inquiry into the Ideas of Beauty and Virtue*, 1725) the famous principle of "the greatest happiness for the greatest number."   Like *Shaftesbury, Hutcheson* was strongly influenced by the ethics of the Greeks, especially as it appears in the later *Stoics*.   This whole trend in modern ethics is, on the whole, an interesting form of the renaissance movement.   *W. R. Scott's* recent monograph on *Hutcheson* contains a suggestive treatment of the whole movement.

According to *Hutcheson*, moral feeling is divinely implanted.   But its operation is not limited to those who believe in God.   Ethics therefore is wholly independent of theology.—The sense of duty arises when moral feeling is momentarily in abeyance but we are at the same time conscious that a proposed act would bring us into conflict with human love and thus rob us of inner peace (serenity) of mind.—*Hutcheson's System of Moral Philosophy* contains a comprehensive elaboration of his ethical theories.

Bishop *Joseph Butler* (1692–1752), in deliberate opposition to the optimism and theory of harmony advocated by *Shaftesbury* and *Hutcheson*, emphasizes the distinction between moral feeling, which he prefers to call *conscience*, and the other human elements and impulses.   Conscience, as a matter of course, acts directly and is combined with a sense of inner satisfaction, as in the case of obedience to a profound impulse. We require a religious sanction (Sermons, 1726), however, in order to resist doubt and the questions which arise in our calmer moods. Whilst *Shaftesbury* bases his optimism on Being or Nature as a whole and assails Christianity on account of its inconceivability and its inhumanity, *Butler* maintains that the view of nature in which so many rudimentary ambitions must perish and the innocent so frequently suffer instead of the guilty violates the belief in a universal harmony, and that the criticisms charged against Christianity must likewise apply to the natural religion which *Shaftesbury* professes. (*Analogy of Religion*, natural and revealed, to the constitution and course of nature, 1737.)

The Frenchman, *Bernard de Mandeville* (c. 1670-1733), who was born in Holland and lived in London as a practicing physician, likewise opposed *Shaftesbury's* optimism. In *The Fable of the Bees* (1705) and in the notes which he afterwards appended to this story he says that private virtues are of no benefit whatever, either from the viewpoint of culture or the general welfare of society. On the contrary, the desire for pleasure, impatience and egoism are motives which inspire effort, culture and social organization. It is the duty of statesmen to strengthen society by a skillful manipulation of the egoistic interests of men. We are naturally disposed, on the other hand, to set ourselves against the public interests when these would suppress egoism and the desire for pleasure. We must therefore choose between morality and culture.—Owing to the fact that this theory apparently supported the doctrine of human depravity and the consequent need of divine revelation, *Mandeville* fared better at the hands of ecclesiastical polemics than the outspoken pagan, *Shaftesbury*.

5. *David Hume* (1711-1776) brought the critical analysis of the process of human knowledge to a provisional
conclusion, especially through his investigation of the
two concepts which had played such an important part
in the seventeenth-century systems of thought, the
concepts of *substance* and *causality*. In order to understand the significance of his criticism we must remember
that the concepts just named are the presuppositions
which are tacitly understood as forming the basis of
natural science, of religious thought, and of ordinary
conversation. *Hume's* problem strikes at the root of
all human thought. He stated a problem which still
continues to bid for solution and of which a final solution
is perhaps impossible. *Hume* is a past master in stating
problems. With this he likewise combines a profound
psychological talent which enables him, when considering
the actual evolution of ideas, to throw light on those
points also in which their objective validity remains
problematical. This twofold gift is valuable to *Hume*
both in the investigation of the problem of knowledge,
as well as in the investigation of the problems of ethics
and religion.

Hume was the son of a landlord in southern Scotland.
His zeal and aptness for learning and reflection showed
themselves at an early age. After several vain attempts
to enter some practical vocation he withdrew into retirement and wrote his chief work, the *Treatise on Human
Nature,* during a residence in France (1739-1740). A
little later he devoted himself to historical and economic
investigations and wrote a history of England, one of
the first historical works which takes account of every
phase of cultural evolution. His *Essays* (1748 ff.),
besides important treatises on economic subjects, include

two monographs (*Enquiry Concerning Human Under-standing* and *Enquiry Concerning the Principles of Morals*) in which the most important problems of his masterpiece are presented in briefer form. He treats the problems of religion from the historico-psychological viewpoint in his *Natural History of Religion* (1757). *The Dialogues on Natural Religion*, written in 1751, but not published until after his death, are a critical study of the problem of religion.—After having held several public offices, *Hume* spent his last years at Edinboro in scholarly retirement.

Whilst *Locke* made a sharp distinction between the problem concerning the origin of our ideas and that of their validity, for *Hume* the two problems, so far as they pertain to ideas in the more restricted sense (ideas as distinguished from perceptions or impressions, i. e. sensations), are identical. He starts with the assumption that an idea can be valid only when it is based on a sensation (perception, impression). He makes no investigation into the origin of sensations because this problem has no epistemological significance: the question whether they proceed from external objects or from God or from the innate powers of the mind has no bearing on the problem of their validity. *Hume* likewise excludes that division of knowledge which is wholly confined to the matter of defining and developing the relations of our ideas—pure logic and mathematics—from his critical investigations entirely. The sole problem of his investigations pertains to the validity of the ideas by means of which we presume to be justified in assuming knowledge beyond what is given in sense-perceptions. The problem growing out of the application of mathematics to empirical science was not formulated until later. This was done by *Kant* on the basis of his studies of *Newton*.

The concept of substance (both in its broader and narrow significance) transcends all sense-perception. We never sense anything beyond single attributes in varying degrees of relationship to each other; but things or substances are never sensed. We sense color, hardness, tone, &c., but sensation never gives us anything possessing these attributes. We perceive within ourselves a multitude of ever-varying sensations, ideas and feelings, but we never sense a soul or an Ego. That is to say we never discover a constant element which is always present and to which we are justified in ascribing the name Ego.—The concept of causality presents a similar case. We perceive distinct phenomena succeeding each other in time; but we do not sense any internal nexus, any necessary connection. Causality is not an object of experience or of perception. (*Hume* regards the concepts of experience and perception as identical.) It is impossible in this instance to appeal to immediate certainty (intuition), for such procedure is permissible only in cases where the simple relation of equality and inequality can be shown to apply. It is just as impossible, furthermore, to demonstrate causality by the method of inference, for all phenomena and occurrences become matters of experience in the form of independent facts, and it is never possible to infer from the concept of the given fact that the concept of another fact necessarily follows. The motion of a ball, e. g., is something altogether different from the motion of another ball; the one motion can very readily be conceived without the other.—The same method of argument applies to the concept of being as to the concepts of substance and causality; no single sensation ever gives us the concept. To take thought about something and to think of it as

existing are not two distinct processes. Things acquire
no new attribute by our thinking of them as existent.

b. We nevertheless employ all these concepts—substance or thing, cause, being! *Hume* undertakes to
explain how this happens, by means of three distinct
psychological factors.—Consciousness naturally tends to
continue the processes which have been produced by an
intense impression even after the impression ceases.
The faculty of imagination continues to be active even
though experience is unable to follow. This gives rise
to ideal representations, e. g. representations of perfect
similarity and perfectly accurate figures, whilst experience
only furnishes suggestions and degrees of approach
towards the perfect. This is likewise the way in which
the representations of absolute substances and absolute
being are formed. The faculty of imagination expands
the relative constancy, which we perceive, into absolute
constancy.

Another peculiarity of consciousness is the tendency
to combine representations which have frequently been
experienced together. When anything happens we are
accustomed to find that something else either precedes
or follows it; hence, when anything occurs, we expect
to find a *"cause"* and an *"effect."* But this is nothing
more than a habit which has become instinctive. It is
impossible to establish the validity of the causal concept
on this basis. This principle of association, which gives
rise to this habit, is likewise an example of causality and
just for this very reason *Hume* says, it, too, is inexplicable.
Observation never discovers more than the separate elements of the content of consciousness, never any "uniting
principle, principle of connection." The problem of
explaining the permanent connection of these elements,

which are absolutely distinct, *Hume* says, is a difficulty which transcends the powers of my understanding.

Consciousness, in the third place, tends to regard its own states as external, objective phenomena. This is the reason for our regarding sensory qualities as objective attributes. And this is why we regard the mental impulse to pass from a sensation to an idea associated with it as due to an objective necessity. We are here guided by instinct, not by reason.—The foundation of science is belief, not knowledge. And the construction of this foundation takes place, as we have seen, by virtue of the expansive, the associative and the objectifying tendencies of consciousness.

c.   *Hume* did not confine himself to the psychology of knowledge. He has likewise treated the psychology of the passions with the same degree of thoroughness. His exposition in many respects reminds us of *Spinoza*. He attaches great importance to the manner in which a passion may be combined with another passion by means of the association of the ideas of their respective objects. He asserts, furthermore, that a passion can only be inhibited by another passion, not by pure reason. Reason is the faculty of comparison and reflection and it can only affect the course of the passions indirectly.

Hume's psychology of the passions forms the basis of his ethics. In ethics he sympathizes with the school of *Shaftesbury* and *Hutcheson*.—Reason cannot furnish the basis of ethics because it establishes only relations or facts. But good and evil are qualities which are ascribed to human actions and characters according to their effect upon the feelings. The fact that we call actions and characters good which are of no benefit to us proves that the passion which forms the basis of approbation cannot be regarded as selfish. In cases of approbation or reproach our viewpoint is social rather than private. If, e. g., we regard justice as a good attribute, it must be due to the fact that we take a sympathetic attitude towards human life as a whole. It may perhaps be that we at first admire justice solely on account of interest in our own security ; but this does not furnish the motive for the appreciation of justice in all those cases which bear no relation to our private welfare. Sympathy or fellow-feeling is therefore the fundamental motive of ethical evaluation.

Hume likewise opposes the intellectualistic conception in the philosophy of religion, just as he does in ethics. He instituted a twofold investigation into the problem of knowledge and he likewise follows the same plan in the matter of religion ; i. e. he investigates both the psychological origin of religion and the validity of religious ideas.

Religion does not originate from purely intellectual motives, but from fear and hope, and from the disposition to think of all other beings after human analogy. Primitive man represents the beings to which he takes refuge in the fearful moments of his life in very imperfect form. But the native disposition to expand and idealize is also in evidence here, and man gradually recognizes that his God must be an infinite being and that there can be but one God. Parallel with this idealizing tendency, which has the effect of elevating Deity far above anything human and placing Him at a great distance from the finite world, there is another counter tendency which endeavors to represent Deity as near at hand, present and intuitively perceivable, and religion reveals a constant tendency to oscillate between these two extremes.

Hume investigates the validity of religious ideas in his *Dialogues*, which is a very important document in the philosophy of religion of the modern period. He adduces several different viewpoints: that of a speculative Supernaturalist, a rationalistic Deist and a skeptical Naturalist. Although the naturalist finally courteously withdraws, it is neverthless clear that *Hume* regarded his arguments as the most important and most conclusive. He denies the right to infer the existence of God from the order and teleology of the universe: Why could the teleology (so far as it really exists!) not have arisen from natural causes and gradual adaptation? We explain the particular phenomena of nature by referring them to natural causes, and the whole series is explained in the explanation of its several parts. At any rate it is impossible to infer, from a world which reveals so many imperfections together with its teleology, the existence of an absolutely perfect being. Furthermore, if we should wish to attribute the origin of the universe to a divine idea, we must not forget that this idea is nowhere given in experience except as a phenomenon combined with other phenomena: with what right therefore can we deduce all the other parts from this single part?— If the naturalist still gets no farther than to discover difficulties in each of the various viewpoints, it is certainly not enough that we regard it merely as a matter of caution, but rather as the expression of *Hume's* constant effort to state the problems clearly and to keep them open.

6. *Hume's* clear statement of the problem of knowledge did not call forth any profound reply immediately. England has not even furnished such a reply.—On the contrary the English literature of the latter half of the 18th century consists of a series of philosophic efforts

which in part continue and supplement and in part
oppose *Hume*.

Adam Smith (1723–1790), a professor at Glasgow and
a friend of *Hume*, elaborated his ethical theory more fully.
In his *Theory of Moral Sentiments* (1759) he describes the
moral sense in its evolution from the mere instinct of sympathy. A spontaneous impulse of imitation causes us to
put ourselves in the place of others, and our feelings and
judgments are therefore primarily determined by environment. But, on the other hand, if the feelings and judgments of others are not of the same kind and intensity
as those which arise in our own minds in their stead, or
would naturally arise, we then experience a feeling of
disapprobation. Again, we approve their feelings and
their judgments (as well as their conduct) whenever,
according to our own experience, they seem to stand in
a fitting relation to the causes which give rise to them,—
and whenever our sympathy for them, for the objects
of their judgments and conduct, is not abnormal. To
illustrate, we cease to approve of acts of revenge whenever
the revenge seems to be too cruel for the circumstances
and the subject. A standard is thus gradually evolved
which is wholly free from any reference to utility. And
we likewise apply this standard to ourselves. We discover that we are criticized by others and not only criticizing others ourselves. We divide ourselves, so to speak,
into two persons, of whom the one criticizes the other in
the capacity of an impartial witness. We unconsciously
idealize this witness; that is we ascribe to him a far more
comprehensive knowledge than it is possible for man to
attain.

It has frequently been observed that *Smith's* ethics
radically contradicts his famous work in economics,

The Wealth of Nations (1776). But, on the other hand, the fact that both works were originally parts of one and the same course of lectures does not harmonize with this view. Moreover the fact has been overlooked, that in his political economy *Smith* assumes the attitude of an "*impartial witness*" of industrial life: his demand for unconditional liberty in commerce and industry rests upon the principle that this is the only way in which capacity can be properly developed and the best methods and instruments of production and of trading be discovered. It frequently happens that the individual serves the community best when he is most concerned about his own interests; he, at the same time, serves a purpose which he has not proposed as if guided by an unseen hand. Sympathy with human life in every phase forms the basis of *Smith's* political economy; it covers the effort of laborers to secure better wages, as well as the effort of employers to increase production. His ethics is therefore in internal harmony with his economics. It is admitted, as a matter of course, that he did not fully appreciate the social problem in its entire scope. His contention was directed against the trusteeship of the reactionary governments, and his optimism led him to expect a large measure of social harmony, even a harmony between ethics and economics, if we should only permit evolution to have free course.

The association of ideas had a profound influence on *Hume's* theory of knowledge. The physician, *David Hartley* (1705–1757), supplemented his theory on this point. He endeavored to explain all the higher mental phenomena by means of the association of simple sensations and ideas. According to *Hartley*, the laws of association are the highest spiritual laws of nature

(*Observation on Man*, 1749). The physiological correlate of association is the combination of various oscillations of particles of the brain. The significance of association manifests itself in three specific forms: it is possible for ideas to so unite internally as to form a new idea with new attributes; conscious activities may, by repetition, be performed entirely automatically; the vividness of an idea may be transferred to the idea which is associated with it. Consciousness can assume an entirely different character from its original by means of these three processes. The most radical metamorphoses become possible in this way, as e. g. when an egoist lapses into complete mystical self-forgetfulness through a series of degrees.—These theories were popularized through the writings of *Joseph Priestley* (1733–1804), the noted chemist. And *Erasmus Darwin* (1731–1802) afterwards went a step farther, and proposed the hypothesis of the transmissibility of such acquired characters (Zoönomia, 1794).

Hume was opposed by what has been called, in the narrower sense, the *Scottish School*. These thinkers aim to quit theorizing and return to the mere description of mental phenomena. As against the results of analytical philosophy they appeal to *common sense*. *Thomas Reid* (1710–1796), Professor at Aberdeen and Glasgow, is the most famous representative of this school. His most important work, *Inquiry into the Human Mind on the Principles of Common Sense* (1764), was written against *Hume*, whom he regarded as the destroyer of all science, religion and virtue.

According to *Reid*, there are certain instinctive presuppositions at the basis of all knowledge, which are unassailable by doubt. These principles of common sense are older than philosophy and proceed from the hand of God. Thus, e. g. every sensation by natural suggestion gives rise to the belief in an external object, as also in an ego as the subject of the sensation. In this way the causal instinct also leads us to the presupposition that the combinations of phenomena which we have perceived will likewise take place in the same way in the future. We likewise have such intuitive evidence in the sphere of morals; we judge a given act good, another evil, intuitively and spontaneously.—*Reid* overlooked the fact that *Hume* had expressly recognized common sense; but *Hume* discovered a profound problem in case one should wish to investigate the foundation of common sense. *Kant* afterwards remarked very pertinently, that instead of making use of common sense as authority, it should rather be used in refutation of objections.

FOURTH BOOK

THE PHILOSOPHY OF THE ENLIGHTENMENT IN FRANCE AND GERMANY

THE great philosophical systems and English empiricism affected a comparatively small circle of thinkers. But about the middle of the eighteenth century an effort was made to popularize the ideas of these solitary thinkers. This movement, which is generally spoken of as the enlightenment, assumed a more definite form in France and Germany than in England. In France, Locke's fundamental principle, that all ideas proceed from experience, furnished the basis for criticizing the existing order of things both in Church and State. The opinion generally prevailed that man had attained the climax of enlightenment and that he was now in possession of adequate presuppositions for the final solution of all the old problems or to dismiss them definitely as groundless. A new dogmatism arose, which was perhaps necessary in order to destroy the old form of dogmatism. In Germany the popularization of the Leibnitzian philosophy, with its reduction of all mental distinctions to the distinction between obscurity and clearness, was particularly influential, and the inference was drawn that enlightenment, and nothing but enlightenment, is the one thing needful. But there were minds both in France and in Germany whose thoughts were centered on the profounder presuppositions of mental life, of which neither the protagonists of the new nor the exponents of the old had the least suspicion. In this respect *Rousseau* in France and *Lessing* in Germany occupied middle ground between the opposing views— and at the same time above them.

A. The French Philosophy of the Enlightenment and Rousseau

1. In France the agitation produced by the enlightenment assumed a decidedly revolutionary character. This was due more particularly to the fact that the old order of things had here reached a greater degree of definiteness and had assumed an attitude of contempt for the new thought to a greater extent than in England and Germany, and that at the same time it was more shallow and corrupt than in the other countries. France was revolutionized by English ideas. The visit of *Voltaire* and *Montesquieu* to England at the close of the third decade of the century became a matter of epochal importance. It was not until then that the English philosophical, religious, aesthetic and political ideas became known in France and on the continent generally. *Voltaire's Lettres sur les Anglais* (1734) marks the beginning of a new period in French thought. *Voltaire* (1694–1778) was not an original thinker. But he possessed the happy faculty of stating scientific ideas and theories with brevity and clearness, and at the same time aggressively. He published a most excellent exposition of *Newton's* natural philosophy, and he used *Locke* with splendid effect in his philosophical works. With *Locke's* principle, that all our ideas proceed from experience, and *Newton's* discovery of the uniformity of nature as his basis, he criticized the theology of the Church. He does not confine himself in the controversy to logical argument, but likewise employs sarcasm and ridicule and— especially when attacking spiritual and physical oppression and intolerance—profound indignation.—The following are his most important philosophical works: *Dictionnaire philosophique portatif* (1764) and *Le philosophe ignorant* (1766).

All ideas proceed from sensations and sensations in turn proceed from matter. What is matter? We do not know, —we are quite as ignorant on this point as on the question concerning the nature of the soul. The Creator endowed us with understanding to the end that we might thereby govern our actions, not for the purpose of penetrating into the nature of things. The eternity of matter represents the limit of our knowledge; and this rests upon the universally accepted principle that nothing can proceed from nothing. The teleology of nature is proof of the existence of God. But the presence of sin and evil in the world (facts which *Voltaire* describes with rare acumen in his *Poeme sur le desastre de Lisbonne*) makes it impossible to believe in the omnipotence of God if we wish to retain our belief in His goodness. *Voltaire* espouses natural religion, but opposes revealed religion by every available means (frequently of course indirectly and secretly). *Voltaire* now applies the principle of simplicity to the explanation of the supernatural in the same way as the thinkers of the Renaissance applied it to the natural world. He refers everything which transcends natural religion to stupidity and deception. Stupidity gives rise to the idea of the supernatural and deceivers afterwards take advantage of this stupidity in order to gain control over men by means of their superstition. The best religion is the one that contains a large measure of ethical culture, but few dogmas.

Montesquieu (1689–1755) is of greater historical significance than *Voltaire*. In his *Esprit de lois* (1748) he advocates the mutual dependence of institutions and of laws upon the natural and moral conditions of the nations. A constitution cannot therefore be transferred from one nation to another without modification. The historical and comparative methods enabled *Montesquieu* to criticize the existing social conditions incisively and systematically. His over-rapid generalizations however are unhistorical. He proposes an ideal form of the English constitution, without observing that the long period of the political development of the English people by means of self-government in smaller groups was its historical presupposition.

Condillac (1715–1780) attempted a simplification of *Locke's* theory of knowledge in his *Traité des sensations* (1754), by means of referring the whole of our conscious experience to absolutely passive sensations. Attention is nothing more than an intense sensation, which precludes the possibility of another sensation arising; memory is simply a secondary effect of sensation, and comparison consists of nothing more than the concomitant appearance of two sensations. The comparison of pleasure and pain gives rise to desires and impulses.—Notwithstanding his endeavor to eliminate every form of activity from psychology, *Condillac* still adheres to the Cartesian theory of the soul and the body as two distinct entities. Sensation cannot be identified with motion, and our ability to make comparisons (i. e., to be conscious of two sensations at the same moment) definitely proves that the vehicle of sensations is a simple substance. *Condillac*, who was a Catholic ecclesiastic, was thus able to harmonize his psychology with his theology. But the spiritualistic element of *Condillac's* theory was devoid of influence. His followers insisted on reducing all psychical phenomena to passive sensations.

La Mettrie (1702–1751), a physician, had even before this time substituted a thorough-going materialism for the Cartesian dualism in his famous work, *L'homme machine*

(1748). The rise of temperature under the influence of enthusiasm and the mental agitation produced by fevers can only be explained on the theory that what we call the soul consists of pure matter. Sensation is an attribute of matter, just like extension and motion. The real nature of matter however transcends the power of our understanding.—Besides these materialistic theories, *La Mettrie's* works (*Système d'Epicure; L'homme planta*) contain interesting anticipations and suggestions of a theory of evolution. The various forms of life evolve from eternal organic germs under the influence of environment. Desire and need are the forms of energy which make for progress, and beings without needs lack the attribute of mind. Man is the highest being, because he is conscious of the greatest amount of needs.

Von Holbach (1723-1789), a German baron living in Paris, published a purely dogmatic and systematic elaboration of materialism. In his *Système de la nature* (1770) he contends that materialism is the only consistent explanation of the facts of natural science. If motion is a primary property of matter (as *Toland* had affirmed), and if material phenomena are only explainable by reference to material causes, it follows that it is unnecessary to assume either one or many minds distinct from matter. An appeal to mind is only a sign of ignorance. Thought or consciousness is simply the agitation of the particles of matter, a motion which is similar to fermentation, which is the common basis of all nourishment and growth, motions which are indeed imperceptible, but which are inferred from what is evident to the senses. There is but one science, physics, i. e. the theory of motion. The assumption of two kinds of nature, spiritual and material, is not only unnecessary, but positively harmful. It is

conducive of superstition and thereby leads back again
to the authority of priestcraft.   Even the so-called natural religion is dangerous; for religion, no matter what the
form, must necessarily have a form of worship, and the institution of forms of worship involves submission to the
authority of priests.   The formation of the concepts of
deity is the product of a profound politics on the part of
the theologians, those *fabricateurs de la divinité!*

Helvetius' (1715–1771) theory of the original equality
of all men, as respects nature and talent, is in a certain
sense closely related to *Condillac's* doctrine of the passivity
of all psychic life.   All distinctions are due to external
causes, to education in its widest sense, i. e. to all the influences which affect us.   Education is responsible for the
tendency which claims our interest and attention.   No
two men ever receive precisely the same kind of education.
The only motive is self-interest, and whether it shall be
actuated by great or small ideas depends entirely upon
education (*De l'esprit,* 1758).   *Helvetius'* posthumous
work *De l'homme* (1773) is a polemic, based on the foregoing presuppositions, against the distinction between
private and public interests, a distinction which is favored
by despotic forms of government, and to which he attributes the misfortune of his native land.   This last observation is of fundamental importance for the understanding of *Helvetius*.   He was a tender-hearted, patriotic
spirit, who devoted his vast fortune, acquired as Farmer-
general, to the service of literature and philanthropy.

The profoundest thinker of this whole group was *Denis
Diderot* (1713–1784), renowned as the energetic editor of
the great Encyclopedia on account of which the French
philosophers of the Enlightenment were called Encyclopedists.   *Diderot* could only express his own ideas in-

directly in the Encyclopedia. In the *Interpretation de la nature* (1754) we find ideas concerning the continuous evolution of life on the earth which are very similar to those of *La Mettrie*. He was profoundly influenced by *Leibnitz*, especially in the matter of his emphasis of the concepts of *continuity* and *force*. The two dialogues, written in 1769, but not published until 1830, *Entretien entre d'Alembert et Diderot* and *Reve d'Alembert*, contain his most ingenious ideas. In direct contradiction of *La Mettrie* and *Holbach*, *Diderot* denies that the psychical processes can be adequately explained as a mere effect of the interaction of material elements. *A transposition of atoms can never produce consciousness*. The only possible explanation of the origin of psychic life is on the presupposition of the presence of germs or dispositions in the lower orders which can be developed to conscious life in the higher orders by means of a process of progressive integration. *Diderot* attributes sensibility to everything in nature, but he makes a distinction between potential and actual sensibility (*sensibilité inerte, sensibilité active*). He likewise emphasizes the difficulty of conceiving how a unitary consciousness could be constructed from a great variety of psychical elements. He does not solve the problem. But he seems inclined to adhere so tenaciously to the idea of continuity, as to leave no room for any actually distinct elements.

2. *Jean Jacques Rousseau* (1712–1778) was intimately associated with the Encyclopedists for a while. His rupture with them—to which, besides their fundamental differences, personal motives certainly contributed not a little—was an event in the history of civilization, a sign that a new problem was forcing its way to the surface. Just as *Hume's* problem pertained to the possibility of

science, so *Rousseau's* problem raised the question concerning the value of civilization.

Rousseau was born in Geneva. His restless spirit, chafing under the restraints of social custom, impelled him to a life of romantic travel and adventure, turning up in Paris in the year 1741, where he became a friend of *Diderot* and *Holbach*. The thought of the contradiction between nature and culture (Kultur), containing the principles of far-reaching consequences, caused him to leave Paris in order that he might live in the country, and the rupture with his Encyclopedist friends soon followed. His writings made him a fugitive and vagabond. He was not even able to find a permanent residence in Switzerland. During his latter years his suspicions and illusion of persecution developed a decidedly morbid character. He spent his last years in seclusion in France.

a. His first essays (*Discours sur les sciences et les arts*, 1750, and *Discours sur l'origine et les fondements de l'inegalité parmi les hommes*, 1755) draw a sharp contrast between nature and culture. Several different classes of ideas are vaguely combined in *Rousseau's* earlier theories of nature, but his ideas are gradually clarified by constant reflection, so that his theory of nature as it appears in his masterpiece, *Emile* (1762), is very clear. In the third dialogue of the remarkable essay entitled *Rousseau juge de Jean Jacques* he calls attention to the fact that his works form a connected series, which leads back step by step to certain fundamental principles. Whoever would wish to read him synthetically, he says, must therefore begin with *Emile*. His object in the first essays was to criticize the existing state of culture and to remove the obstacles which impede natural development. The direct and positive elaboration of his principles must necessarily come later. The paradoxes to which his introductory theories had led would likewise then be removed by the positive presentation.

Three distinct classes of ideas (as may be seen from the preface to the *Discours de l'inegalité*) influenced *Rousseau* from the first in the formation of his theory of nature: a theological, a zoological and a psychological. Nature is a divine product, but civilization is a human product. The state of nature is therefore a state of perfection, of "heavenly and majestic simplicity." We are here reminded of the Garden of Eden. But other passages describe the state of nature as a life of pure instinct, in which no needs beyond the purely physical exist, and in which reflection and imagination are wholly undeveloped. *Rousseau* passes from the department of theology to that of zoology without being aware of it. The real source of his theory of nature however is psychological. As a matter of fact *Rousseau* is not concerned about any far distant past, but with a matter which he was able to discover within his own soul. "Nature" consists of the immediate, total energy of life, spontaneous development, rather than the restraint and complexity which civilization so readily brings with it. Man has a natural tendency to assert himself, to develop aptitudes and impulses. And this spontaneous tendency is so powerful, the hidden source of life is so rich, that self-assertion in itself in nowise contradicts sympathy, or resignation and self-denial. The individual originally made no distinction between himself and others. The stream which issues from within extends to all beings which are similarly constituted to the individual himself: *La force d'une ame expansive m'identifie avec mon semblable.* Kindness and love are therefore natural. Even religious emotion—in the form of gratitude, admiration and reverence—is a natural consequence of this spontaneous expansion.

However when the distinction between individuals makes itself felt, due to the rise of comparative reflection, self-assertion (*amour de soi*), in itself free and noble, becomes egoism (*amour propre*). Dependence, discontent, vanity, envy and lust for power manifest themselves. And to this must be added the division of labor which social life evolves. Faculties and accomplishments are specialized and the perfect, harmonious and all-round development of personality is suppressed. Mental life is broken to pieces and rendered artificial. With *Rousseau* the demand to return to nature is therefore identical with the demand that man shall once more become a unit; *Rendez l'homme un!*—This sense of completeness and unity, experienced in the freedom of nature with which he became so well acquainted during the vagabond journeys of his youth, grew upon *Rousseau* with an extraordinary power and freshness. He is the first to have given enthusiastic expression to the genuine joy to be found in the solitude of nature and in the appreciation of the beauties of nature.

The more profoundly he reflected upon his ideas the clearer it became to *Rousseau* (as had also been the case with *Shaftesbury* before him) that the contradiction between nature and culture could be only a matter of degree. When he declaims against science and art, he really means only the science and art of his own age which was so utterly devoid of originality, whilst he praised the great investigators of the Renaissance and the seventeenth century. Even genius is likewise a form of spontaneous development, rather than the product of imitation or discipline. Culture is a good thing and natural in itself, so long as it harmonizes with the stage of human development; indeed it then even becomes a means to the proper development of natural powers. A given type of culture however can never be transferred from one people to another without modification. There is no culture which is adapted to all men, to all ages and in all places. *Rousseau* vigorously opposes the opinion that the Parisian enlightenment and culture of the middle of the eighteenth century should be regarded as typical of culture in general; and it was exceedingly vexatious to him that *Voltaire* and the Encyclopedists were endeavoring to introduce this culture into his beloved Switzerland. (The author of this text-book has endeavored to elaborate this conception of *Rousseau's* theory of nature more fully in his book entitled *Rousseau und seine Philosophie.*)

b. The psychology then in vogue still retained, in adherence to *Aristotle*, the twofold division of psychical elements into intelligence and will, the theoretical and the practical faculties. The question of a different division of the mental functions was agitated to a certain extent by *Spinoza* and the English psychologists of the eighteenth century (*Shaftesbury* and his disciples). But the real credit for securing the recognition of feeling as manifesting a distinct phase of psychic life nevertheless belongs to *Rousseau*. As a matter of fact, feeling possesses the character of immediacy and expansion which *Rousseau* regards peculiar to nature, whilst cognition consists of comparison, volition of preference or choice. It is feeling, furthermore, according to *Rousseau*, that constitutes the real value of human life. It is almost wholly independent of knowledge; in its climaxes, when it rises to ecstasies, it excludes clear ideas entirely. And it changes less rapidly than knowledge. (See, besides *Emile: Reveries d'un promeneur solitaire.*)

c.   *Rousseau* makes a strong defense for Nature in his pedagogy. He decidedly prefers to leave education to nature, because he has implicit confidence in the growth and the natural improvement of the various organs and faculties. The fact however that children are constantly exposed to external social influence imposes the necessity of protecting them against harmful impressions, so as to give free course to nature. Education should be predominantly negative, i. e. it should rather consist in the removal of obstacles than in the making of positive impressions. His splendid apology for *Emile,—Lettre a Beaumont, archeveque de Paris,*—contains a full development of this idea of a negative pedagogy. Its supreme necessity rests upon the fact that we are utterly ignorant of the nature of the child at the beginning of its career. We cannot begin positive discipline until after we have become acquainted with the disposition of the child by means of observation. The period of infancy is quite as distinct and important a part of life as the later periods and it should be regarded as more than a mere preparation for the latter. The child should therefore be as free from restraint as possible, giving itself to the joy of life without reserve. It were decidedly the best if the child could acquire all of its knowledge independently, discover all the established truths for itself.

The negative period of discipline is an exceedingly difficult task. It requires the pedagogue to be observant, alert, inspiring and yet reserved and self-denying, all at the same time: *tout faire, en ne faisant rien!*—This idea represents one of the most important modifications in the history of pedagogy.

d.   In his attitude towards religion *Rousseau* presents a very peculiar contrast to *Voltaire,* even though both practically agree in their religious ideas,—the dogmas of "Natural Religion." In agreement with *Voltaire*, *Rousseau* believes in a personal God, who is good, but not omnipotent; and he likewise explains the fact of evil and sin by reference to the resistance of matter. Like *Voltaire*, he also repudiates the materialism of *La Mettrie* and *Holbach*. But he nevertheless experienced a profound antipathy towards *Voltaire's* position. For him, the roots of religion are to be found entirely within the realm of the emotions. As we have observed, it springs from the yearning for self-assertion and self-development. This yearning is capable of such intensity as to transcend the possibility of satisfaction by any finite object. It is especially true in the solitude of nature that, according to *Rousseau*, this yearning rises to an affection, to an ecstasy of love, of admiration, of superabundant life. No idea is commensurate with religion; it transcends every conceivable object, every effort of expression. J'étouffle dans l'univers, says *Rousseau* (in a letter to *Malesherbes*). The fact that religion proceeds from the "deeper emotions": j'ai laissé là la raison, et j'ai consulté la nature, c'est-à-dire le sentiment intérieur qui dirige ma croyance (Letter to *Vernes*).

However, even though religion has its origin in a source which is independent of reason, according to *Rousseau*, it is still not in conflict with reason. He is convinced that the fundamental truths of natural religion can be established by rational proofs. He regards materialism absurd because neither motion, nor the uniformity of nature, nor the origin of psychic life is capable of explanation from mere matter. In his philosophy *Rousseau* is a Cartesian. But he does not believe in a creation out of nothing. Nothing can come into being through a sheer act of will.

And the only way of explaining the evil and the sin in the world is on the assumption of a constant resistance to the divine purposes; i. e. the eternity of matter.

Rousseau objects to the positive religions on the ground that they set up authorities and books between man and God, and that they detract from the dignity of the divine relationship by their "clumsy worship." He regards himself a Christian, even though he cannot accept the dogmas and miracles.

Rousseau elaborates his religious ideas in fullest detail in the *Emile*, in the famous section entitled "Profession de foi du Vicaire Savoyard." He would postpone religious instruction until the adolescent period, because children should not accept ideas which are incomprehensible to them. And the aim of religious instruction should be above all else to satisfy the needs of the heart. "What does it matter to me whether the world is eternal or created?" In the *Contrat Social* he advocates natural religion as the state religion. Here, speaking from the viewpoint of the state, he takes strong ground against Christianity, because it regards man's highest duty and his highest aim to pertain to the next world and thus paralyzes the energy which the state must require of its citizens.

e. *Rousseau* elaborated his political ideas in the *Contrat Social* (1762). He advocates popular sovereignty with an enthusiasm unknown since the days of *Althusius*. The universal will (la volente generale, rather than la volente de tous) must be the final court of appeal. It represents the inner yearning, the governing tendency of the people which is concerned for the common interests, the welfare of the whole as well as the individual in the constantly changing generations. It finds expression in the sentiment of patriotism and is analogous to the desire for self-assertion (amour de soi) in the individual. Subjection to it does not involve any limitation of liberty, because it combines the wills of all the individuals: each individual is membre du souverain.

Rousseau distinguishes between the form of the state and the form of the government, just as *Bodin* and *Althusius* had done. The former can be only one, since sovereignty always belongs to the people; but the forms of government vary with the stage of culture and the character of the people. *Rousseau* had a decided preference for small states, for the simple reason that in them, custom and popular usage, the spontaneous expression of the popular will, could shape the course of public policies without conscious interference and without formal legislation. These offer the most favorable conditions for the development of sympathy and humanity. They furnish a larger degree of liberty and it is unnecessary that governmental authority should be so rigid. Furthermore, the citizens can here maintain their control of the affairs of the government more easily than in a larger state. The only way a great nation can maintain its freedom is by forming a union of a number of smaller states.

The unlimited division of labor is detrimental to society as a whole. This, as we have observed, is the real source of the problem of civilization, which, for *Rousseau*, is identical with the social problem. He was the first to form a clear conception of the social problem. The division of labor results in a one-sided development of the individual, producing a state of unnatural dependence on others. *Rousseau* extols rural life because the division of labor is much farther advanced in the cities, and the country likewise brings one closer to nature. He regards the country-folk as really constituting the nation and looks with grave apprehension on the strong drift from the country to the city.

B. The German Philosophy of the Enlightenment and Lessing

1. *Christian Wolff* (1679–1754) was the first to give a detailed exposition of modern philosophy in the German language. He popularized the philosophy of *Leibnitz*. The wide range of his systematic writings drove scholasticism out of the advanced schools of Germany. However, it was not metaphysical idealism and the doctrine of monads that was prominent in his system, but the theologically more acceptable theory of preëstablished harmony. But even this doctrine made him a martyr. King *Frederick William I* dismissed him from his professorship at Halle on account of his apparent fatalism, and even drove him into exile on the short notice of forty-eight hours. He went to Marburg, but was recalled to Halle during the first year of *Frederick II.*—His *Vernünftige Gedanken von Gott, der Welt, der Seele der Menschen, auch allen Dingen Überhaupt* (1719) contains a general outline of his philosophy. His attempt to derive the principle of sufficient reason from the principle of contradiction—because he thinks that origin from nothing involves a contradiction—brings the dogmatico-rationalistic philosophy to its culmination in him. Many of his disciples nevertheless tried to accord due recognition to experience. This led to a combination of the Lockian and Wolffian philosophies in a more 'or less eclectic fashion. They were especially disposed to place great emphasis on empirical psychology (in which indeed *Wolff* himself was a famous

example). In relation to psychology metaphysics fell more and more into the background.

The psychology of the enlightenment, in its more characteristic development, held that the clearness or obscurity of ideas is all that it is possible to assert. In Germany however, like *Shaftesbury* in England and *Rousseau* in France, *Sulzer* (in the *Essays of the Berlin Academy*, 1751-2) and *Mendelssohn* (*Briefe über die Empfindungen*, 1755) held that the sentiments (above all the aesthetic sentiment) possess an independent significance and that they cannot be resolved into purely intellectual elements. *Kant* (in his writings during the sixties) and *Tetens* (*Philosophische Versuche über die menschliche Natur und ihre Entwickelung*, 1777) likewise adopt this view.

The eighteenth century was not only the century of enlightenment, but likewise the century of sentimentality. The natural sentiments demand satisfaction just as well as the natural understanding. And it frequently happened that these two tendencies came into conflict with each other, just as in the "*storm and stress period*," the period of ferment, whence the most brilliant products of art and of science were ultimately destined to proceed. On the other hand, however, the ferment did not permeate public life there as it had done in France. Neither were the religious antitheses so sharply drawn in Germany as in France. Protestantism had already departed from barren orthodoxy through the influence of pietism, and adherents to rationalism were even found within the church itself. Influential churchmen accepted the Wolffian philosophy, frequently (as e. g. at Königsberg) in its characteristic combination with pietism.

Moses Mendelssohn (1722-1786), a Jewish author noted for clearness and elegance of style, a disciple of *Wolff* and

Locke, who defended the doctrine of immortality (*Phädon,* 1767) and the existence of God (*Morgenstunden,* 1786) on rational grounds, exerted a profound influence on the worldly classes. *Mendelssohn* is convinced that the dogmatics of Judaism contain nothing which transcends natural religion (*Jerusalem,* 1783). Many Protestant theologians likewise held similar views with reference to Christianity. It was only in exceptional and isolated cases that the relation between natural and positive religion became more hostile. Thus, for example, *J. Chr. Edelmann* (1698–1767), who has given an interesting account of his doctrinal evolution in his *Autobiography* (published 1849), passed from orthodoxy to pietism and finally to a Spinozistic type of rationalism. He translated "*Logos*" at the beginning of the Gospel of John "*Reason,*" and, like Spinoza, he regarded God only as the immanent, not as the transcendent cause of the world. The only way in which he could find true religiosity in the biblical writings was by historical criticism and symbolic interpretation. Professor *Reimarus* (1694–1768) of Hamburg, the author of the *Wolfenbüttel Fragments* published by *Lessing,* was unable to conceive this relation so simply and harmoniously. He thinks that the human understanding and conscience are in irreconcilable conflict with the content of the Scriptures. Revelation is a physical and moral impossibility. The only possible explanation of the origin of the biblical traditions is on the hypothesis of a series of self-deceptions.

The German philosophy of the enlightenment did not confine itself to psychology and the philosophy of religion, but was likewise active in the department of epistemology. *C. A. Crusius* (1712–1775) showed that the distinction between sense-perception and pure thought is not identical with the distinction between obscure and clear conception; sense-perception can likewise be perfectly clear. He makes a sharp distinction between the ground of cognition and the ground of reality, and criticizes *Wolff's* attempt to establish the principle of causality by purely logical methods. He also exposes the error at the root of the ontological argument (*Entwurf der notwendigen Vernunft-wahrheiten*, 1745). In the problem of methods, *J. H. Lambert* (1728–1771) drew a sharp and clear distinction between the analytical and the constructive methods in philosophy (*Neues Organum*, 1764). *J. N. Tetens* (1736–1805) (in the work mentioned above) finally demonstrated that every act of the intellect, just as every act of attention, at once assumes a relation of difference or similarity. —These three investigators are *Kant's* immediate predecessors. *Tetens* may even have had access to *Kant's* earlier writings.

2. It is evident from the foregoing presentation that the so-called philosophy of the enlightenment contains many implications which transcend its essential doctrines. But *Gotthold Ephraim Lessing* (1729–1781) stands out especially as the thinker of the German enlightenment who projects himself beyond the conflicting antitheses of the age. Despite his wide divergence from *Rousseau* as respects character and talent, his position in the history of thought is nevertheless analogous. As a matter of fact, he was not a productive writer himself, but he had a keen and fine sense for originality in thought as well as for that internal consistency, which can never be exhausted in the definitely expressed forms of life. His attitude towards both the rationalists and the orthodox was therefore that of a critic. As a theological critic he appealed to primitive Christianity which is older than the much discussed Bible

(*Über den Beweis des Geistes und der Kraft*). He likewise
places the everlasting search for truth upon a higher plane
than the slothful possession of it (Duplik). The continuity of spiritual evolution does not consist in results and
dogmas, but in the inner strivings to which the former
owe their origin.—In aesthetics he is likewise guided by the
sense for the original and characteristic. In his *Hamburg-
ischen Dramaturgie*—contrary to the dominant classicism
—he refers to *Shakespeare* as the unrivalled model of dra-
matic poetry, and in his *Laokoön* he attempted to define
the sphere of sculpture and poetry.

Lessing's own religious attitude is best described by the
statement that it is impossible to base our knowledge of the
eternal uniformity of reality upon particular historical
events. The various positive religions must be understood as stages of human spiritual evolution, or, as *Lessing*
expresses it figuratively, as disciplinary forces. Revelation bears a relation to the human race similar to that of
education to the individual. The Old and New Testa-
ments are "*the primers of the human race.*" The time will
come when such books will be unnecessary. For the
present it is important that the pupil should regard his
Primer as the highest science,—but the third kingdom, the
new everlasting Gospel will come (*Erziehung des Menschengeschlechts,—Gespräche über die Freimaurer*).

From the purely philosophical point of view *Lessing*
(according to *Jacobi's* account in his *Briefe über die Lehre
des Spinoza*) is closely related to *Spinoza;* if he were to
name himself after anyone, he knows of no one else
more suitable. He wanted a purely natural theory
of the universe and of life, free from any transcendental leaps. (Cf. *Chr. Schrempf: Lessing als Philosoph.*,
1906.)

FIFTH BOOK

IMMANUEL KANT AND THE CRITICAL PHILOSOPHY

WE have found investigations into the nature of knowledge as early as the philosophers of the Renaissance and in the great system builders. But they were nevertheless decidedly under the spell of the constructive tendency. As a result of the English empirical philosophy regarding the investigation of knowledge as the distinctive problem of philosophy, we have the extreme statement of the problem by *Hume*. It was this statement of the problem that furnished the occasion which led *Kant* to undertake a comprehensive investigation of the conditions and presuppositions of our knowledge and of our mental functions in general. Such an investigation constitutes the task of what he has called the *Critical Philosophy*. The critical philosophy has nothing to do with a theory of the evolution of knowledge, in the modern sense of the word. Its distinctive task is to discover the necessary principles which must be presupposed—howsoever human nature may be constituted—if a mental function, no matter whether it be cognition, aesthetic or ethical evaluation, or religious trust, is to attain any *valid* results. It investigates the conditions of the *validity* of knowledge, not those of its origin. The success of and the purely scientific element contained in this philosophy consists in its penetrating beneath the finished products and results of the human mind to their efficient causes. Just as we can only understand a man's real nature by penetrating beneath his outward acts to his real character, so likewise the only way

to understand the phenomena of mental life is to penetrate to its original sources.—By founding the critical philosophy, in this understanding of the term, *Kant* defined
the problem and method of the science of mind. The
entire product of the nineteenth century in the department
of the mental sciences is based upon the view-points which
he has marked out.

According to *Kant's* theory, primitive human thought
is *dogmatic*. Man begins with an implicit confidence in
his intellect and he believes himself capable of solving all
problems. He wishes to comprehend and coördinate
everything. It is this desire that leads to the dogmatic
systems, which proceed from the demand for unity so
deeply imbedded in human nature. But eventually, when
disillusionment supervenes, and the systems are found to
contradict each other, there arises a *tendency towards
sceptical* reflection. The third step however is the specific
investigation of knowledge or the understanding, i. e.
critical reflection. It is this endeavor, at once the sign
of philosophic maturity and self-limitation, that *Kant*
wishes to introduce.

The life of the thinker who bequeathed this profound
thought to the world was confined within narrow circles,
but it is a life of simple majesty. *Immanuel Kant* was
born of poor artizan parents at Königsberg on the 22d of
April, 1724. His parents were moderate pietists, and the
mother especially exerted a profound influence upon the
son. At the University in Königsberg he studied the
Wolffian philosophy and the Newtonian physics. Through
the former he became acquainted with the dogmatic
method of philosophy, and in the latter he discovered a
pattern of exact empirical science. After having spent
several years in various families of the nobility in East

Prussia as private tutor, he habilitated as *Privatdozent* at the University, in which capacity he labored for a long period with pronounced success. Not until 1770 did he receive an ordinary professorship. He never left his native province of East Prussia. He devoted his whole life to the elaboration of his works and to his academic instruction. Notwithstanding this however he participated actively in the social life of Königsberg and had the reputation of being a most agreeable companion. He belongs to the period of the enlightenment, but he regarded "*enlightenment*" as a process, a problem, rather than as a finished product. And finally, when his critical principle led him into profound depths, unknown to the ordinary enlightenment, he possessed a sense for the sublime in harmony with the conception of the aesthetic, ethical and religious which furnished the guiding principle of his mental life. In his old age, under the clerical reaction which followed the death of *Frederick the Great*, he suffered persecution. The publication of an essay on religious philosophy in 1793 brought forth a royal rescript against him with a threat of severer measures in case he persisted in the same tendency. *Kant* replied with the declaration that he would thenceforth neither speak nor write anything whatsoever on religious matters. He did not renew his activities in the philosophy of religion until the beginning of a new administration when he published the whole of the controversial proceeding (in the preface to the *Streit der Facultäten*, 1798). His last years present a case of the gradual disintegration of a mighty spirit. He apparently became a victim of dementia senilis. Isolated moments of mental brilliance are the only reminders of his former greatness. He died on the 12th of February, 1804.

A. THE THEORETICAL PROBLEM

1. *Kant's* philosophical reflections matured very slowly. There are two distinct periods of development, in his theoretical writings, before the appearance of his masterpiece; the first extends from 1755 (the year of *Kant's* habilitation) to 1769, the second from 1769 to 1781 (in which latter year his masterpiece appeared).—In describing the historical development of the Kantian philosophy (both as respects the theoretical as well as the practical problems) the author of this text book follows his essay on *Die Kontinuität im philosophischen Entwicklungsgange Kant's* (Archiv für Gesch. der Philos., VII, 1894).

a. The dominant characteristic of *Kant's* first period is the firm conviction that an all-pervasive uniformity of nature rigidly determines the phenomenal universe. His famous hypothesis of the evolution of our solar system is elaborated in his *Allgemeine Naturgeschichte und Theorie des Himmels* (1755). *Newton* had declared that a scientific explanation of the origin of the solar system is impossible. But *Kant* now shows that such an explanation is possible. He starts with the assumption of a rotating nebulous sphere, and then deduces the logical consequences according to the known laws of nature. He furthermore regards the denial of nature's capacity to evolve order and purpose from its own inherent laws as an erroneous presupposition. He discovers the proof of deity in the very fact of the uniformity of nature itself.—*Kant* elaborated this theory more fully in the essay *Einzig möglicher Beweisgrund einer Demonstration Gottes*. Whilst he had even then already lost confidence in the validity of the traditional "*proofs*" of the existence of God, he at the same time found a basis for his religious conviction in the ultimate postulate of all real science—the postulate of the uniformity of nature. He stood quite close to *Spinoza* in this respect without being aware of it.

Kant's mind was likewise occupied with various other problems during this period. His conclusion concerning the distinction between philosophy and mathematics is noteworthy, namely, that philosophy cannot create its concepts as mathematics does. It derives its concepts from experience. Hence, inasmuch as experience is never universal, philosophy is limited to imperfect concepts. The concept of soul, for example, is an imperfect concept; experience furnishes no warrant for speaking of a psychical substance. In the ingenious brochure, *Traume eines Geistersehers, erlaütert durch Traüme der Metaphysik* (1766), *Kant* shows, partly in satire, how easy it is to construct a system of the supersensible world. The only requirement is a naïve implicit confidence in our concepts as complete and final.

The concept of causality is another example of an incomplete concept. How can the analysis of a given phenomenon reveal the necessity of another phenomenon? But the concept of causality assumes precisely this necessity! *Kant* therefore (even in the essay: *Versuch den Begriff der negativen Grösse in die Weltweisheit einzuführen,* 1762) approaches the problem of causality in precisely the same form in which it had been stated by *Hume.* *Kant's* later remark that it was *David Hume* that roused him from his dogmatic slumbers, with its evident reference to *Hume's* criticism of the concept of causality, would indicate that this awakening took place as early as 1762. (Students of *Kant* differ widely on this point however.) It is impossible to describe the years in which *Kant* was occupied with the study of the causal concept and

The Dreams of a Ghost-seer, as spent in "dogmatic slumber."

b. *Kant* is led to the first step from his inquiring, sceptical attitude towards criticism by the discovery that space and time, with which the exact natural sciences operate, are not real objects or attributes in the absolute sense; but schemata (schemata coordinandi) which are abstracted from the forms in which our sensations are arranged. Space, which *Newton* regarded a divine sense, thus becomes a human sense (*De mundi sensibilis atque intelligibilis forma et principiis*, 1770). He makes the discovery that many propositions which we regard as objective only express the conditions under which we perceive or conceive the objects. For the time being he applies this observation only to space and time as the forms of sense-perception. This was nevertheless the discovery of the fundamental thought of the critical philosophy. *Kant* had thus already discovered the theoretical method which he afterwards called the Copernican method. Just as our perception of the rotation of the firmament around the earth is due to our position in the universe, so, according to *Kant*, it is likewise due to our method of sense perception that we apprehend things under the relations of time and space. This explains therefore—and this is the essential matter so far as *Kant* is concerned—how it happens that pure mathematics, which is after all a purely intellectual science, can be valid for every possible sense-perception. We experience everything in time and space, and everything must therefore conform to the mathematical laws of time and space.

Kant was still of the opinion that the understanding could grasp the absolute nature of things. But he soon saw that the Copernican principle must likewise apply to the understanding. His letters and notes enable us to follow the gradual development of this deeper insight. We are active in the operations of our own thought, i. e. we act in a manner peculiar to our mind; but how can the products of our own mental activity retain their validity when applied to the perceptions which are objectively produced?—As to the nature of this mental activity, an investigation of the fundamental concepts of our understanding, especially the causal concept, reveals the fact that the understanding is likewise a uniting, synthetizing faculty like sense-perception. The uniting principle (*Hume's*), which was the stumbling-block of *Kant's* English predecessor, now became *Kant's* fundamental presupposition of knowledge. He could now say of the fundamental concepts of the understanding (*categories*), after the analogy of what he had previously said of the forms of intuition: *Knowledge exists only when what is given* (the matter) *in the forms of our thought is united.* The concept of *synthesis* is therefore the fundamental concept of all knowledge and the profoundest thought of the Kantian philosophy. This constitutes *Kant's* real discovery, which will justify its value, even if *Kant's* particular theories are to a considerable degree subject to criticism. We must apply his own method in the study of *Kant*. We must penetrate the finished forms in which his philosophy is cast and discover their primary principles—realities.

According to his own statement, *Kant* wrote out the results of his reflections covering a period of twelve years quite hastily. His chief work, *Kritik der reinen Vernunft* (1781), is therefore a very difficult book.—In presenting its contents we shall follow a clearer order than that given by *Kant* himself.

2. *Kant* distinguishes a subjective and an objective deduction in his investigation of the problem of knowledge.

a. It is the business of *subjective deduction* to discover the forms of our intuition and reflection. These forms represent what is constant and universal,—that which is capable of maintaining its identity, even though the qualitative content, the matter, changes. They are discovered by a psychological analysis which distinguishes between the changeable and the permanent. In this way we discover extension (space) and succession (time) as constant elements of sensory intuition, magnitude and causality as constant elements of thought. The *Forms of intuition* are forms of our receptivity. As a matter of fact they too are a kind of synthesis, a combining together; but at this stage our own activity does not yet attain the prominence that it does in thought; here the only concern is the arrangement of the sensations in immediate intuition. We develop a higher level of activity whenever we place these intuitional images in relation to each other. This function is more fully conscious than the involuntary process of intuition. *Kant* calls it *apperception*. Whenever we pass from a given spacial or temporal intuition to another, we are trying to affect our own inner unity, in the fact that we combine together the antecedent and consequent in a definite manner. Thus, e. g. I know a line only when I draw it, i. e. when I combine its several parts according to a definite law. Or, e. g. I know a fact, e. g. the freezing of water, only when I am in position to combine the antecedent state (the water in liquid form) with its consequent according to a definite law.

Kant believes that he has thus discovered a method which proves the necessity of a certain number of con-

cepts of the understanding (categories). He says the
function of the understanding is judgment; every judgment consists of a combination of concepts. There must
therefore be as many different categories as there are kinds
of judgments!—He thus discovers, on the basis of the
traditional logic (of course somewhat modified by himself), twelve categories, neither more nor less. This was
certainly a profound illusion. For the customary classification of judgments is logically untenable, it is at least
impossible to justify the inference from them to different
kinds of fundamental categories.

Kant divides the twelve categories, which we will not
here repeat, into two classes: *mathematical* and *dynamic;*
the concept of *magnitude* and the concept of *causality*
might be regarded as representative of these two classes.
All our judgments express either a relation of magnitude
(greater or less) or a relation of real dependence (cause
and effect). The concept of continuity is common to
both relations: all magnitudes arise continuously from
smaller magnitudes, and cause passes continuously into
effect.

We have thus far discovered two groups of forms: the
forms of intuition and of the categories. But there is still
a third group. We are not satisfied with simply arranging
sensations in space and time, and afterwards arranging
the intuitional forms which have thus arisen according to
their relations of magnitude and cause. The synthetic
impulse, the combining activity, is so deeply imbedded in
our nature that we are constantly in search of higher uni-
ties and totalities and finally demand an absolute completion of the synthesis. This is the sphere of *ideas*, the
forms, in which man attempts to conceive absolute uni-
ties and totalities. *Kant* calls the ideational faculty

reason in its narrower significance. (In its broader significance understanding and intuition likewise belong to
reason.) Those synthetic impulses together with these
ideational faculties give rise to the dogmatic systems
which deal with the ideas of God (as the absolute being),
the soul (as substance) and the world (as absolute totality). *Kant* attempts to prove, by a very artificial method,
that these three are the only ideas: they are to correspond
with the three forms of inference of the traditional logic.

b. *Objective deduction* investigates the right of apply-
ing our cognitive forms to given sensations. The fact
that we are able to become conscious of the content of our
intuitions and concepts does not constitute the problem.
Neither does the fact that we can deduce new content
from experience constitute a problem. But *Kant's* problem rather consists in this, namely, the fact that we are
able to use our intuitional forms and categories in such a
way as to form, with their help, valid judgments which are
not found in experience. He expresses it in his own language as follows: How are synthetic judgments a priori
possible? By analytical propositions we become aware
of the content of our intuitions and reflections; by syn-
thetical propositions a posteriori we include new content
derived from experience; but synthetic propositions a
priori extend our knowledge independently of our experience. The following are examples of such propositions:
every perception has extensive and intensive values, and
every event has a cause (or better: every change takes
place according to the law of the connection between
cause and effect).

According to *Kant* the validity of such judgments rests
upon the fact that *experience*—in the sense of the fixed and
necessary relations of phenomena—is possible only in

case the mathematical laws and the concepts of magnitude
and causality are valid for all perceptions.   Only such abstract propositions as formulate *the very conditions of
experience* are synthetic propositions a priori.   Whenever
we are able to discover and express the conditions of experience we come upon propositions which are propositions
of pure reason, because they are based on the pure forms
of our knowledge, and which must nevertheless be valid
for all experience.

The whole content of experience is conceived in *space
and time*.   Hence since pure mathematics really does
nothing more than develop the laws of space and time, it
must be valid for every possible content of experience,
every possible perception.   But this demonstration likewise involves a limitation: namely, mathematics is valid
only for phenomena, i. e. only for things as we conceive
them, not for things-in-themselves.   We have no right
to make the conditions of our conception the conditions
of things-in-themselves.   Time and space can be conceived only from the view-point of man.

Experience not only implies that we conceive something
in space and time, but likewise that we are able to combine
what is given in space and time in a definite way, i. e. as
indicated in the concepts of magnitude and causality.
This is the only means of distinguishing between experience and mere representation or imagination.   All extensive and intensive changes must proceed continuously,
i. e. through every possible degree of extension and intensity, otherwise we could never be certain of having any
real experience.   Gaps and breaks must be impossible
(non datur hiatus non datur saltus).   The origin of each
particular phenomenon moreover must be conditioned by
certain other phenomena,—analogous to the way in which

the conclusion of a syllogism is conditioned by the premises. In any purely subjective representations or in dreams, images may be combined in every variety of ways; we have experience however only when it is impossible to permit the members of a series of perceptions to exchange their places or to pass from one perception to another by means of a leap. In my mind I can at will, e. g. conceive of a house being built from the roof downward or from the foundation upward; but in the case of the actual construction of a house there is but a single possible order of succession. Wherever there appear to be gaps in the series of perceptions we assume that further investigation will discover the intervening members. This demonstration of the *validity of the categories* of magnitude and causality likewise involves a limitation: The validity of the categories can only be affirmed within the range of possible experience; they cannot be applied to things which from their very nature cannot become objects of experience. Experience is the empirical synthesis which furnishes validity to every other synthesis.

The principles of demonstration by which we obtain our results when dealing with the forms of intuition and the categories are inapplicable to the realm of *ideas*. The ideas demand an unconditionality, a totality, finality; but experience, which is always limited, never furnishes any such thing. Neither God, nor the soul (as substance), nor the universe (as an absolute whole) can be given in experience. There is here no possibility of an objective deduction. It is impossible to construct a science of ideas.

When *Kant* bases the real significance of the rational sciences upon an analysis of the conditions of experience, it must of course be remembered that he uses the concept of experience in its strict sense. Experience consists of the fixed and necessary relation of perceptions. But in this sense experience is an idea (in *Kant's* meaning of the term) or an ideal. We can approach this ideal to infinity, but it was a piece of dogmatism when *Kant* here failed to distinguish between the ideal and reality. *Kant* had not, as he believed, solved the problem propounded by *Hume;* for the thing concerning which *Hume* was skeptical was just the matter as to whether any experience in the strict sense of the term really exists.—This dogmatic tendency is peculiarly prominent in *Kant's* special works, especially in his *Metaphysische Anfangsgründen der Naturwissenschaft* (1786).—*Kant's* chief merit consists in referring all knowledge to synthesis and continuity. These fundamental principles enable us to anticipate experience. But all anticipations are only hypotheses.

3. As we have observed, the demonstration of the real validity of abstract knowledge (of pure reason) is closely related to the limitation of this validity. *Kant* states this as follows: We know only experiences, but not *things-in-themselves*. Whenever he expresses himself concisely, he calls the concept of the thing-in-itself an ultimate concept or a negative concept. In this way he gives expression to the permanently irrational element of knowledge. Speaking exactly, the concept of the thing-in-itself indicates that we cannot deduce the matter of our knowledge from its form. For *Kant* however the concept of the thing-in-itself imperceptibly assumes a positive character. The thing-in-itself is regarded as the cause of phenomena (especially in reference to the matter, but likewise also in reference to the form). Here (as *F. H. Jacobi* was the first to show) *Kant* falls into a peculiar contradiction; he has limited the real validity of the concept of causality to the realm of experience (in which the thing-in-itself can never be pres-

ent) and then conceives the thing-in-itself as cause!—
Here again we discover a remnant of dogmatism in *Kant*.

4. *Kant* proves the impossibility of constructing a
science of "*Ideas*," both by the fact that ideas contain
none of the conditions of experience (as is the case with the
forms of intuition and the categories), and by means of a
criticism of the attempts which have been made to establish such a science.

a. *Criticism of speculative (spiritualistic) psychology.*
There is no justification for concluding from the unity of
psychic life, which manifests itself in synthesis, the fundamental form of consciousness, that the soul is a being which
is distinct from the body or a substance. Synthesis is
only a form, which we are not permitted to regard as a
separate substance. It is impossible for psychology to
be more than a science of experience. There is no ground
for interpreting the distinction between psychical and
physical phenomena as a distinction between two entities: It is possible indeed that one and the same essence
should form the basis of both kinds of phenomena.

b. *Criticism of speculative cosmology.* Every attempt
at a scientific theory of the universe conceived as a totality
is ever and anon confronted with contradictions. Our
thought here culminates in antinomies; the universe must
have a beginning (in space and time), else it were not a
totality. But it is impossible to conceive the beginning
or the end of space and of time, because every place (in
space and in time) is thought in relation to other places.—
Furthermore the world must consist of parts (atoms or
monads) which are not further divisible, otherwise the
summation of the parts could never be complete. But
everything conceivable is divisible; we can think of every
body as divided into smaller bodies.—The series of causes

must have a first member if the universe is to be regarded
as a complete system, and if a complete causal explanation
of particular phenomena shall be possible. But the assumption of a first cause is in conflict with the law of
causality, for this cause would itself have no cause, and at
what moment should it begin its operation?

According to *Kant* the only way to avoid these antinomies is to distinguish between phenomenon and the
thing-in-itself and limit the validity of our knowledge to
phenomena. We meet with contradictions the moment
we attempt to apply our concepts to the things which
transcend our circumscribed experience. *Kant* therefore
regards the antinomies as a demonstration of his theory
of knowledge.

c. *Criticism of speculative theology.* Reflective thought
aims to find in the concept of God an absolute resting-
place for all its effort. This concept is supposed to contain the ground of the concepts of soul and universe. In
it knowledge would attain its ideal: all ideas would be referred to a single idea which in turn contains the ground
of its existence within itself and hence implies nothing beyond it! According to *Kant* the concept of God is fully
justified as an ideal; but we must not confuse an ideal of
knowledge with knowledge actually attained. The traditional arguments for the existence of God however rest
upon such a confusion of terms.

The most popular argument rests upon the adaptation
of nature and thence infers the existence of an all-wise,
all-loving and all-powerful Creator (the *physico-theological
argument*).—But by what right do we presuppose that the
order and adaptation of nature should not be explainable
as the effects of natural causes operating according to natural laws? And at any rate this argument can only lead to

the assumption of an architect or governor of the universe, not to that of a creator.

The cosmological argument goes into the matter more profoundly: the universe must have a cause (both as to its matter as well as to its plan).—But the law of causality leads only from one member of the causal series to another —it only furnishes causes which are in turn conditioned, i. e. effects, and hence never establishes the assumption of an unconditioned, necessary being.   In the case of every existing thing, even the highest, it always remains not only possible but necessary to inquire: Whence doth it come?

The ontological argument, if it were tenable, is the only one that would lead to the desired goal.   It is also the tacit presupposition of all the other arguments.   This argument proceeds as follows: to think of God as non-existent were a contradiction, because He is the perfect being and existence belongs to perfection!—But existence or being is a predicate which differs from all other predicates.   The concept of a thing does not change because the particular thing does not exist.   My concept of a hundred dollars is the same, no matter whether I possess them or only think of them.   The problem of existence is independent of the problem of the perfection of the concept. And, as the investigation of the categories has shown, we have but a single criterion of existence or reality: namely, the systematic uniformity of experience.

B.   The Ethico-Religious Problem

1.   There is a sense in which *Kant's* ethical ideas develop along parallel lines with his ideas of theoretical knowledge.   *Rousseau's* influence evidently affected him on this point at two different periods with telling effect. *Kant* declares, in an interesting fragment, that *Rousseau*

taught him reverence for mankind, to ascribe a certain dignity to all men which is not merely based on the degree of their intellectual culture. He had previously been an optimist whose basis was an intellectual and spiritual aristocracy. And in addition to *Rousseau, Shaftesbury, Hume* and especially *Hutcheson* likewise influenced him at this period. During the sixties *Kant* bases his ethics on the sentiment of beauty and the dignity of human nature. (*Beobachtungen über das Gefühl des Schönen und des Erhabenen,* 1764.) Even here *Kant* already emphasizes the necessity of fundamental principles of morality; they are however only the intellectual expressions of the content of the sentiments: "*The fundamental principles are not abstract laws, but the consciousness of an affection that dwells in every human breast . . . of the beauty and dignity of human nature.*"

Kant afterwards abandoned this identification of ethics with the psychology of the affections. In his *Essay* of 1770 he declared that it is utterly impossible to base moral principles on sentiment, i. e. empirically. It is also evident, from a fragment discovered by *Reicke*, that at the period during which he was engaged with the *Critique of Pure Reason* he based the ethical impulse on the self-activity which we exercise in our striving for happiness. The matter of happiness is empirical, but its form is intellectual, and the only possibility of realizing our freedom and independence rests upon maintaining the constant harmony of our will with itself. Morality is liberty under a universal law which expresses our self-consistency. Even here *Kant's* ethics attains that purely formal character which is so peculiar to it. In ethics as in epistemology he regards the form as the constant factor in contrast with its ever-varying content.

But in the fragment just cited *Kant's* ethics was still individualistic: The moral law demands only that the individual be in harmony with himself. The specifically Kantian ethics springs from an expansion of this principle. He elaborates it in the *Grundlegung zur Metaphysik der Sitten* (1785) and the *Kritik der praktischen Vernunft* (1788). Here he formulates the moral law as follows: *Act according to the maxim that you could at the same time will that it might become a universal law!*—The viewpoint is therefore no longer individualistic, but social. His elaboration of the theory of knowledge evidently affected his ethics at this point. The fundamental moral law must be quite as universal and objective as the theoretical fundamental principles, as e. g. the principle of causality! But there are other theoretical motives likewise here in evidence.

In the interval between the fragment just cited (1780) and the first draft of the ethics (1785) another noteworthy essay appeared, namely, *Idee zu einer allgemeinen Geschichte in weltbürgerlicher Absicht* (1784), in which *Kant* shows that the only viewpoint from which history is comprehensible and of any value is from that of the human race as a whole, but not from that of the individual citizen. Reason is an evolutional product of the process of history. The antagonism of interests brings the capacities of man to maturity, until he finally organizes a society in which freedom under universal laws is possible. And it is only then that genuine morality becomes possible! *Kant* observes that *Rousseau* was not wholly in error in preferring the state of nature, so long as this stage has not been reached. —It is evident that, from the viewpoint of history, the moral law which *Kant* formulated in 1785 contains a sublime anticipation. The individual citizen is expected to regulate his actions here and now, precisely as all actions shall finally be regulated in that ideal society. Morality, like history, is likewise incomprehensible from the viewpoint of the individual.—*Kant* returns to this theory two years later (1786 in the essay on *Muthmasslicher Anfang der Menschengeschichte*). Civilization and nature are contradictory principles (so far *Rousseau* was right) "until perfect art becomes nature once more, which is the final aim of the moral determination of the human race." *Kant* therefore arrived at this definitive ethical theory by the historical or social-psychological method, and *Rousseau's* conception of the problem of civilization influenced him at this point, just as it did at an earlier stage of his ethical reflection.—But in the mind of *Kant* that sublime anticipation appears with such ideality and absoluteness that he regarded the fundamental moral law as a manifestation from a super-empirical world and he forgot his historical and psychological basis. (Cf. the author's essay: *Rousseau's Einfluss auf die definitive Form der Kant'schen Ethik*, in Kantstudien, II, 1898.)

2. In the first draft of his ethics (1785) *Kant* discovers the fundamental moral law by means of an analysis of the practical moral consciousness. That action alone is good which springs from pure regard for the moral law. Neither authority nor experience can be the source of this sense. Moral principles reveal the inmost, supersensible nature of our volition, and neither psychology nor theology can here furnish the basis. The fact is the more evident in that there are elements in human nature which impel us in directions which are contrary to the moral law. The moral law manifests itself in opposition to these empirical and egoistic tendencies in the form of duty, an unconditional command, *a categorical imperative*. The distinc-

tively moral element appears most clearly in cases where duty and inclination stand out in sharp contrast. *Kant* even says in a certain place that a state of mind in which I follow duty even though it is in conflict with my purposes is the only one which is really good in itself.

The moral law must be purely formal. Every real content, every purpose would degrade it to the level of the empirical and hence to the material. The moral law can do nothing more than indicate the form of the fundamental principles which our actions are intended to express,— that is to say, that these fundamental principles are capable of being based on a universal principle of legislation in such manner as to enable all rational beings to obey them under similar circumstances. I must, e. g. return borrowed property even though no one knows that it does not belong to me; because the contrary course will not admit of generalization, and in that case no one would make a loan to another. *Kant* however here clearly presupposes that man is a member of society. This maxim is therefore not purely a priori. He likewise realizes the need of a more realistic formulation of the maxim and the necessity of a real object of human action. The highest object can be given only through the moral law, and *Kant* discovers this object in the very dignity which every man possesses in the fact of being capable of becoming conscious of the moral law. From this he deduces the principle: "*Act so as to treat humanity, in thyself or any other, as an end always, and never merely as a means!*"

The moral law is not objective, but deeply imbedded in the nature of man and identical with the essential nature of volition. Law and liberty are not separate concepts. They express only the autonomy of man viewed from opposite sides. As an empirical being man is subject to psychological laws, but as a rational being he is elevated above all empirical conditions and capable of originating a series of changes absolutely. But man possesses this capacity only as an *"intelligible character,"* as a "thing-in-itself." And since things-in-themselves can never be given in experience, it is impossible for intelligible liberty and empirical necessity ever to conflict with each other. *Kant* here introduces a positive use of the concept of the thing-in-itself.

Kant elaborated the special problems of ethics in his *Rechtslehre* and his *Tugendlehre.* Both works appeared in 1797 and bear the impress of old age.—Right, according to *Kant,* consists of the aggregate conditions under which the will of the individual can be united with the will of another according to a universal principle of liberty. As a matter of fact man's only original right is liberty, i. e. immunity from the arbitrary demands of every other individual in so far as it can obtain together with the liberty of others according to a universal law. Even though *Kant* makes a sharp distinction between the Right and the Moral (Legality and Morality), he nevertheless regards our obligation to regulate society as far as possible according to principles of Right to rest upon a categorical imperative.

In the Theory of Virtue he finds the highest duty in the realization of the dignity of man, which is based on autonomy and consists in the complete development of personal qualities. To be useless and superfluous is to dishonor humanity in our own person. Besides personal perfection the happiness of others is a matter of fundamental importance. The perfection of others on the other hand can only be realized through their own efforts; and we provide for our own happiness even through a natural instinct.

3. *Kant* aimed to establish the pure autonomy and spontaneity of the moral sense, and especially as independent of all theological presuppositions. But he was nevertheless convinced that religion and morality are vitally related. He finds the transition from morality to religion to rest on the fact that man is destined to realize the unconditional moral law in the empirical world, i. e. in the world of finitude, limitation and conditionality. Ideal and reality here appear in sharp contrast to each other, which gives rise to a demand for harmony between liberty and nature, virtue and happiness, and it is just because experience offers no guarantee, that religious postulates, which contain the conditions of such a harmony, are formulated. Besides the freedom of the will previously cited, there are according to *Kant* two additional postulates: viz. the immortality of the soul and the existence of God. *Kant* is convinced that these postulates reveal a universal human need. Faith is the natural consequence of the sentiment of morality, even though faith is not a duty.

The possibility of faith rests upon the fact that knowledge is limited to phenomena. The native element of the dogmas of faith is the thing-in-itself. But these dogmas add nothing to our knowledge. This follows even from the fact that our intellectual and intuitional forms do not pertain to the thing-in-itself. Religious ideas are nothing more than analogies or figures of speech. *Kant* even goes so far as to say that if the anthropomorphisms are carefully discarded from the psychological attributes ascribed to God, nothing remains but the empty word.

This fact, which even applies to the ideas of natural religion, is still more pertinent to the ideas of positive religion. In his treatise on *Religion innerhalb der Grenzen der blossen Vernunft* (1793) *Kant* shows that important ethical ideas are hidden within the Christian dogmas. In the dogma concerning sin he discovers the experience of an inclination, deeply imbedded in human nature, which strives against the moral law; which he calls "*radical evil.*" *Kant* regards the Bible story of the Fall as a subjective experience on the part of each individual, not as an historical event. So is the Bible story of the suffering Christ likewise experienced by every serious human being; regard for the moral law gives rise to a new man who must endure the suffering due to the constant opposition of the old man of sensual inclination.—The significance of a purely historical or "*statutory*" faith is only provisional; but we respect "the form which has served the purpose of bringing a doctrine, the acceptance of which rests on tradition, —which is irrevocably preserved in every soul and requires no miracle,—into general influence."

4. *Kant* maintains a sharp antithesis between the world of experience and things-in-themselves both in his theory of knowledge and in his ethics. In fact, his whole philosophy is characterized by these sharp antitheses. This was necessary to his purpose, if he would demonstrate the validity of knowledge and the unconditionality of ethical ideals. But the question must naturally arise— even in consequence of the critical philosophy—Must not even these distinctions and antitheses be ascribed to the method of our human understanding? The fact that this point also occurred to his mind with more or less definiteness is a splendid testimony to *Kant's* profound critical acumen. He felt the need before concluding his reflections, of investigating whether there might not be viewpoints which—more directly than the religious postulates —would transcend these profound antitheses. He thus

discovers certain facts which show us how existence by virtue of its own laws and even our ethical ideals become matters of our knowledge. There are two such facts: the one is of an æsthetic nature, the other biological (*Kritik der Urtheilskraft*, 1790).

In the phenomena which we call beautiful and sublime the object inspires in us a sense of disinterested satisfaction. In the case of the beautiful this rests on the fact that our intuitional faculty or our understanding is induced to harmonious coöperation, in that the parts of a phenomenon are readily and naturally combined into a single unit. *Kant* places special emphasis on the pure immediacy and involuntariness of the impression of beauty,—what he calls *free* beauty (e. g. the beauty of a flower, of an arabesque, of a musical fantasy). He does not regard the "secondary" beauty presupposed in the concept of an object (e. g. the beauty of man as such) as real beauty.—In contemplating the sublime our faculty of comprehension is overwhelmed and the sense of self subdued in the consciousness of being confronted by the immensity, the immeasurable in content and energy; but even in this very vanquishment, the consciousness of an energy superior to all sensible limitations arises in our consciousness: the consciousness of ideas and of the moral law as transcending all experience. The really sublime, according to *Kant*, is not the object, but the sentiment to which it gives rise.

Just as we behold the activity of Being in harmony with our spiritual dispositions in the beautiful and the sublime, even so the genius acts his part as involuntarily as a process of nature, and nevertheless produces works which have the value of patterns or types. Genius is a talent by means of which nature furnishes rules of art,—it is typical originality.

Organic life presents an analogy to the beautiful, the sublime, and the ingenious. Nature employs a method in the organic realm for which we really have no concept. Here we do not discover a being originated by the mechanical articulation and interaction of parts; nor have we the right, scientifically, to assume an antecedent plan according to which the parts are afterwards combined (as in the case of human architecture). The organism is therefore unexplainable either teleologically or mechanically. But perhaps the antithesis between the mechanical and the teleological explanations of nature rests merely on the peculiarity of our knowledge. Our understanding proceeds discursively, i. e. it proceeds from the parts to the whole, and if the parts are to be regarded as defined from the viewpoint of the whole, we are obliged to apply the anthropomorphic analogy with human purposes. But in pure being the same regulation which provides for the causal unity of things might perhaps also account for the possibility of the origin of organic forms capable of adaptation. It might be that the principles of mechanism and of teleology are after all identical in the unknown grounds of nature.

The same might be true also of the antithesis of pure reason which formulates natural laws, and the practical reason which propounds ethical ideals. Such being the case it would follow that it is one and the same principle which is revealed in the laws of nature and in the principles of ethics!

Here *Kant* reverts at the conclusion of his career, to a theory which had engaged him considerably during his early life (*Allgemeine Naturgeschichte und Theorie des Himmels. Einzig möglicher Beweisgrund*), and which certainly had never left him. He suggests the possibility of a monistic theory, which, according to his conviction, was incapable of scientific elaboration.

C. OPPONENTS AND FIRST DISCIPLES

If *Kant* himself felt that the stupendous critical task made it necessary to appeal to a fundamental unity behind the variety of distinctions, such demand must necessarily become even more insistent to independent thinkers who assumed a critical attitude to his own investigations. Independent disciples, if they had seriously studied the doctrines of the master, must likewise have felt the need of a greater unity and harmony. The difference between the opponents and the disciples consists in the fact that the former assumed a purely polemical attitude, whilst the latter endeavored to forge ahead to new viewpoints on the basis of the critical philosophy; the former oppose the necessary totality of life and faith to philosophical analysis, whilst the latter seek to realize a new idea of totality by means of a thorough analysis.

1. Foremost among the opponents, stands *John George Hamann* (1730–1788), "*The Wise Man of the North,*" who was one of *Kant's* personal friends. After a restless youth he settled in Königsberg in the office of Superintendent of Customs. His external circumstances were poor and he experienced profound mental struggles. He was a foe to every kind of analysis because of a morbid demand in his own nature for a complete, vital and undivided spiritual reality. He finds the ground of religion in our total being and it is far more comprehensive than the sphere of knowledge. The life of pure thought is the most abstract form of existence. *Hamann* refers to *Hume* as not having been refuted by *Kant* (the Prussian Hume).

In harmony with *Giordano Bruno* he thinks existence consists of a coincidence of opposites (coincidentia oppositorum), which are compatible with life, but in reflective thought remain forever incompatible. This explains the futility of analysis. In direct antithesis to *Kant* he holds (in the posthumous treatise *Metakritik über den Purismus der reinen Vernunft*) that reason, apart from tradition, faith and experience, is utterly helpless. He directs his attack more particularly against *Kant's* distinction between matter and form, intuition and reflection. What nature has joined together man must not put asunder!

John Gottfried Herder (1744–1803) likewise emphasizes the helplessness of reason: It is a product, not an original principle. He makes the racial character of poetry and religion prominent, regarding them as the immediate products of the human mind, in contrast to clear conception and volitional conduct. He extols the ages in which the mental faculties operated in unison rather than in isolation from each other, in which poetry, philosophy and religion were one. He aimed to penetrate behind the division of labor in the realm of mind. During the sixties he was an enthusiastic student of *Kant*, whom he attacks rather indirectly in the *Ideen zur Philosophie der Geschichte der Menschheit* (1784–1791), which is his most important work, more directly in his later, less significant treatises (*Metakritik*, 1799, *Kalligone*, 1800). As opposed to *Kant*, he denies the opposition between the individual and society. The individual is identified with the entire race by innumerable unconscious influences, and his inmost being is modified by historical development. On the other hand the goal of history is not alone determined by the race as a whole but likewise by the individual. *Herder* was no less opposed to the distinction between mind and nature,

God and the world, than to the sharp distinction between the individual and society, or between the conscious and the unconscious. God can no more exist apart from the world than the world can exist apart from God, and, like his friend *Goethe*, he was an admirer and exponent of *Spinoza*, to which *Lessing* referred in the famous conversation with *Jacobi*. His ecclesiastical position did not prevent him from expressing his thoughts freely and courageously. (*Gott*, 1787.) On this point he disagreed with his friends *Hamann* and *Jacobi*, notwithstanding their common emphasis of the total and indivisible life.

Friedrich Heinrich Jacobi (1743–1819), the third member of this group, as already observed, exposed the contradiction resulting from the Kantian theory of the "thing-in-itself" (*David Hume über den Glauben, oder Idealismus und Realismus*, 1787). Like *Hamann* and *Herder*, he likewise fails to find in the Kantian philosophy, and in all philosophy for that matter, the complete, total, undivided unity which can only be found in life and in unmediated faith. He contends that philosophy, if it is to be consistent, must annul all distinctions, combine everything into a single series of causes and effects, and thus not only the perfect and the vital, but even all originality and individuality, would be annulled. He used this argument in his *Briefen über Spinoza* (1785) against the philosophy of the enlightenment. In his *David Hume* he used the same argument against *Kant*, and later he made similar objections to *Fichte* (*Jakobi an Fichte*, 1799) and *Schelling* (*Von den göttlichen Dingen*, 1811). He regards even direct perception a miracle, since it is utterly impossible to furnish any demonstrative proof of the reality of the objective world. We are born into faith. *Jacobi* defends the rights of the individual both in the realm of morals and of religion. It is perfectly right for a beautiful soul to be guided by the affections, even though it should thus contradict abstract moral law.

2. The Kantian philosophy was first introduced into wider circles through the *Briefe über die kantische Philosophie* (1786) by *Karl Leonhard Reinhold* (1758–1823). *Reinhold* had become a monk in his early youth; but when the conflict between his rationalistic philosophy and the Catholic faith became too strong, he fled the cloister, became acquainted with the Kantian philosophy at Weimar and was shortly afterwards called to a Professorship at Jena (later at Kiel). Jena now became the center of the philosophical movement inspired by *Kant*. In contrast to *Kant's* multiplicity of distinctions and forms *Reinhold* proposed the derivation of everything from a single principle as the true ideal of philosophy (*Versuch einer neuen Theorie des menschlichen Vorstellungsvermögens*, 1789). He deduced this principle from the postulate that every idea sustains a twofold relation, to a subject as well as to an object. Consciousness, as a matter of fact, consists of such a relationship. That which *Kant* called Form is that element of an idea by means of which it is related to the subject. It is necessary to assume a thing-in-itself, because it is impossible for the subject to produce the object. The fact that he conceived the thing-in-itself as something entirely distinct from consciousness subjected *Reinhold* to a contradiction similar to that of his master. This contradiction is clearly elaborated in *G. E. Schultze's Aenesidemus* (1792).

The clearest exposition of the error resulting from postulating the thing-in-itself as a positive concept however is by *Salomon Maimon* (1754–1800). The thing-in-itself is intended to be the cause of the matter of our knowledge,

—but we never discover any absolute, i. e. entirely unformed matter, in our consciousness, and it would therefore be impossible even to inquire concerning the cause of the matter! The pure matter (pure sensation) is an "idea" like the pure form, the pure subject.

Maimon, the Lithuanian Jew, following the example of *Reinhold* in quitting the Catholic cloister, abandoned his native village with its limitations and poverty, in order to satisfy his intellectual hunger in Germany. *Kant* admitted that *Maimon* was the man who best understood him; but the venerable master was nevertheless dissatisfied with the criticisms and corrections offered by his brilliant disciple.

Maimon saw clearly that the mere reference to the conditions of experience is not the solution of *Hume's* problem: for what *Kant* calls experience, the permanent, necessary coherence of impressions, is the very thing that *Hume* denies. By experience *Hume* understands nothing more than impressions. That which is given in experience is never anything more than a succession of impressions, and it is useless to appeal to the categories, for they are nothing but rules or ideas used in our investigations. The concept of causality, e. g., enables us to attain the highest possible degree of continuity in the series of our impressions.

It is not reason that impels us to transcend experience, but the imagination and the desire for completeness. These are the motives that give rise to the ideas (in the Kantian sense), to which we afterwards ascribe objective reality. It is not the objects which are believed to exist on these grounds, but rather the constant striving after totality—which is the source of faith—that constitutes the highest reality. (*Versuch einer Transcendentalphilosophie*, 1790. *Philosophisches Wörterbuch*, 1791. *Versuch einer neuen Logik*, 1794.)

There is a close analogy between *Reinhold, Maimon* and *Friedrich Schiller* (1759–1805). *Schiller*, like the others, ran away from his cramping environment (the Military school at Stuttgart). And then, after the writing of his first sentimental essays, he devoted himself more thoroughly to the Kantian literature. He greatly admired *Kant's* indefatigable research and the exalted, ideal character of his ethics. But from his point of view *Kant* had nevertheless over-emphasized the antitheses of human nature, and severed the moral nature too completely from the actual development and ambitions of men. Duty appeared to be a kind of compelling force which man's higher nature exercises over his lower nature. *Schiller* therefore asserts that *harmony is the highest criterion in life as well as in art.* All the elements in the nature of man must coöperate in his actions. In order to be good, an act must not only bear the badge of dignity, but likewise of gracefulness. Morality is slavish as long as it consists of self-command (*Über Anmut und Würde*, 1793). *Schiller* elaborates this theory more fully in his *Briefen über aesthetische Erziehung* (1795) which shows a decided agreement with *Rousseau's* problem of civilization (which likewise exerted a profound influence on the reflections of *Kant*). The important thing is to surcharge the spontaneous fullness of the natural life with the independence and freedom of human life, the devotion to ever-changing circumstances with the unity of personality, the matter-impulse with the form-impulse. The solution of this problem is found in *play*, which is the beginning and prototype of art. It is only in the free play of his energies that man acts as a totality. The æsthetic state is therefore the highest perfection of culture: it is at once the end and the means of development, which transcends all coarseness and all harmony.

SIXTH BOOK.

THE PHILOSOPHY OF ROMANTICISM.

The history of philosophy, from the Renaissance onward, has revealed the fact that philosophy is not an exclusive world. It was in fact the new theory of nature and the new methods of natural science that, in all essential respects, determined the problems and the character of modern philosophy; to these must be added the new humanistic movements. And later on *Kant* was not only influenced by the opposition between *Wolff* and *Hume*, but likewise by the *Newtonian* natural science and *Rousseau's* problem of civilization. The development which followed during the first decades after *Kant* furnishes a new type of thought,—the romantic tendency of thought at the transition to the nineteenth century exercised a profound, in part even a fatal, influence on philosophy. Philosophy here reveals an undue susceptibility to the influences of other departments of thought. Otherwise the philosophy of *Romanticism* would have been unable to supplant the critical philosophy.

Kant had indeed aroused a profound enthusiasm, and he had a large following in his own age. But this was largely due to the seriousness and the depth of his fundamental principles of ethics. The new age was consciously opposed to the eighteenth century, the period of the *Enlightenment*, to which *Kant*, despite his profounder conception, nevertheless belonged. It now became necessary to institute a profound investigation of nature and history directly. Men were anxious to enjoy spiritual life in its unity and totality. Science, poetry and religion were no longer to be regarded as distinct or even hostile forces, but merely as different forms of a single life. *Novalis* proclaimed this gospel with fervent zeal. All antitheses must be transcended. *Kant's* philosophy abounded in antitheses; the profound antithesis between thought and being especially now became a rock of offense. *Kant's* suggestion of a unity at the basis of all antitheses was taken as the starting-point. According to *Kant* this conception represented one of the boundaries of thought; but now this was to furnish the starting-point whence all else is derived. *Reinhold* had already made the start. He proposed the ideal of knowledge assumed by *Romanticism*. No one inquired whether such an ideal were logically tenable: does not every inference in fact presuppose at least two premises! The intensity of their enthusiasm led men to believe that they could dispense with the traditional methods of thought and of science. As *Goethe's Faust* (this work appeared just at this time and the Romanticists were the first to applaud it), dissatisfied with everything which previously passed for knowledge, resorted to magic, in the hope of thus attaining an explanation of "the secret which maintains the universe in harmony," so the philosophers of *Romanticism* believed it possible to discover a new avenue to absolute truth. They resorted to intellectual magic. An attempt was made to sever the relationship which had existed between natural science and philosophy since the days of *Bruno* and *Descartes*. Despite the intense enthusiasm, the sublime sentiment and the profound ideas of the *Romantic* school, it nevertheless represents a vain attempt to discover the *Philosopher's Stone*. But just as the ancient *Alchemists* were not only energetic students, but in their effort to produce gold

likewise acquired important ideas and experiences, so
the significance of German idealism must not be estimated
alone by the results of its keen speculation. The fact is
indeed patent, that profound ideas neither stand nor
fall with the demonstration which men seek to give them.
The kernel may persist even though the husk decays.
The persistence of values is no more identical with the
persistence of certain special forms in the realm of thought
than in the realm of energy.

A. The Speculative Systems.

1. *John Gottlieb Fichte* (1762–1814), the son of a
Saxon peasant, took an enthusiastic interest, during
his school period, in the spiritual struggles of *Lessing,*
and later, after struggling with extreme poverty during
his university life, was led to philosophy by the writings
of *Kant.* His service at the University of Jena met with
great success, not only because of his intellectual keen-
ness and his eloquence, but likewise on account
of the impression made by his moral earnestness.
Having been dismissed on account of his religious
views he went to Berlin, where he afterwards received an
appointment. He takes first rank among those who,
in the disastrous period following the battle of Jena,
labored for the preservation of the sentiment of patriotism and of hope, especially by his *Addresses to the
German Nation,* delivered during the winter of 1808–9,
while Berlin was still in the hands of the French.

a. *Fichte's* philosophy is inspired by the criticism of
the Kantian theory of the thing-in-itself in which *Jacobi,
Schulze* and *Maimon* were already engaged. The motives
at the root of *Fichte's* reflections however were not purely
theoretical. Action constituted his profoundest motive

from the very beginning, and he even regarded thought as action. It was perfectly consistent therefore for him to say, in the clearest exposition of his doctrine which he has given (*Erste Einleitung in die Wissenschaftslehre*, 1797), that *a man's philosophy depends primarily on his character*. *Fichte* contends that there are two fundamental divisions in philosophy: *Idealism*, which takes the subject, the ego, as its starting-point, and *Dogmatism*, which takes the object, the non-ego, as its starting-point. This follows from the nature of the problem of philosophy, i. e. the explanation of experience. But experience consists of the knowledge of objects. And this admits of but two alternatives, either to explain objects (things) from the standpoint of knowledge (the ego), or knowledge (the ego) from the standpoint of objects (things). Persons of an active and independent nature will be disposed to choose the former method, whilst those of a passive and dependent nature will adopt the latter method. But even then idealism, from the purely theoretical point of view, has the advantage of dogmatism (which is liable, either as Materialism, Spiritualism or Spinozism, in all three cases to resolve itself into a theory of substance or things). Because it is impossible to deduce knowledge, thought, the ego, from things (i. e. regarded either as material, spiritual or neutral). But idealism makes knowledge, thought, the ego, its point of departure and then proceeds to show how experience, i. e. certain definite forms of knowledge, arises. The ego can contain nothing (known or thought) which is not posited by the activity of the ego.

In his chief work (*Grundlage der gesammten Wissenschaftslehre*, 1794) *Fichte* starts with the activity of the ego. The non-ego exists for us only by virtue of an activity of the ego; but the ego posits itself. Every idea involves this presupposition in a peculiar and special form. But the only method of discovering it is by abstract reflection, for immediate consciousness reveals nothing more than its products. We are never directly conscious of our volitions and activities; we take note of our limitations, but never of the thing which is thus limited. Free, unconstrained activity, which transcends the antitheses between subject and object, can only be conceived through a higher order of comprehension, through intellectual intuition. That is to say, it transcends every concept because every concept presupposes an antithesis.

But it is impossible to deduce definite, particular objects from this free activity, i. e. from the pure ego. In addition to the presupposition of self-activity by means of which the ego posits itself, we must therefore postulate a second presupposition: The ego posits a non-ego. Both propositions, notwithstanding their opposition, must be combined, and thus by thesis and antithesis we arrive at synthesis; so that our third proposition must be stated thus: The ego posits a limited ego in antithesis to a limited non-ego. This finally brings us to the level of experience. The limited ego is the empirical ego, which is constantly placed in antithesis to objects and must constantly overcome limitations.

Fichte moreover seeks to deduce the universal forms of experience (the Kantian intuitional forms and categories) from these fundamental principles. Thus, e. g. time is a necessary form whenever several acts of the ego are to be arranged in a definite order with reference to each other, and causality comes under the third fundamental principle (concerning the mutual limitation, i. e. the reciprocity between the ego and the non-ego). All such forms are forms of the activity of the pure, unlimited ego, which forms the basis of the empirical antithesis between ego and non-ego, but which can never manifest itself in experience.

But how is it possible to deduce this antithesis of an empirical ego and a non-ego from the pure ego? How does it happen that this unlimited activity is resisted and broken?—These questions are theoretically unanswerable according to *Fichte*. Whence this opposition, whence this impetus comes we do not know, but it is necessary to the explanation of actual (empirical) consciousness. And the limitation, as a matter of fact, does not even concern us theoretically, it pertains only to the practical reason! "An object possesses independent reality only in so far as it refers to the practical capacity of the ego." The only explanation of the existence of a world of non-egos is that we are intended to act: activity and effort as a matter of fact presuppose opposition (resistance) and limitation. Our task consists in realizing our liberty and independence through the successive transcendence of limitations. But the ultimate presupposition forever remains that pure activity which is revealed in us under the form of an impulse to act for action's sake. This presupposition furnishes the only possible explanation of the unqualified obligation which *Kant* expressed in the categorical imperative.

This complete subordination of the theoretical to the practical resulted in a complete refutation of fatalism. For the dependence of the whole system of our ideas rests far more profoundly on our volition than our activity on our ideas.

b.   The empirical ego is dependent even as limited.   It experiences an impulse to transcend the objects in order to transform them into means of pleasure.   Activity reveals itself at first as mere natural impulse.   But the impulse to act for action's sake can never be satisfied by a finite object, and hence consciousness will forever strive to transcend what is merely given.   Man gradually learns to regard things merely as means towards his own self-development.   It follows therefore that the highest moral obligation is expressed in the law: *realize the pure ego!* And this realization comes to pass by virtue of the fact that each particular act belongs to a series which leads to perfect spiritual liberty. (*Sittenlehre*, 1798.)

Radical evil consists of the indolence which holds fast to existing conditions and resists progress.   And moreover it leads to cowardice and treachery.   The first impulse in the development towards liberty comes from men in whom natural impulse and liberty are in equilibrium, and who are consequently regarded as types. The spontaneous respect and admiration accorded to such typical characters is the primitive form of moral affection.   The man who is still incapable of self-respect may nevertheless perhaps respect superior natures.   *Fichte* elaborated this idea in considerable detail in his famous *Reden an die deutsche Nation* (1808) as the foundation of a theory of national education. The spontaneous adoption or creation of ideal types forms the middle term between passive admiration and perfect liberty.

According to *Fichte* the religious consciousness is really implied in the moral consciousness.   For the very fact that I strive to realize my highest ideal assumes at the same time that the realization of this ideal by my own activity is possible. I must therefore presuppose a world-order in which conduct based on moral sentiment can be construed consistently. Religion furnishes an immediate validation of the confidence in such a world-order. It is not necessary that I should collect the experiences which reveal my relation to this world-order and formulate from them the concept of that unique being which I call God; and ascribing sensible attributes to this Being and making Him the object of servile and egoistic reverence, may even be positively harmful. This were indeed real and actual atheism. The fact that I conceive of God as a particular Being is a consequence of my finitude. The act of conceiving involves limitation and every supposed concept of a God is the concept of an idol! (*Über den Grund unseres Glaubens an eine göttliche Weltregierung*, 1798. *Appellation an das Publicum gegen die Anklage des Atheismus*, 1799.)

c. *Fichte* was never satisfied with the expositions which he had given of his theory. He was constantly trying to attain greater clearness both for himself and for his readers. He modified his theory unconsciously by these repeated restatements. In his later drafts he discarded the scholastic method of proof which he had employed in the first exposition of the *Science of Knowledge*. He then placed more stress on the immediate states and facts of consciousness. But the more he delved into the inexpressible ideas of absolute reality and no longer conceived this reality as active and infinite, but as at rest and superior to all effort and activity, the more his theory likewise assumed a mystical character. His religion was no longer mere practical confidence, but it now became a matter of devotion, of absolute self-surrender. This idea is quite prominent in his *Anweis-*

ung zum seligen Leben (1806). *Grundzüge des gegenwärtigen Zeitalters* (1806) is likewise of vast importance on
account of the incisive polemics against the eighteenth
century as "*the age of enlightenment and impoverishment*"
(*Auf-und Ausklärung*). Here we find a clear statement
of the antithesis which was later (in the school of *St.
Simon*) described as the antithesis between the organic
and critical age.

2. *Friedrich William Schelling* (1775–1854) is the
typical philosopher of *Romanticism*. Having no critical
prejudices whatever, in this youthful treatises which
constitute the exclusive basis of his philosophical significance, he proclaims a new science which is intended to
transcend all the antitheses still confronting the traditional
science. He labored first at Jena, afterwards at Stuttgart,
Munich and Erlangen. His youth was characterized by
great productiveness, which was however followed by
a remarkable period of stagnation in his productivity.
After the death of *Hegel*, when nearly seventy, he was
called to Berlin by *Frederick William IV*, for the purpose
of counteracting the radical tendencies arising from the
Hegelian philosophy. His lectures at Berlin, which had
aroused great anticipations, were however a complete
disappointment.

a. *Schelling* began his philosophical career as a col-
laborator of *Fichte*. His first essays constitute a further
development of the Fichtean science of knowledge. But
he could not accept the subordinate position ascribed
to nature in *Fichte's* philosophy (as mere limitation
and means). He undertakes to show in his *Ideen zu
einer Philosophie der Natur* (1797) and in various essays
in natural philosophy, that it is impossible that nature
should assume such a mechanical relation to mental life.

He states his problems very clearly; the romantic character consists in the treatment and the solution. Whilst the natural scientist lives in the midst of nature as in the immediate presence of reality, the philosopher of nature inquires how it is possible to know nature: "How nature and the experience of it is possible, this is the problem with which philosophy arose." Or as it has also been expressed: "*The phenomenality of sensibility is the borderland of all empirical phenomena.*" (*Erster Entwurf eines Systems der Naturphilosophie*, 1799.) This setting of the problem recalls the observation of *Hobbes*, namely, that the most remarkable of all phenomena is the fact that phenomena do exist. The realist and the romanticist agree in the statement of the problem, however widely they differ in their respective solutions. *Schelling* wishes to explain nature from the viewpoint of mind and thus substitute a new science instead of the natural science founded by *Galileo* and *Newton*. The natural scientist cannot explain how nature can be known. The natural philosopher explains it by construing nature as *unconscious mind*. *Fichte* had even distinguished a twofold tendency in consciousness: an infinite, unconditioned activity (the pure ego) and limitation (by the non-ego). Hence if there is to be any possible way of understanding the origin of mind from the forces of nature, it follows that these two tendencies must already be manifest in nature, only in lower degrees, or, as *Schelling* puts it, in lower potentialities. And since nature differs from mind only as a matter of degree, in which the tension of those tendencies, the polarity of opposites, as *Schelling* calls them, is manifested, it follows that the various phenomena of nature likewise show only quantitative differences.

Gravity, light and the organism represent the various levels through which nature ascends to mind. The relation of contraction and expansion varies on the different levels; in the organism they coexist in inner unity, and as a matter of fact we are then likewise already at the threshold of consciousness. Whilst mechanical natural science, with its atoms and laws of motion, reveals to us only the external aspect of nature, as lifeless objectivity, it is the business of natural philosophy to explain nature as it really is in its inmost essence, whereby it at the same time appears as the preliminary step to mind. On the lower levels the objective element predominates, on the higher levels the subjective element. These three levels of nature correspond to knowledge, action and art in the realm of mind (*System des transcendentalen Idealismus,* 1800). Art portrays directly and concretely what philosophy can describe only abstractly. Here therefore the two tendencies of being manifest themselves in perfect unity. *Schelling* could no longer regard the Absolute as pure ego because the relation of the latter to the non-ego was wholly external. The distinction between the subjective and the objective vanishes entirely in the Absolute; it is pure identity. *Antitheses exist only for finite mind.*

Schelling's Philosophy of Nature is really nothing more than a symbolic interpretation of nature, not an explanation of nature. He is even conscious of this fact himself. In one of his best essays (*Methode des akademischen Studiums,* 1803) he remarks: "Empiricism contemplates being as an object apart from its meaning, because the nature of a symbol is such as to possess its own peculiar life within itself. In this isolation it can appear only as a finite object, in an absolute negation of

the infinite." That is to say *the natural scientists are
not aware of the fact that nature is a symbol, but they
regard it as a thing-in-itself. The Philosopher alone
understands* (because he starts from within or from
above) *the symbolic significance.* But then *Schelling's*
philosophy likewise really amounts to nothing more
than a system of analogies and allegories which are
very arbitrarily applied. It is not without justification
that the term *"Philosophy of Nature"* has acquired a
suspicious sound in scientific ears.

Notwithstanding the fact that *Schelling* speaks of levels
and transitions, he is nevertheless not an evolutionist
in the modern significance of the term. He does not
accept any real development in time, but regards
nature as a magnificent system which reveals at once
the profound antithesis of subjectivity and objectivity
in the greatest variety of nuances and degrees, whilst
none of these differences pertain to the absolute ground
of his system. Time is nothing more than a finite form.—
Schelling's ideas have nevertheless contributed much
towards producing the conviction of the inner identity
of the forces and forms of nature.

b. *Schelling's* philosophy, with various modifications
which we cannot here discuss, bore the character of
"Philosophy of Nature" throughout its first period
(until 1803). But a problem now arises which all speculative philosophy must eventually take up: namely, if
the Absolute is to be regarded as an absolute unity or
indifference, how shall we explain the origin of differences,
of levels or (as *Schelling* likewise remarks) of potencies?
How can they have their ground in an absolute unity?
He treats this problem in his essay on *Philosophie und
Religion* (1804), which forms the transition from *Schelling's*

period of the philosophy of nature to that of the philosophy of religion. If experience reveals not only differences, but even antitheses which cannot be harmonized, it must mean that a fall from the eternal harmony must have taken place. *Historical evolution implies the mastery of disharmonies and the restoration of harmonious unity.* Just as he had made nature the preliminary of mind in the *Philosophy of Nature*, he now likewise construes history as a series of stages; not only the former but the latter is likewise an *Odyssey of the soul.*

Schelling elaborated this idea more fully in the treatise *Philosophische Untersuchungen über das Wesen der menschlichen Freiheit und die damit zusammenhängenden Gegenstände* (1809). *Schelling's* philosophy of religion was considerably influenced by the writings of *Jacob Böhme*, as this treatise in particular shows. *Schelling* seeks to prove that the only way God can be conceived as a personal being is to assume in Him an obscure principle of nature which can be clarified and harmonized by the unfolding of the divine life. The infinite personality must contain the antithesis within itself, whilst the finite personalities discover their antitheses outside themselves. But without opposition and resistance there can be no life and no personality. Hence God could not be God if there were not something within him which is not yet God.

Just as *Schelling* had read mind into nature in his Philosophy of Nature, so he reads nature into the absolute mind in his Philosophy of Religion. But that obscure principle contains the possibility of evil, according to *Schelling* even as for *Böhme*. That which was merely intended to be principle and matter may separate, i. e.

isolate itself. We can thus understand egoism, the sin and evil in nature, the irrational in general, which refuses to conform with ideas.

Thus *Schelling* passes into mythical mysticism. He elaborated his philosophy of religion in greater detail in works which appeared after his death, and which constituted the content of his Berlin lectures (*Philosophie der Mythologie* and *Philosophie der Offenbarung*). He regarded the history of religion as a great struggle with the Titanic elements which had been isolated by the Fall. This struggle takes place in the religious consciousness of mankind, which ascends through the various mythologies to Christianity, and finally through the development of Christianity to the religion of pure spirit.—In addition to brilliant ideas and points of view, we find here also, just as in the Philosophy of Nature, a large measure of fantasy and arbitrariness.

3. *George William Frederick Hegel* (1770–1831) is the systematizer of *Romanticism*, just as *Fichte* was its moralist and *Schelling* its mystic. He too labored at the University of Jena in his youth. Later on he went to Bavaria, first as an editor and afterwards as the director of a gymnasium. He appeared again in the capacity of university professor at Heidelberg, but soon accepted a call to Berlin where he founded a large and influential school.

a. *Hegel* undertook to construe the ideas which, according to his conception, express the essence of the various phases of existence in a progressive series based on logical necessity. What he called the dialectical method consisted in the discovery of the inherent necessity with which one concept leads on to another concept until at last all the concepts constitute one great, system. Notwithstanding this however, this purely logical character, which is so prominent because of the severely systematic form of *Hegel's* works, is not the fundamental characteristic of Hegelian thought. *Hegel* was naturally a realist. His supreme ambition consisted in penetrating into the real forces of being, and abstract ideas were intended to express only the forms of this content. He was of course convinced that the elements of reality in every sphere are essentially related to each other in the same way as ideas are in the mind. In this way the twofold character of his philosophy as realistic penetration and logical system becomes clear. Epistemologically this might be stated as follows: namely, that *he once more annuls the distinction between ground and cause (ratio and causa) which Hume and Kant had insisted on so strongly*. To this extent he returns to pre-critical dogmatism.

The realistic character is still quite dominant in *Hegel's* earlier works, with which we are acquainted through his manuscripts which have been used by a number of investigators. During his youth he was much occupied with historical studies and reflections, especially those of a religious nature. He paid high tribute of praise to the periods in which men dwelt in natural fellowship, because the individual still constituted an actual part of the whole, and had not yet asserted itself with subjective reflection and criticism as is the case in modern times. Even Christianity appeared to him as a sign of disintegration because it was a matter of individual concern, whilst on the other hand he regarded classical antiquity as fortunately situated because the individual lived and wrought completely and spontaneously within the whole. Like *Fichte* (in the *Grundzüge des gegenwärtigen Zeitalters*) *Hegel* likewise experienced a profound sense of antagonism towards the enlightenment, notwithstanding the fact that he too belonged to this period. But it was not *Hegel's* affair to revel in ecstasies over the ideals of the past. According to him ideal and reality, reason and actuality, are not real opposites.

He stood quite close to *Schelling* for a considerable period, during which time they published a paper in partnership. But important differences gradually arose and *Hegel* assails his former colleague openly in the preface to his first important treatise, *Phänomenologie des Geistes* (1807). He admits of course that *Schelling* understood that the problem consists in discovering the harmony between the antitheses. But he operates with a mere schema (subject-object), which he applies to everything mechanically, instead of showing how the one member of the antithesis effects the transition to the other by an inherent necessity, and how a higher unity of both is then formed. The absolute cannot be an immobile indifference; it is process, life, mind.—He showed, even in this book, how ordinary, practical consciousness rises to speculative consciousness through a series of steps, each of which leads to its successor by means of the contradictions discovered within itself. The reader is thus brought to the point from which he may grasp the pure system of ideas. This evolution takes place in the individual as well as in the human race as a whole; the *Phenomenology* is both a psychology and a history of civilization. The same law pertains to both realms, the same progressive dialectic.

b. According to *Hegel* dialectic is not only characteristic of thought, but it is likewise a fundamental law of being, because one form of existence always implies another and things are members of one grand totality.

No single idea is capable of expressing the totality of

being. Each idea leads to its own negative, because it reveals itself as limited and to that extent untrue. Negation then brings a new concept into existence. But since this one is likewise determined by the first, the necessity of a higher unity is evident, a unity within which both find their explanation, because they are *"annulled"* in a two-fold significance,—namely, negated in their isolation and at the same time affirmed as moments of the higher unity. Hence, according to the dialectical method, thought proceeds in *triads*, and *the system of all these triads constitutes truth. Truth can never be particular, but must always be totality.*

The fact that dialectic constitutes the process of being is revealed by the fact that every phenomenon of nature and of history leads beyond itself and exists only as an element of a totality. It is evident that *Hegel* here construes all being after the analogy of consciousness; the things which constitute the universe are supposed to sustain the same relations among themselves as ideas sustain in our minds. But he likewise makes use of other analogies. The effects of contrast show how the antitheses may oscillate from one to the other. And organic growth shows how it is possible for the earlier stages to determine the later and to continue their existence in them. *Hegel* constructs his theory of universal dialectic upon such analogies without being clearly conscious of the fact himself. Everything perishes and yet there is nothing lost. The memory of the universal mind preserves everything. And it is because of its inherent identity with the universal mind that the human intellect is capable of evolving the pure forms of the universal dialectic. *Kant's* doctrine of the categories is transformed into a world-system (*Wissenschaft der Logik*, 1812–1816).

Pure logic however is only the first part of the system. This follows from the fact that the pure forms of logic constitute the antithesis to real nature. We are led from logic to the philosophy of nature (likewise the profoundest problem in *Hegel's* system), i. e. to the doctrine of the phenomena which occur in time and space, by a dialectical necessity. As a matter of fact we have here to deal with *Schelling's* "Fall." *Hegel's* exposition of the philosophy of nature is, so far as particulars are concerned, quite as arbitrary and fantastic as that of *Schelling*. He likewise regards nature as a series of levels: we approach physics through mechanics, and thence to the organic sciences, but always under an "*inherent necessity.*" *Hegel* has no more room for a real development in time than *Schelling.*— The philosophy of nature brings us to the philosophy of mind, the "higher unity" of the first two parts of the system. The struggle incident to the objective distraction of space and time matures the abstract idea and it now returns within itself. Dialectic likewise leads through a series of steps in this case. Subjective mind (in a series of steps known as soul, consciousness and reason), the mental life of the particular individual, leads to objective mind, which is manifested in the triad of right, individual morality (conscience) and social morality (social and political life). The higher unity of subjective and objective mind is absolute mind, the totality of mental life, in which the antithesis of subject and object is annulled. Absolute mind is revealed in art, religion and philosophy (*Encyclopädie der philosophischen Wissenschaften*, 1817).

c. We shall discuss two divisions of the philosophy of mind somewhat more in detail; the doctrine of objective mind, which *Hegel* elaborated in his *Philosophie des Rechts* (1821), and the *Philosophy of Religion* as treated in the

Vorlesungen über die Philosophie der Religion, published posthumously.

Although *Hegel* no longer refers to the ancient character of the state with the same romantic fervor that characterized his early youth, his theory of the state nevertheless assumes an antique character. Actual morality appears in the life of the family, political society and the state, and not only forms an antithesis to abstract and objective right, but also to "morality," to subjective conscience in its isolation from the historical forms of society. The good exists in moral association and does not depend upon individual caprice and contingency. The moral world reveals the activity of something which is superior to the consciousness of the individual. The individual can only realize the highest type of development by a life in and for society. "*The moral substance*" is the mind which governs the family, the political society, and above all the state. The state is the complete actuality of the moral idea: the fact that the state exists is the witness of God's course in the world. The constitution of the state is a necessary consequence of its nature, and individual construction is here quite as much out of place as individual criticism. The modern state as a matter of fact is an organization of liberty; but this does not imply that the individual can participate in the government according to his individual caprice. The wise shall rule. Governmental authority belongs to the enlightened, the scientifically educated bureaucracy. The fact that the systematic development of the Hegelian philosophy of right shows a striking correspondence with the constitution of Prussia at that time (as far as it may be called a constitution) is not to be explained as a mere accommodation, but it was rather a consequence of *Hegel's* realism. *Hegel* thinks the divine idea is not so feeble as to be unable to permeate reality—of the state as well as of nature—and it is not the business of philosophy to contrive new ideals, but to discover the ideality of the vital forms realized hitherto.

The contrast between formalism and realism in the Hegelian philosophy appears perhaps most clearly in the sphere of religion. Here too it is *Hegel's* sole purpose to penetrate the facts; even here the sole business of philosophy consists in understanding what is actually given. He was convinced that philosophy which is developed to perfect clearness has the same content as religion. Philosophy indeed seeks the unity of being through all antitheses and at every step,—and religion teaches that everything has its origin in the One God. The only difference is this: that *what philosophy expresses in the form of the concept, religion expresses in the form of idea*, of imagination. Philosophy states in the language of abstract eternal concepts what religion proclaims concretely and enthusiastically in sublime symbols. The relation (as *Hegel* remarks, borrowing an illustration from *Hamann*) is like that between the closed fist and the open palm. Religion, e. g., speaks of the creation of the world as a definite act in time, accomplished once for all, whilst philosophy conceives the relation between God and the world as eternal and timeless (like that of ground and consequence). In the religious doctrine of reconciliation God becomes incarnate, lives as a man, suffers and dies on the cross: according to philosophy this too is an eternal relationship: the incommensurability of the finite and the infinite which must constantly be annulled in consequence of its finite form, if it is to describe an infinite result.—In the fervency of his zeal *Hegel* failed to see that this distinction of form might be of decisive importance. He describes the distinction between two world theories—the theory of monism or immanence and the theory of dualism or transcendence. *Hegel* reveals his romanticism in the naïve conviction that values are never destroyed by transposition into new forms. The problem which he thus neglected, as we shall presently see, was very clearly defined by his disciples.

B. CRITICAL ROMANTICISTS

The critical philosophy was not wholly suppressed during the romantic period. There were certain thinkers, who, whilst profoundly affected by the romantic tendency, had nevertheless not rejected the results of the critical philosophy. Although critics in epistemology, they endeavored at the same time by various methods to secure a theory of life which would transcend the limitations of science. Among these we mention *Schleiermacher, Schopenhauer* and *Kierkegaard*.

1. *Friedrich Daniel Ernst Schleiermacher* (1768–1834) completed his first courses of study at a Moravian institution, and even there already laid the foundation of his distinctive theory of life. The desire for a broader and more critical training took him to the university at Halle, where he later, after serving a number of years in a pastorate, became professor of theology. After the battle of Jena he went to Berlin, where, as professor and preacher, he labored not only on behalf of science and the church, but in the interest of public questions and the affairs of the nation.

He came to the conclusion early in life that the real characteristic feature of human life, its real nature, has its seat in the affections, and that in them alone man experiences the totality of his personal self. In addition to this he acquired, both by independent reflection and by the study of the works of *Kant*, a clear insight into the limits of human knowledge. He did not join the circle of romanticists until later. *Dilthey* has described this course of the development of the critical romanticist in his *Leben Schleiermachers*. *Schleiermacher's* position in the history of philosophy is characterized by the fact that he keeps the spirit of the critical philosophy alive within the ranks of romanticism. His Socratic personality, in which the capacity of complete inner devotion was united with a remarkable degree of calm discretion, furnished the basis for the combination of romanticism and criticism. According to his view the things which criticism destroyed and would no longer regard as objectively true did not necessarily lose their religious value if they could be supported as the symbolic expression of an affective personal experience. *Schleiermacher* reveals his romanticism especially in the fact that he does not distinguish sharply between symbol and dogma. He failed to see that as a matter of fact he assigned to religion a different position in the spiritual life than that which the church could accept. In his *Reden über die Religion an die Gebildeten unter ihren Verächtern* (1799) he defined immediate intuition and feeling, by which man is enabled to experience the infinite and the eternal, as the psychological basis of religion. Here every antithesis is annulled, whilst knowledge must forever move from idea to idea and volition from task to task. The only method by which intellectual, æsthetic and moral culture can attain their completion is by finally resting on subjective concentration such as is given in feeling alone. Hence *Schleiermacher* defines religion from the standpoint of human nature, not vice versa. He seeks to show the value of religion for life.

Schleiermacher's philosophical labors cover the departments of *epistemology, ethics* and the *philosophy of religion.*

a. He investigates the presuppositions of knowledge in his *Dialectik* (which was published only after his death). Knowledge exists only in the case where every single idea is not only necessarily combined with all other ideas, but where an actual reality likewise corresponds to the particular ideas. The relations between ideas must correspond with the relations between things. Particularly does the causal relation of objective reality correspond to the combination of concepts expressed in judgments. Here *Schleiermacher* presents a mixture of criticism and dogmatism. He forgets that the only knowledge we have of reality is by means of our thoughts, and furthermore that reality and thought forever remain incomparable. He nevertheless assumes that the identity of thought and being is a presupposition of knowledge, but not in itself knowledge. He thus opposes *Schelling*, for whom in fact that very identity constituted the highest kind of knowledge. But, according to *Schleiermacher, Schelling* offers nothing more than abstract schemata.—The pathway from that presupposition, which forms the starting-point of knowledge, to the idea of a complete totality of all existence, which would be the consummation of all knowledge— or, as it may likewise be expressed, from the idea of God to the idea of the universe—is a long one, and it can never be compassed by human knowledge. *Knowledge is only provisional.* We are always somewhere between the beginning and the end of knowledge and neither the one nor the other can be transformed into actual knowledge. But beyond the confines of knowledge the unity of being can be directly experienced in the affections and expressed in symbols. Here dialectic justifies every symbol which maintains the inseparability of the beginning and the end (God and the world). It is impossible to construe either of these from the standpoint of the other. But dialectic insists, in opposition to the religious method of representation, on the symbolic character of all expressions which are supposed to describe God, the world, and their respective relationship. Thus, e. g. the term *"person,"* when applied to God, is nothing more than a symbol.

b. Just as knowledge presupposes the unity of thought and being, so action likewise presupposes the unity of will and being. Action would be impossible if the will were absolutely foreign and isolated in the world. The former presupposition can no more be a fact of knowledge than the latter. We are thus led from dialectics to ethics (cf. a series of essays published in Complete Works, III, 2, and *Philosophische Sittenlehre*, published by *Schweizer*, 1835). According to *Schleiermacher* ethics is a theory of development in which reason and desire cultivate and govern nature. This development would be impossible if reason and will were not already present in nature. Nature is a kind of ethics of a lower order, a diminutive ethics. Will reveals itself by degrees—in the inorganic forms, in the life of plants and of animals, and finally in human life. There is no absolute beginning of ethical development. Here *Schleiermacher* in direct opposition to *Kant* and *Fichte* coördinates ethics with nature and history. But it is nevertheless only within the realm of humanity that he accepts an actual, real development.

Ethical capacity consists partly of organization, i. e. of constructive and formative power, partly symbolizing, i. e. expressive and descriptive power. Its organizing activity is shown in material culture and in commercial and legal business. In its symbolizing activity man objectifies his inner experiences in art, science and religion. —Whilst in his youth *Schleiermacher* (*Monologe*, 1800) was impatient with the prominence ascribed to material culture, and as a matter of fact wanted to recognize the "symbolizing" activity alone as ethical, later on he tried to recognize both forms of activity in their distinctive significance.

He disagreed with *Kant* and *Fichte* not only in the matter of the intimate relation of ethics to nature, but likewise in his strong emphasis on individuality. The nature of the individual is not exhausted in the universal and social. The only way an individual can possess any moral value is by means of the fact that he expresses what is universal in human nature in an individual way. His acts must therefore necessarily contain something which could not pertain to another individual. The individual could not have been fully active in the case of any act of his which lacked the distinguishing marks of his individuality.

c. In his conception of religion *Schleiermacher* is inclined both to intellectualism and to moralism. He assigns religion to the point where the division of the mental faculties has not yet become active, and where that which is individual is just in process of differentiating itself from the universal, without however as yet having attained the antithesis of subject and object. This point is given in an immediate feeling, which he at first (in the *Reden über die Religion*) described as a sense of unity, later on (in *Der christliche Glaube*, 1821) rather as a sense of dependence. *It is the birth-place of personality.* In this feeling we are at once personal and dependent: it is here that we acquire the basis of our personality. The sense of dependence becomes a consciousness of God at the moment when reflection begins; the term "God" implies *"the source of our susceptible and independent being."*

Religious ideas and concepts are all secondary. They are deduced by reflection on the immediate states of feeling in which the essence of religion consists. The demand for expression and communion furnishes the impulse to clothe the subjective experiences in word and symbol. Such words and symbols constitute dogmas, i. e. symbolical expressions of religious states of mind. Each separate dogma must bear a direct relation to some feeling, and the dogmatician must never deduce a dogma from another dogma by purely logical processes. *Whenever dogmatic statements are taken literally, dogmatics becomes mythology.* This appertains, e. g. to the ideas of the personality of God, personal immortality, creation, the first human pair, etc. It likewise applies to the idea of miracle. The interests of religion can never place God and the world in opposition to each other. The Christian-religious feeling is characterized by the fact that Christians experience a purifying and an enlargement of their own circumscribed feelings through the type expressed in the congregation; in this way they experience Christ as the Redeemer.

Schleiermacher's philosophy marks an important advance, especially in its psychological aspect. But he is likewise disposed to identify symbolic statement and causal explanation in the same way as he identifies dogma and symbol. On these points the philosophy of religion receives further development at the hands of *Strauss* and *Feuerbach.*

2. *Arthur Schopenhauer* (1788–1860) is a Kantian in epistemology, but he claims to have discovered a direct revelation of the thing-in-itself. He discovers the solution of the riddle of the universe with romantic precipitancy

by means of an intuition which instantly drops all limitations. His great importance rests on his psychological views and on his philosophy of life which is based on personal experience.

Schopenhauer, the son of a wealthy Dantzig merchant, enjoyed a well-rounded education and became acquainted with the world early in life by means of travel and a variety of social intercourse. His complete independence enabled him to devote himself entirely to his studies and to the elaboration of his theory of life. After an unsuccessful attempt in a professorship at the University of Berlin, he withdrew into private life at Frankfort-on-the-Main where he spent the rest of his days. From his own inner experience he had very early become acquainted with the mysterious, conflicting energies and impulses of life; and the things which he saw around him at times aroused his anger, and again his sympathy. He concluded from these experiences that the beginning of philosophy is not wonder, but confusion and despair, and he endeavored to rise above them by reflective thought and artistic contemplation.

a. *Schopenhauer* elaborated his critical theory already in his first essay (*Über die vierfachen Wurzeln des Satzes vom zureichenden Grunde*, 1813). The principle of sufficient reason receives its four different forms from the fact that our ideas may be inter-related in four different ways: as ground and consequence, as cause and effect, in space and time, and as motive and act. Contemporaneously with *Hegel's* attempt to annul the distinction between ground and cause, emphasized by *Hume* and *Kant*, *Schopenhauer* shows clearly the importance of this distinction.

The first book of his chief work (*Die Welt als Wille und Vorstellung*, 1819) contains his theory of knowledge. He differs from *Kant* especially on account of the intimate relation between intuition and thought which he maintains. Sensation, which is the correlate of a bodily change, is the only thing which is directly given. But the faculties of understanding and intuition likewise coöperate instinctively; we conceive the cause of sensation as an external object, distinct from our body, by an act which reveals the theory of causality. Space, time and causality coöperate in this projection. Experience never modifies this act, which indeed even forms the basis of the possibility of experience.

Cognition (sensation, understanding, intuition) is a product of our physical organization. The methods of natural science never get beyond materialism. Just as we discover the cause of a sensation in a physical object distinct from our body, so we likewise find the cause of such object, as well as its states, in a third object, etc. The law of inertia and the permanence of matter are the direct implications of the law of causality. The insufficiency of materialism however rests upon the fact that the principle of sufficient reason pertains only to the objective correlate of the idea; matter itself, which is the cause of the sensation and of the idea, is present only as the object of the idea. *For cognition the world is nothing more than idea.* We are not concerned with anything beyond the relations of ideas to each other. It is impossible, on the basis of theoretical knowledge, to get beyond this circle.

But *what* is being? What really constitutes the aggregate of these objects of ideas? *Schopenhauer* believes that he has discovered a method of unveiling the "thing-in-itself." The principle of sufficient reason appertains only to us as cognizing beings. *As volitional beings we ourselves are thing-in-itself.* An aspiration and yearning, an impulse towards self-assertion, is active in the profound depths of our being, beneath every idea, which is manifest in pleasure and in pain, hope and fear, love and hate,— *a will, which constitutes our inmost nature, the primary phenomenon!* We understand the inmost nature of the world by our own inmost nature. Thus, with the help of analogy, an analogy whose justification, due to his romantic temper, he never questions, he makes the transition to metaphysics.—The fact that all volition is a temporal process and that all we know about it is merely phenomenal, of course constitutes a real difficulty. (*Herbart* called attention to this difficulty already in a review in 1820.) *Schopenhauer* concedes this difficulty in the second volume of his chief work (which appeared twenty-five years later than the first), but thinks that volition is nevertheless the phenomenon with which we are really identical. But in that case the principle of sufficient reason, which applies to all phenomena, must likewise apply to volition,—and then the thing-in-itself still remains undiscovered!

It was a matter of profound importance for the development of psychology that volitional life was emphasized so vigorously—and in its details frequently so ingeniously—in contrast to the Hegelian intellectualism.—Beyond this *Schopenhauer* is evidently affected by *Fichte*, not only in his theory of will, but likewise in his projection theory which forms an essential part of his theory of knowledge (especially by *Fichte's* lectures *Über die Thatsachen des Bewusstseins*).

Our knowledge of will does not rest upon direct introspection alone. It likewise possesses phenomenal form, because our whole body is the material expression of will. Body and will are one. *Schopenhauer* could therefore call knowledge (the idea and its object) a product of the will quite as consistently as a product of the body. The body is the same thing seen objectively (physically) as the will seen subjectively (metaphysically). The operation of will is manifest throughout the whole of physical nature—in organic growth, in the functional activity of muscles and nerves, in fact in all the forces of nature. *Schopenhauer* endeavors to prove this in detail in his book, *Der Wille in der Natur* (1836), and in the second volume of his master-piece, because here he likewise operates with analogies. We behold the operation of will in nature through a series of steps (which are however no more to be regarded as temporal, real evolutional steps than in *Schelling* and *Hegel*). The steps accordingly vary to the degree of difference between cause and effect. On the level of mechanism cause and effect are equivalent, showing a slight degree of dissimilarity already in chemism, whilst in the organic realm the cause dwindles to a mere dis-charging stimulus, and where consciousness enters it simply furnishes the motive. The dissimilarity is greatest when we come to the last step—and here indeed the causal relation is revealed as an act of will!

Will manifests itself everywhere as the will to live—for the mere sake of living, of pure existence. Here the ques-tion, why, no longer occurs; the principle of sufficient reason does not apply to the will itself. The multiplicity of forms and energies in nature, the movements which are forever renewed, and the everlasting unrest in the world reveal the presence of the ever-active energy of the impulse of self-assertion. This vague impulse involves us in the illusion that life is good and valuable. The will employs this illusion as the inducement for us to maintain our existence at any cost. Existence understood in its real nature, just because it consists essentially in a restless and insatiable impulse, is pain, and pleasure or satisfaction only arises as a contrast-phenomenon, namely, when this infernal fire is momentarily quenched. ⟨All pleasure is illusory, a zero, which only appears to have positive value by contrast. In a vivid portrayal of human and animal life *Schopenhauer* describes the torture of existence, "the rush and confusion," in which living beings fight and destroy each other.

The vast majority are under the illusion, produced by the desire to live, of the value of life. Those of profounder vision, especially the geniuses, lift the veil of the *Maya* and discover the profound disharmonies.—The question arises, is there then no way of escape, no means by which we can rescue ourselves from this torture?

b. He devotes the last two books of his chief work to answering these questions. *Schopenhauer* finds some real difficulties on these points: for if will is everything, identical with the "world," whence shall the energy proceed by which the will itself is to be annulled? And if the will should be annulled, would it not follow that everything would then be annihilated? *Schopenhauer* replies that the will is not annihilated by some cause other than itself, but that it simply subsides (in such a manner that *velle* is supplanted by *nolle*). And the state which supervenes is merely a relative nothing, i. e. as respects our idea; in itself it may quite as readily be a positive reality. It is the Nirvana of the Buddhists; were it not for the danger of abuse of the term, *Schopenhauer* would not have objected to apply the word "God."

There are three ways by which the will-to-live may be sublated. It is possible to assume the attitude towards life of a mere spectator, in which case he devotes himself wholly to aesthetic or intellectual contemplation. ⟨If e. g. we are completely absorbed in the contemplation of some work of art, the will is subdued and we forget that we are denizens of the world. Art everywhere represents the climax. The agony of life subsides in the presence of the image of life.—This is the course taken by *Schopenhauer* himself.—In the case of human love, which—because all life is full of agony—necessarily assumes the character of sympathy, the individual will vanishes from the fact that it is lost in its identity with its object. This thought forms the basis of *Schopenhauer's* ethics (*Die beiden Grundprobleme der Ethik*, 1841).—It is after all only the saints, the ascetics, for whom every motive has vanished, who are capable of an absolute suppression of the will. *Schopenhauer* finds the best practical solutions of the riddle of life and of the agony of life in Buddhism, in primitive Christianity, and in mysticism, and he has the most profound regard for the chief representatives of asceticism,—the more so, because of the consciousness that he was not a saint himself.

3. The romantic philosophy made a profound impression in the Scandinavian North, differing according to the different character of the northern peoples.—In Sweden the romantic opposition to empirical philosophy is particularly evident. The fundamental principle of the philosophy characteristic of Sweden was this, namely, that truth must be a perfect, inherently consistent totality, and since experience merely presents fragments, and such forsooth as are constantly undergoing change, a constant antithesis of ideal and empirical truth must follow. After this idea had been elaborated by a number of thinkers, the most noteworthy of whom are *Benjamin Hoyer* and *Eric Gustav Geyer*, the school attained its systematic culmination in the philosophy of *Christopher Jacob Boström* (1797–1866), professor of the University of

Upsala, according to whom time, change and evolution are illusions of the senses, whilst true reality consists of a world of ideas which differ from Platonism by the fact that the ideas are construed as personal beings.—Denmark reveals the influence of *Schelling* and *Hegel* to a marked degree, especially among the writers in æsthetics and the theologians. The more independent thinkers however have devoted themselves almost exclusively to the problems of psychology, ethics and epistemology and assumed an attitude of decided opposition to abstract speculation. *Frederick Christian Sibbern* (1785–1872), who labored at Copenhagen in the capacity of professor of philosophy for more than fifty years,—in opposition to *Hegel* and *Boström*—placed great stress on a real evolution in time. Experience reveals that evolution has a number of starting-points, and the contact of the various evolutional series with each other gives rise to strife, "*a stupendous debate of everything with everything,*" which in turn accounts for progress. This idea of sporadic evolution has likewise an important bearing on the theory of knowledge: each cognizing being has the viewpoint of one of these beginnings and hence cannot survey the entire process. *Sibbern* devoted himself more particularly to psychology, for which he was specially adapted by his gift of observation and his enthusiastic interest in human life.

We shall consider *Soren Kierkegaard* (1813–1855) only as a philosopher, leaving out of account his æsthetic and religious activities, which have taken such deep hold on the life of the North. The author of this text-book has given a general description of this thinker in his book *Soren Kierkegaard, als Philosoph* (in Frommann's Klassiker).

Kierkegaard is a "subjective thinker" in the sense in which he used that word (in the book *Unwissenschaftliche Nachschrift*, 1846, *Kierkegaard's* chief philosophical work). The ideas of the subjective thinker are determined by the interplay of all the elements of psychic life,—by emotion and reflection, by hope and fear, by tragic and comic moods. *And this thinking takes place in the midst of the stream of life, whose boundaries we cannot see and whose direction we can never know, at least not in the fantastical and impersonal world of abstraction.* *Kierkegaard* is the Danish *Pascal*, and his position in relation to the philosophy of his age possesses a certain analogy to *Pascal's* relation to *Cartesianism.*—This predominantly personal character of his thought however does not preclude the possibility of his making valuable contributions to epistemology and ethics (or better, to a comparative philosophy of life) as he has actually done.

Sibbern had already observed that the fruitful ideas of *Kant* had not received their just dues at the hands of his successors. *Kierkegaard* renews the problem of knowledge with still greater definiteness, and declares that *Hegel* had not solved the Kantian problem. We can arrange our thoughts in logical order and elaborate a consistent system. It is possible to elaborate a logical system, but a finite thinker will never be able to realize a complete system of reality. We deduce the fundamental ideas from experience and experience remains forever imperfect. We understand only what has already taken place; *knowledge comes after experience. We cognize towards the past—but we live towards the future.* This opposition between the past and the future accounts for the tension of life and impresses us with the irrationality of being. The denial of the reality of time by abstract speculation is the thing that constitutes the thorn in the problem of knowledge.

What is thus true of scientific thought is even more so in the reflections on the problems of practical life. In this case it is personal truth that takes first rank, i. e. the important matter to be considered here is the fact that the individual has acquired his characteristic ideas by his own efforts, and that they constitute an actual expression of his personality. Subjectivity constitutes the truth. Whoever prays to an idol with his whole heart and soul, prays to the true God, whilst he who prays to the true God from mere force of habit and without having his heart in it, is really worshipping an idol. *Kierkegaard* shows his romanticism in the fact that he sharply contrasts the heart with life as it is actually experienced and entirely disregards intellectual integrity, which is an essential condition, if personal truth is to escape identification with blindness.

Kierkegaard outlined a kind of comparative theory of life—partly in poetic form (*Entweder—Oder; Stadien auf dem Lebensweg*), partly in philosophical form (in his chief philosophical treatise mentioned above). He distinguishes various "Stadia," which however do not constitute stages in a continuous line of evolution, but sharply severed types. The transition from the one to the other does not follow with logical necessity, nor by means of an evolution explainable by psychological processes, but by a leap, an inexplicable act of will. *Kierkegaard* maintains the qualitative antitheses of life in sharp contrast to the quantitative continuity of the speculative systems.

According to *Kierkegaard* the principle of evaluation and construction of theories of life consists in the degree of opposition which spiritual life is capable of comprehending. The particular moment and the totality of life, time and eternity, reality and the ideal, nature and God—constitute such antitheses. The tension of life increases in direct proportion to the increasing sharpness of the manifestation of these antitheses, and the energy which is supposed to constitute life must therefore likewise be correspondingly greater. The professional artist who is absorbed in the pleasure of the moment represents the lowest degree; the writer of irony already discerns an element of the inner life which is incapable of expression in a single moment, or in a single act; the moralist develops this inner life positively by real influence on the family and in the state; the humorist regards all the vicissitudes of life as evanescent as compared with eternity and assumes an attitude of melancholy resignation, which he preferably makes the subject of jest; the devotees of religion regard the temporal life as a constant pain because finite and temporal existence is incommensurable with eternal truth; the Christian finally regards this pain as the effect of his own sins, and the antithesis of time and eternity can only be annulled by the fact that the everlasting itself is revealed in time and apprehended in the paradox of faith.

Kierkegaard wanted to show by this scale how comprehensive an ideal of life was possible even outside of Christianity. He likewise wanted to put an end to the amalgamation of Christianity and speculation in theology. But the anguish occasioned by the tension finally became his standard for the sublimity of life, and he had sufficient courage of consistency to draw the inference, *that the sufferings of no one are equal to those endured by God!*— This brings him into direct conflict with the romantic theory of the reconciliation of all antitheses in the "higher unity," as well as with the accepted conception of Christianity. This furnished the motive for the deplorable controversy with the state church, which occupied the latter years of his life.

C. THE UNDERCURRENTS OF CRITICAL PHILOSOPHY IN THE ROMANTIC PERIOD.

It is important for the continuity of the history of philosophy that there were philosophers, even in the period of romanticism and speculation, who undertook to carry out a strictly critical and empirical treatment of the fundamental concepts. Two of *Fichte's* students at Jena deserve mention in this connection as belonging to the first rank. These men soon protested that the method by which *Fichte* and his disciples were trying to develop the Kantian philosophy was not correct. The significance of *Fries* and *Herbart* however does not depend alone upon the fact that they are representatives of the critical philosophy, but likewise upon their scientific method of treating the problem of psychology. This latter fact makes them, especially *Herbart*, the forerunner of modern psychology. *Beneke*, who had been considerably affected by the English school, likewise joins them.

1. *Jacob Friedrich Fries* (1775–1843), like *Schleiermacher*, was educated at a Moravian college, and, despite the fact that a native impulse for untrammelled science had carried him far beyond the ideas of his early teachers, he nevertheless continued his adherence to them to the end, especially in the matter of the emphasis which he placed on the emotions. While professor at Jena, *Fries* participated in the Wartburg celebration, on account of which he was forbidden to continue his lectures in philos-

ophy. The fact that he was then able to accept a professorship in physics was a tribute to the breadth of his scholarship.

According to *Kant* the critical philosophy must consist of self-knowledge; *Fries* deplored the lack of a psychological foundation for such knowledge. According to him the problem of psychology consisted in discovering and describing the spontaneous forms with which our knowledge operates. Those fundamental concepts which constitute the scientific expression of these forms must then be deduced from psychological experience by the method of abstract analysis. Notwithstanding the fact that *Fries* clearly saw that we can have no guarantee that the fundamental concepts discovered by this empirico-analytic method are adequate, he was nevertheless convinced that *Kant* had succeeded in enumerating all of the fundamental concepts (categories). He accepted *Kant's* table of categories and of ideas.—On the other hand however he departs from *Kant* on one important point, namely, on the matter of establishing the objective validity of knowledge. Here he agrees with *Maimon* that *Kant* had failed to establish the right to apply the categories. *Kant* only answered the *quæstio facti*, not the *quæstio juri*. Truth can only consist in the agreement of mediate knowledge (of reason) with immediate (of perception), and beyond this it is impossible for us to transcend the subjective demonstration of knowledge. *Fries* regards the denial of this situation as the cause of the ultra-speculative tendency of the Romanticists (*Neue Kritik der Vernunft*, 1806–7).

According to *Fries* the real problem of philosophy consists in the application of the regressive, analytical method, which seeks to discover the fundamental concepts, which condition all understanding from the facts of experience. The method is more important than the system. This analytic method demands a strictly scientific treatment of the problems of psychology. Psychology must be a strictly causal science, whose correlate constitutes an exact science of the corporeal side of nature. This standpoint of *Fries* is Spinozistic. He presumes, by way of analogy, that all existence everywhere possesses an inner, spiritual phase as well as an external, material phase (*Psychische Anthropologie*, 1820–1).

Even the most consistent causal method only leads from the finite to the finite. There is no scientific path to the infinite and the eternal. But the same reality which the natural sciences regard as the world of phenomena, faith construes as supported by an eternal principle. But the only way we can describe this principle is negatively. Whenever faith makes use of positive expressions, it must be understood that these can only have symbolical significance. *Fries* carries out the idea of symbolism far more purely and consistently than *Kant* and *Schleiermacher* (*Handbuch der Philosophie der Religion*, 1832).

2. *John Friedrich Herbart* (1776–1841), who was an instructor in the universities of Königsberg and Göttingen, calls himself a "Kantian of 1828." He thus described both his relation to *Kant* as well as his critical advance beyond him. He would start from experience—but he regards it impossible to remain on the empirical basis. For experience contains contradictions which—owing to the logical principle of identity—must be corrected: things change but they are nevertheless supposed to remain the same things! One and the same thing

possesses a variety of attributes! And the concept of the ego, which *Fichte* endeavored to make the basis of the speculative philosophy, contains both contradictions: the ego develops and is nevertheless supposed to remain identical with itself, and the ego is supposed to be a unity, but it nevertheless possesses a manifold content!—The correction of contradictory experience should however adhere to experience as closely as possible; for we are obliged to maintain the principle: *every phenomenon contains its proportionate implication of reality!* (*Hauptpunkte der Metaphysik*, 1808). The contradictions vanish whenever we assume a manifold of existing entities (realities): when a thing changes it must be explained from the fact that it is being observed in relation to different things (different realities) than before; when a thing possesses a number of attributes it must be explained from the fact that is being observed in relation to different things (realities). Thus experience is corrected by "*the method of relations.*" But the relations do not pertain to things as such; they are wholly contingent, and the method of relations can therefore likewise be called "*the method of contingent views.*" Each particular Real constitutes an absolute position, independent from all other Reals.—The peculiarity of the Herbartian philosophy is expressed in two propositions: 1. *In the realm of being there are no events.* 2. *Every continuum is excluded from reality* (*Allgemeine Metaphysik*, 1828).

What then do we know about the Reals? Herbart, in opposition to metaphysical idealism, holds that, if it is possible to form an idea of the Real, the experiences in the realm of spiritual nature have no prerogatives above the experiences in the realm of material nature. But when he calls the identity of a Real "*self-preservation*" notwithstanding its relation to other Reals, and since the only example of self-preservation of which we can have any knowledge is contained in our own sensations, he nevertheless likewise really makes use of the analogy with our psychical experiences in the same manner as the metaphysical idealists.

Even the soul is Real. Ideas arise in the soul as forms of self-preservation in distinction from other Reals. And since, according to Herbart, the Real which supports psychical phenomena must be different from the Real which supports material phenomena, he attains a spiritualism which differs from the Cartesian by the fact that the interaction does not take place between dissimilar entities, but between similars. *Herbart* therefore partly bases his psychology on his metaphysics (*Psychologie als Wissenschaft, neu gegründet auf Erfahrung, Metaphysik und Mathematik*, 1824–5). But he bases the necessity of assuming a psychical Real largely upon the fact that our ideas present a mutual interaction and combination. Sometimes they blend (by assimilation), i. e. when they are internally related; sometimes they combine into groups (aggregations), i. e. when they are heterogeneous (as colors and tones) but still occur coincidently; sometimes they inhibit or obscure each other, i. e. when they are homogeneous without however being able to blend. That which we call our ego is the controlling group of ideas, which is formed by assimilation and aggregation, and upon which the determination of what shall have psychological permanence depends; for only that can persist which can be blended with the controlling ideas (i. e. be apperceived).—*Herbart* here recalls the English associational psychology founded by *Hume* and *Hartley*.

But *Herbart* would not only base his psychology on metaphysics and experience, but likewise upon mathematics. He discovered the possibility of this in the fact of inhibition. Mathematical psychology aims to discover definite laws governing the reciprocal inhibition of ideas. Psychical energies cannot be measured by movements in space like those of physics; but *Herbart* thought it possible to start from the fact that, inasmuch as all ideas strive to preserve themselves, the sum of inhibition in any given moment must be the least possible. The problem therefore consists in determining how to divide the inhibition among the various coincident or aspiring ideas.— This presupposition rests upon *Herbart's* metaphysical theories, according to which every idea is a self-preservative act of the psychical Real. *Herbart* failed to attain clear results and such as could be harmonized with experience on the basis of this presupposition by the method of calculation, and his significance as a psychologist does not rest upon this attempt to reduce psychology to an exact science.

Herbart excludes ethics—here he is an out-and-out Kantian—completely from theoretical philosophy. He is of the opinion that there is no scientific principle which can at once be subsumed as the explanation of reality and the guarantee of value.—Our value judgments are spontaneously and often unconsciously determined by certain practical ideas. Such ideas are patterns which hover before the mind whenever we judge of the harmonic or disharmonic relation between the conviction and the actions of a man or between the strivings of a number of men in relation to one another. Whenever we discover disharmony between a man's conviction and the trend of his actual desires, it conflicts with the idea of inner

freedom; whenever the conviction or its practical execution is too feeble, it conflicts with the idea of perfection.
And the ideas of right, of equity, and of benevolence in
the mutual relations of a number of men find their application analogously. We discover the practical ideas by
means of an analysis of our judgments concerning human
actions, in cases where the relations are clearly present,
and where irrelative interests are in abeyance. *Herbart*
even refers to *Adam Smith's "disinterested observer"*
(*Allgemeine praktische Philosophie*, 1808).

3. *Frederick Edward Beneke* (1798–1854) quietly
fought a hard battle at the University of Berlin for the
empirical philosophy against the dominant speculative
philosophy. For a while he was even deprived of the
privilege of lecturing. Notwithstanding the fact that he
exercised a profound influence upon the development of
psychology and pedagogy, he nevertheless regarded his
effort as useless, and discouragement apparently caused
his death.

Beneke is especially influenced by *Fries* and *Schleiermacher*. He would base his philosophy on psychology,
i. e. elaborate a psychologism. Here he is radically
opposed to *Herbart*, who even endeavored to partly base
psychology on metaphysics. *Beneke* approaches closely
to the English school and even calls himself a disciple
of *Locke*. His psychology has a biological character.
He describes the development of consciousness as a
growth of innate germs or rudiments, which he calls
original faculties; these are the faculties of sensation and
of motion. The original faculties are conjoined with a
tendency; the objective stimuli through which the original
faculties are enabled to attain a complete development
are sought out spontaneously. The experiences which are

thus acquired leave traces or dispositions behind, which furnish the possibility of the origination of new, derived faculties. An incessant interaction between the conscious and the unconscious is therefore in constant progress.—Of the more specific psychical phenomena *Beneke* describes especially the significance of the relation of contrast for the emotions, and the tendency of psychical elements to extend their impress over the whole psychical state ("liquidation"). The distinction between the higher and lower levels of consciousness is to be explained by the great multiplicity and variety of the elements and processes coöperating in the development of consciousness (*Psychologische Skizzen*, 1825–7; *Lehrbuch der Psychologie als Naturwissenschaft*, 1833).

Beneke passes deliberately from psychology to metaphysics by means of an analogy: In our inner experience we become acquainted with a part of being as it is in itself, and we afterwards naturally conceive that part of being which we only know as external, objective being (material nature), after the analogy of our own self. But this analogy does not mislead him into the substitution of an idealistic interpretation for the mechanical explanation of nature (*Das Verhältniss von Seele und Leib*, 1826).

According to *Beneke* ethical judgments arise through reflection concerning the kind and manner in which our feelings are set in motion by human actions. This viewpoint dominates his youthful essay, *Physik der Sitten* (1822). Strongly influenced by *Bentham*, he placed greater emphasis on the objective side of ethics later on, in the fact that he took special account of the way in which the actions affect the welfare of living beings (*Grundlinie der Sittenlehre*, 1837).

D. The Transition from Romanticism to Positivism.

1. *The Dissolution of the Hegelian School.* The profound influence and the wide dissemination of the Hegelian
philosophy is due more particularly to the supposed
successful reconciliation of faith and knowledge, of
ideality and reality. But these alleged results were put
to the test shortly after *Hegel's* death. There was some
doubt whether the belief in a personal God and in a
personal immortality could be reconciled with Hegelian
philosophy (*Fr. Richter: Die Lehre von den letzten Dingen,*
1833), and it was claimed that the logical consequence
of the Hegelian philosophy of religion was not the Chris-
tology of the church, but the mythical theory of the
Person of Christ (*D. F. Strauss: Leben Jesu, kritisch
bearbeitet,* 1835).

The Hegelians divided on this question, and we soon
hear of a Hegelian right and a Hegelian left. Those on
the right (represented particularly by *Göschel, Rosen-
karanz* and *J. E. Erdman*) held that the theory of the
master, properly understood, was in harmony with positive faith and with the doctrine of the Church. Those on
the left, on the other hand, drew most radical conclusions from the teaching of the master who was apparently
so very conservative, both in the department of the philosophy of religion (*Strauss* and *Feuerbach*) and in that of
the philosophy of law and society (*A. Ruge, Karl Marx,
Ferdinand Lasalle*).

There were also men however who granted to the
Hegelian left that Hegelianism was incapable of defending
theism, but who at the same time thought it possible to
vindicate theism by the method of pure thought. They
endeavored to show that all fundamental ideas (cate-

gories) finally combine in the idea of personality, and that this idea must be accepted as the expression of the highest reality. *C. H. Weisse* (*Das philosophische Problem der Gegenwart*, 1842) and *J. H. Fichte*, the son of *J. G. Fichte* (*Grundzüge zum System der Philosophie*, 1833–1846) were the chief representatives of this tendency. *Lotze* and *Fechner* joined them later so far as pertained to their ideas on the philosophy of religion.—As we have previously observed, the ideas of *Schelling* had been moving in the same direction for a long time already.—We find a peculiar combination of theistic philosophy of religion and humanistic philosophy of law in the voluminous writings of *Ch. Fr. Krause*, of which we can only mention *Das Urbild der Menschheit* (1811).

The most thorough criticism of the Hegelian philosophy, which is at the same time an important positive contribution to the theory of knowledge, is from the pen of the judicious and profound thinker, *Adolph Trendelenburg*, in his *Logischen Untersuchungen* (1840).

2. *Ludwig Feuerbach* (1804–1866), under the influence of *Hegel*, gave up theology for philosophy. After serving in the capacity of Privatdocent at Erlangen for a time, he withdrew to the solitude of country life where he developed a fruitful activity as an author. In his latter years he struggled with poverty and sickness.

Within the Hegelian school the foremost problem was whether religious ideas could be transformed into scientific concepts without losing their essential meaning. *Feuerbach*, on the other hand, as soon as he had definitely renounced the school, assumed the task of discovering the source of religious ideas in human affections and impulses, in fear and hope, in yearning and wish. He aims to explain the origin of dogmas psychologically, and in so doing he enters upon a line of thought in which *Hume* and—less historically—*Kant* and *Schleiermacher* were his forerunners. He appeals from the official documents of religion to the spiritual life which has found expression in them. His most important work in the sphere of the philosophy of religion is *Das Wesen des Christenthums* (1841). He however himself attaches more importance to the *Theogonie* which appeared in 1857.

The break with the speculative philosophy gave *Feuerbach* occasion to develop an entirely new conception of philosophy. After he had even insisted on an "analytico-genetic" philosophy in his elegant treatise on *Pierre Bayle* (1838), he announced a program for the philosophy of the future in a brief essay (*Grundsätze der Philosophie der Zukunft*, 1843) in which he especially emphasized the concrete distinction of every particular reality. The subject-matter of philosophy has nothing to do with the things which transcend experience, but consists entirely of man as given in experience and nature as furnishing the basis of his existence. He seeks, by painstaking studies in the natural sciences, to determine the more intimate relation between man and nature. In his last essay (*Gott, Freiheit und Unsterblichkeit*, 1866) he elaborates his view of the relation of the spiritual to the material universe. He was occupied during his last years with studies in ethics, the results of which unfortunately exist only in interesting fragments. *Fr. Jodl* has published a valuable monograph on *Feuerbach* (in Frommann's *Klassikern der Philosophie*).

a. According to *Feuerbach* the characteristic phenomena of religion arise from the fact that the impassioned aspiration towards the fulfillment of the wishes of the heart breaks through the boundaries fixed by reason.

This explains the anti-rational character which religious phenomena assume, especially those of the most exalted kind. The wish is the fundamental principle of theogony.

At the beginning man has no grounds upon which to impose limits on his wishes and the ideas conditioned by such wishes; he therefore ascribes unqualified validity to them. It is in the very nature of the affections to eternalize its object and at the same time always regard it as real. Doubt arises only after man has come to discover his limitations. He then begins to distinguish between the subjective and the objective.

Religious predicates represent the contents of human wishes. Heaven and the attributes of the gods are evidences of the things which have occupied the human heart: God is personal, i. e. the personal life is valuable, "divine." God is love, i. e. love is valuable, "divine." God suffers, i. e. suffering is valuable, "divine." Hence, in order to understand religion we must transform its predicates into subjects and its subjects into predicates. This is most clearly apparent in Christianity. Here affection attains an inwardness and an intensity, and at the same time moreover a boundlessness, wholly unknown to paganism. Both suffering and love are felt more profoundly, and they are therefore also projected with greater fervency and greater confidence as divine things.

But no sooner has man transferred everything valuable to heaven than he begins to feel the more his own emptiness and insignificance. This accounts for the sense of finitude and sinfulness. As long as we hold fast to its original forms we find that religion lives and moves in these sharp contrasts. The theogonic wish is at its best only in these forms; later on it becomes exhausted. Hence we must make a distinction especially between primitive Christianity and *"the dissolute, characterless, self-satisfied, belletristic, coquettish, Epicurean Christianity of the modern world."*

There is an inverse relationship existing between religion and civilization. They represent two opposite methods by which man hopes to realize his purposes, and just in proportion as he confides in the one he is ready to surrender the other. The relation of ethics and religion is similar. Just in proportion as the distinction between God and man is emphasized, the attributes (love, righteousness, etc.) which are ascribed to God are accordingly used in an entirely different sense than when they are applied to man, and man must then surrender his natural conscience and his natural reason in order to obey the divine will even though the latter should command something which is in conflict with human love and righteousness.

No real values are ever lost by the surrender of religious faith. The projection is annulled, nothing more. We retain in the form of subject what was predicate in religion.

b. In his general conception of philosophy *Feuerbach* approaches the psychologism of *Fries* and *Beneke*. His conception has likewise certain points of contact with the positivism of *Comte*. He does not as a matter of fact expressly treat of the problems of epistemology. But notwithstanding this it is impossible to understand his attitude towards materialism without the epistemological presuppositions. His viewpoint with respect to materialism is analogous to that which he assumed towards theology. Just as he would not regard man as a creation of God, but inversely the idea of God as a creation of man, neither would he regard man as a creation of matter, but inversely matter as a concept formed by man. We must, so he affirms, start with man. Life, sensation, thought is something absolutely original, ingenious, incapable of being copied or transferred! Man must be conceived of as being at once spiritual and corporeal, and the resulting problem is to find an Archimedian point between spiritualism and materialism.

c.   *Feuerbach* had forcefully asserted the independence of ethics from religion already in his *Pierre Bayle* (1838).   In *The Essence of Christianity* he refers to human love as the affection in which the unity of the race reveals itself in the individual.   Later on he emphasized the individual desire for happiness, not however as purpose, but as fundamental principle: only those who know from personal experience what it is to suffer need and wrong can have sympathy with others.   Ethics however knows of no striving for happiness in isolation. Nature itself has solved the problem of the transition from the egoistic desire for happiness to the recognition of duties towards others by the relation of the sexes to each other.   The feelings of community and fellowship arise by virtue of the fact that the existence of the individual is shown to stand in the most intimate relation to the existence of other individuals.

SEVENTH BOOK.

A. Positivism.

The two great intellectual tendencies of the nineteenth century are *romanticism* and *positivism*. The former starts with the forms and ideals of the intellect, the latter with given facts: "positive" signifies first of all the "actual, established, given." Despite their wide divergence, even opposition, they both nevertheless indicate, each in its own way, a reaction against the century of the enlightenment, of criticism, of revolution. The supreme aim of both tendencies is to attain a more thorough mastery of the profound realities of nature and of history. —*Positivism* did not originate as a reaction against *romanticism*, even though it only came into prominence just as the prevalence of *romanticism* began to decline. The roots of both tendencies can be traced back historically to the beginning of the nineteenth century.

Whilst Germany is the home of the romantic philosophy, positivism belongs more particularly to France and England. We are here using the term positivism in the broad sense, according to which not only *Comte*, but likewise such men as *Mill, Spencer, Dühring* and *Ardigo* are positivists.

1. *French Philosophy in the Nineteenth Century before Comte.*

At the beginning of the nineteenth century we can distinguish three philosophical schools in France, one resting on the principle of authority, another psychological ("ideological"), and a third sociological. The first represents a radical reaction against the eighteenth century; the second represents a continuation and correction of the French enlightenment; the third represents a new formation which contains the germ of positivism.

1. *Joseph de Maistre*, the most important exponent of the principle of authority, assails both philosophy and natural science, the moment they presume to undertake anything beyond wholly specialized investigations. And yet he has a philosophy of his own, which is closely affiliated with that of *Malebranche*. Whatever is material cannot be a cause; every cause is essentially mental and the type of all causality is given in the immediate consciousness of volition. Our world theory is not to be determined by investigators and thinkers, but by the authorities instituted by God in state and church. Has not history indeed sufficiently exposed the impotence of human reason! The philosophy of the eighteenth century was indeed a veritable conspiracy against everything sacred. The only thing which can put an end to human misfortune and establish social peace is the acknowledgment of the infallibility of the Pope (*Les Soirees de St. Petersbourg*, written 1809, not published until 1821).

2. Amid the storms of the revolution there was a small group of thinkers who remained loyal to philosophical investigation. These had been disciples of *Condillac*, but they introduced important corrections into his doctrine. Thus, for example, the physician, *Cabanis*, places special emphasis on the influence of the inner organic states upon the development of mind. He describes vital feeling as something which is only indirectly determined by external impressions, and hence forms a basis for psychic life which is relatively independent of

the external world. The instincts which presuppose an original motive equipment are intimately related to vital feeling. Hence man is not entirely passive in the presence of the objective world as *Condillac* had taught (*Rapport du physique et du moral de l'homme*, 1802). There are a number of separate passages in which he appears to approach closely to materialism—as, e. g., when he says that the brain secretes thought like the liver bile. But it was not his intention to furnish a metaphysics, and in another treatise, posthumously published, he rather expressed himself spiritualistically (*Lettre sur les causes premières*).—The *Élements d' Idéologie* (1801) of *Destutt de Tracy* shows a tendency similar to that of *Cabanis*. By the term ideology he simply means the theory of ideas. *Napoleon*, who found the men of this school the pronounced opponents of his despotism, on the other hand used the term "Ideology" sarcastically to describe a visionary and abstract idealism. *Picavet* has written a learned monograph on the theoretical and practical significance of this whole movement (*Les idéologues*, 1891).

Maine de Biran (1766–1824) at first likewise coöperated with *Cabanis* and *Tracy*. *Biran* held high legislative and administrative positions under the republic, the empire and the restoration; but his talents and inclinations were directed towards the inner life. Introspection and analysis gradually led him to ascribe far greater importance to psychical activity than *Condillac* and the ideologists had done. He held that immediate self-consciousness (apperception immediate) refutes *Condillac's* theory of passivity. He describes the antithesis of passive states and of inner activity by very interesting analyses. His native temperament seems to have been peculiarly adapted

to experiences of this kind (*Journal intime*, by *Naville;
Maine de Biran, sa vie et ses pensées*, 1857.—Cf. also
Rapports du physique et du moral, Œuvres philos., IV).—
Maine de Biran takes issue with *de Maistre* and his
school as well as with *Condillac*. According to them
in the last analysis the soul is likewise passive, because
it receives everything from the authorities (just as,
according to *Condillac*, from external objects).

De Biran discovers both the origin of the categories
(especially causality) and the basis of morality in the
consciousness of volitional activity.—Later on his
psychologism culminated in mysticism, on account of
the fact that he—in adherence to *Kant's* distinction
between phenomena and thing-in-itself—regarded "la
vie de l'esprit" as an immediate participation in something
which transcends every phenomenon, and places this "life
of the spirit" above "la vie humaine," the active life of
reason and of will (*Nouveaux essais d'anthropologie*, 1859).

The famous physicist, *A. M. Ampère* (1775–1836),
with whose philosophical ideas we are acquainted more
particularly from his interesting correspondence with
Biran (published by Barthelemy St. Hilaire in *Philosophie des deux Ampères*), was led, by the theory of his
friend, to investigations concerning the combinations of
sensations and ideas which are independent of our conscious activity. He distinguishes blending (concretion) and
association of independent ideas (commemoration); to the
first he ascribes immediate recognition. In epistemology he departs from *Biran* (and *Kant*) by ascribing
absolute validity to the relative concepts (causality,
number, time, space) and discovers in them a bridge from
phenomena to things-in-themselves (*Essai sur la philosophie des sciences*, 1834–43).

The so-called *eclecticism*, which was for a long time regarded as the official philosophy of France, started originally with the psychological school. After *Royer Collard*, with *Reid's* philosophy of common sense as his basis, had attacked the theory of *Condillac* at the Sorbonne, *Victor Cousin* (1792–1867) began his brilliant professional career, in which he first undertook to combine the theories of *Reid* and *Biran*, and later offered a popular and rhetorical exposition of the ideas of *Schelling* and *Hegel*. He thought it possible to attain to a point by psychological observation where universal reason would be evident and truth could be directly conceived. He finds it possible, by means of this intuition, to abstract the true and the sound elements in the various systems, each of which is one-sided in itself, and organize them into a single system (*Du vrai, du beau et du bien*, 1838).

3. The origin of positivism must be sought within the sociological school founded by *Saint Simon* (1760–1825). The task of *Saint Simon* was to prepare the way for a social reformation. But he thought that the only possibility of such a reformation involved the founding of a new world-theory which might accomplish for the present age what Christianity had done for the Middle Ages. Such a new world-theory, in the opinion of *Saint Simon*, must be constructed on the foundation of an encyclopedia of the positive sciences. This is all the more true, because it must now transpire that men shall make common cause in the exploitation of nature instead of the mutual exploitation of each other. The history of the sciences reveals the fact that they begin with theological presuppositions, but gradually build upon purely natural presuppositions. As soon as this development is completed it will be possible to establish the

positive philosophy (*Doctrine de Saint Simon, par Hippolyte Carnot,* 1829).—It was under the influence of *Saint Simon* that *Auguste Comte* produced his first important work: *Plan des travaux scientifiques pour reorganiser le société* (1822).

B. AUGUSTE COMTE (1798–1857).

Comte was a student at the polytechnic institute in Paris. But when this was closed by the Bourbons on account of the revolutionary ideas still prevalent there, he continued his studies privately, at the same time giving them an encyclopedic character, to which his association with *Saint Simon* contributed. This association came to an end because, according to *Comte's* opinion, the master wanted to subordinate science too completely to his reformatory ideas. *Comte* then carried forward his encyclopedic exposition of positive philosophy with marvellous energy and concentration. During the latter years of his life his reflections assumed a more subjective and mystical character, so that he regarded himself as the founder of a religion of humanity and even instituted a kind of worship.

a. Our modern civilization is suffering,—and on this point *Saint Simon* and *Comte* are agreed,—from an excess of the critical and revolutionary spirit. There is a lack of fellowship in the mode of thought and sentiment, and hence also in coöperation towards common ends. Society, under the old order of things, had a common foundation in theology. Now positive science is the only thing which can serve as such a foundation. There must be a thought structure erected which can speak with the same authority as the special sciences within their respective spheres. History reveals the fact that there is an intimate relation between the evolutional stages of society and the evolutional stages of science. It is this therefore that accounts for the tremendous importance of the evolution of the sciences through the three stages, *the theological, the metaphysical and the positive*. In his chief work, *Cours de philosophie positive* (1830–42), *Comte* develops the law of the three stages by furnishing both a classification of the sciences and an encyclopedic exposition of the positive knowledge of his age.

At the *theological stage* human knowledge governs but a very small portion of experience, and hence the imagination plays an important part. The bond which at this stage unites the facts for the human mind is the idea of gods and spirits. The only way of explaining the events which transpire in the universe is by reference to these ideas, and the importance of theology in the history of civilization rests upon the fact that it was the intellectual bond upon this primitive stage of science. It was likewise of practical importance, because morality was essentially founded on religious authority. Within the theological stage the transition from fetichism to polytheism is especially significant because, by the removal of divine beings from the particular phenomena of nature, it became possible to subject these phenomena to an empirical investigation.

At the *metaphysical stage* the explanation of natural phenomena is no longer found to consist of personal beings, but in universal energies or ideas. There are just as many distinct energies postulated as the number of distinct groups of phenomena require; thus we speak of a chemical energy, a vital energy, etc., and finally we postulate the idea of nature (an abstract equivalent of the idea of God) for the total aggregate of phenomena.

Speculative reflection has taken the place of religious imagination. The advance consists in this, namely, that energies or ideas indicate a greater degree of uniformity and invariability than was to be expected of deities and spirits. But the metaphysical stage is still predominantly negative and critical. It destroys the authorities and yet fails to attain to a new basis of certitude. It is the period of individualism.

At the *positive stage* both imagination and reflection are subordinated to experience. The only criterion of truth consists of the agreement with the facts. Positivism does not however permit the facts to remain in isolation; it seeks after the laws, i. e., the constant relations of the phenomena. Science builds on the invariability of natural law, which was anticipated already by the Greeks, but clearly expressed in modern times by *Bacon*, *Galileo* and *Descartes*, the real founders of positive philosophy.—It is impossible to refer the numerous laws to a single law. Our knowledge cannot attain objective unity,—unity is only subjective. Subjective unity consists in the fact that the same method—the explanation of facts by facts—is consistently applied everywhere. This unity of method furnishes a basis for the fellowship of minds, which has not existed since the Middle Ages.

The point of difference between these stages is partly due to the difference in the range of experience, partly to the different viewpoints which are postulated in the explanation of nature. Before this explanation could be found in the facts themselves it was necessary to postulate imagination and speculation in the interpretation of nature.

b. The classification of the sciences coincides with the theory of the three stages. It rests first of all upon the serial order in which the various sciences entered the positive stage. Mathematics comes first, which had even become positive already among the Greeks, then successively Astronomy, Physics, Chemistry, Biology and Sociology (theory of society). But this serial order likewise presents a successive passage from the simplicity of the objects considered to their complexity: the simpler the objects of a given science, the sooner it will become positive. The serial order furthermore reveals a constant passage from universality to particularity: the laws of mathematics are valid of all phenomena, whilst the astronomical, physical, chemical and biological laws apply to an increasingly smaller group, and those of sociology to the most circumscribed group of all. Finally we likewise find in this serial order a gradual passage from the predominance of the deductive method to the predominance of induction.—These four principles of classification, as may be readily observed, are closely related.

The various departments of experience corresponding to the different sciences are not connected in a single continuum. Discontinuity manifests itself even within one and the same department, as e. g., between the various physical energies, between the organic species, etc.,—*Comte* was not acquainted with the law of the conservation of energy, which however did not receive general recognition during his lifetime, and he did not survive the appearance of *Darwin*.

His classification omits logic and psychology, of which the former should be placed before mathematics and the latter between biology and sociology.—In his later years *Comte* himself added ethics as a seventh science. According to his conception, ethics is more specialized than

sociology, because it goes more into details, especially in
the fact that it places special emphasis on the affections,
which receive but little attention in sociology.

c. *Comte's* positivism is not empiricism. As a matter
of fact the theory of stages presupposes that the facts
must always be combined; the only question is, whence is
the combining instrument to be derived. In the positive
stage the combination can be effected in two ways. We
associate phenomena which are given simultaneously
according to their similarity of structure and function.
We naturally arrange phenomena which follow in succession in a temporal series. The former is a static explanation (*par similitude*); the latter is a dynamic explanation
(*par filiation*). We satisfy our mind's native impulse for
unity by both methods and thus discover the constant in
the midst of change (*Discours sur l'esprit positif*,
1844).

Of this combining function of the mind, which *Comte*
here presupposes, he made no further investigation. His
works contain no epistemological nor psychological
analyses. His conception of knowledge is biological.
Our knowledge is determined by the interaction of our
organism with the objective world, of our understanding
with the milieu. The elaboration of the impressions
received from without follows the laws of our organization, and all knowledge is therefore determined by a
relation of subject and object. *Comte* is of the opinion
that in this biological theory of knowledge he is a fol-
lower of *Kant* and *Aristotle.*—In his later years he came to
emphasize the subjective character of our knowledge
more and more, until he finally proposed a subjective
system instead of the objective system given in the
Cours de philosophie positive.

d. The term sociology was formulated by *Comte* and, despite its philological indefiniteness, it has gradually come to mean the rights of citizenship in scientific terminology. In *Comte's* sense, the term sociology covers what has generally been called the philosophy of history, and in addition thereto, political economy, ethics and the major portion of psychology. Just as in other departments of science, so likewise in sociology we must distinguish between statics and dynamics.

Social statics includes the doctrine of the reciprocal relation of the factors of society, e. g., ideas, customs and institutions. The business of institutions is simply to regulate whatever has been evolved in the course of unconstrained coöperation. As compared with spontaneous development, law and the state are of subordinate importance, and the concept of law is subordinate to the concept of duty. The concept of duty originates from the individual's consciousness of being a member of the social whole. And this consciousness arises at the moment when the solidarity of the human race is first felt and recognized. Mankind spontaneously follows the social impulse, and only later discovers the advantages which thus accrue. On this point *Comte* regards *Hume* and *Adam Smith* as his predecessors. He discovers the first germs of solidarity in biology: in the sexual instinct and in the instinct to care for offspring. In the realm of mankind there is a constant progressive discipline towards altruism (which term was likewise formulated by *Comte*). The individual, considered by himself and in isolation, is a mere abstraction. The family is the social unit; here we have more than a mere association, it is a complete union. In larger societies the coöperation of individuals towards common ends and under the inspiration of common ideas is of peculiar importance. The supreme idea is the idea of humanity, to which all individual and social development should be subservient.—*Comte* challenges the distinction between private and public functions. This distinction belongs to modern thought; it was unknown to the Greeks and to the Middle Ages. It is the duty of positive philosophy to develop a sentiment by means of which all should be enabled to regard themselves as co-laborers of the one great body of humanity. It is especially important to incorporate the proletariat, which has arisen since the abolition of slavery, into the social system.

The law of the three stages, with which we are already acquainted, belongs to *social dynamics*. The various stages of intellectual development correspond to definite stages of social and political development. Militarism corresponds with the *theological stage*. This is the period of regulative authority. The control of the jurists ("legislators") corresponds with the metaphysical stage; their specific task consists in regulating the rights of the various classes, particularly the rights of the middle class, of the military and of the clergy. Industrialism corresponds with the positive stage; the distribution of power is now determined by productive capacity, and social problems take the place of the political problems.

e. In a later work (*Politique positive*, 1851–4) *Comte* undertook to lay the foundation of a new religion, the Religion of Humanity. (The complete title therefore reads as follows: *Politique positive, ou traité de sociologie instituant la religion de l'humanité.*) Whilst in his *Cours* he made the world or nature his starting-point and aimed to attain an understanding of man on the basis of the knowledge of nature, he would now replace this objective method by a subjective method. Nature as a whole must be construed from the human standpoint and humanity described as the highest being (*le grand être*). The affections and not merely the understanding are now to be the final arbiter, and synthesis, i. e., the conception of unity, is to be regarded as superior to analysis and specialization. The new religion is to be a worship of humanity, of which we are all members,—those now living as well as those who have died and those as yet unborn. Every thought and action is to be directed towards the development of this *Grand être*. The constitution of the future is to be a *Sociocracy*, a social community without fixed institutions. The patricians direct production, whilst the proletariat represent the dynamic, the philosophers the reason, and the women the affections of the social body. Public opinion and the right of refusal to coöperate will furnish an adequate check against any misuse of power on the part of the spiritual or temporal authorities.—Thus the founder of positivism ends up as a *Utopian romanticist*. His school divides on this point, several of them (as e. g. *Littré*) maintaining the theory of the *Cours*, whilst others (such as *Lafitte* and *Robinet*) regarded the *Politique positive* as the actual culmination of the positive philosophy.

C. English Philosophy in the Nineteenth Century before John Stuart Mill.

Both in Germany and in France the transition from the eighteenth to the nineteenth century was effected by a revolution—in Germany by the romantic revolution in the sphere of thought, in France by the political revolution. In England on the other hand there were a number of energetic philosophic thinkers who endeav-

ored to make a practical application of the principles discovered by the eighteenth century to the problems of the
nineteenth century. The English philosophy of the
nineteenth century therefore, in its chief representatives,
bears the stamp of radicalism and empiricism. *Jeremy
Bentham* and *James Mill*, pronounced adherents of the
radical enlightenment, produced a profound impression
on the first decades of the century. *John Stuart Mill*
afterwards undertook on the one hand a consistent
development of their principles, and on the other to
adapt them to the changed setting of the problem,—
namely, that brought about by the romanticism
represented by *Coleridge* and *Carlyle* and the criticism
represented by *Hamilton* and *Whewell*.

1. *Jeremy Bentham's* (1748–1832) most important
philosophical writings had appeared already in the
eighteenth century (*A Fragment on Government*, 1776;
Principles of Morals and Legislation, 1789). But they
did not make much of an impression until after the
dawn of the new century. *Bentham*, who, as a private
scholar, devoted himself uninterruptedly to his efforts for
social and legislative reform, assumed as his chief task
the reform of English legislation. He demanded a
codification of the laws (he formulated the term *codification* himself), a reduction in the costs of legal processes,
prison reform and an extension of political franchise.
Theoretically he assumed the principle of the greatest
happiness to the greatest number, previously advocated
by *Hutcheson*, as the fundamental principle of morality.
This principle, which to his mind is self-evident, is to
govern our judgment of every institution, every action,
every quality and every motive. *Bentham* attacks the
so-called natural rights as well as the morality which is

founded on authority and tradition. He examines the
intensity, persistence, certainty, intimacy, purity and
fruitfulness of pleasurable feelings which follow our
acts and which condition the value of an act. He investigates the motives of action in order to discover what
motives should be fostered and what others should be
restrained. He regards self-interest, properly understood, as the most reliable motive, because he believed
that self-interests, properly understood, are harmonious,
so that the individual must necessarily be interested in
the general welfare even for prudential considerations.
This idea is expressed very one-sidely and harshly in a
work (*Deontology*) that was published posthumously,
and perhaps interpolated by the publisher.

Bentham's friend, *James Mill* (1772–1836), was a
zealous exponent of the radical application of the principle
of utility. This energetic man, whose high official
position in the East India Company excluded him from
Parliament, acted as counsellor of the radical politicians
who were working for parliamentary reform, and above all
else the emancipation of the middle classes. He undertook the theoretical task of furnishing a psychological
basis for *Bentham's* ethical theory, the so-called *utilitarianism*. He discovered such a basis in the *Associational psychology* founded by *Hume* and *Hartley*,
which he greatly simplified by referring all combinations
of ideas to association between such ideas as frequently
take place together (association by contiguity) (*Analysis of the Human Mind*, 1829). He attaches special
importance to the fact that the association may be so
completely subjective that an entirely new totality may
arise, without containing any traces of the original
elements whatever. By this method he aims to show,

i. e. to explain, how selfless (*"disinterested"*) feelings may arise. Such feelings are secondary; they arise from the fact that something which is at first capable of exciting pleasure only as a means afterwards becomes an end and then acts as a pleasurable stimulus directly. This is the psychological explanation of the immediacy of conscience. (The best exposition of this theory is given by *James Mill* in appendix B. of his polemical essay, *Fragment on Mackintosh*, 1835.)

2. Against these enthusiastic advocates of empirical and analytical psychology and ethics there arose a romantic tendency, under German influence, whose most noted representatives were *Coleridge* and *Carlyle*.

Samuel Taylor Coleridge (1772–1834) in his early youth was an ardent disciple of the associationist psychology. But he later became an opponent of all analysis and of every effort to explain mental life by elementary principles, and, in adherence to *Schelling*, he proclaimed the awe-inspiring totality of all things as intuitively apprehended, in opposition to the empiricism which breaks everything to pieces. He however attaches special importance to the Kantian antithesis of "understanding" and "reason." He charged all religious criticism to the account of the pure "understanding," and then refuted it by an appeal to the higher court of "reason," the faculty of ideas and the theory of totality. He not only hurls his polemics against the free-thinkers, but likewise against the theology which has degenerated into barren dogmatic formulas. His great work which was intended to show the agreement of Christianity and philosophy was never written. We gather his ideas from his essays on *Church and State* (especially the appendix) and from his *Biographia Literaria* and his *Table Talk*.

Thomas Carlyle (1795–1881) did not care to attain any "higher" knowledge. He satirized *Coleridge's "transcendental moonshine."* He proposed a new basis of faith and for the guidance of life to which he was led by the study of *Goethe* and the romantic philosophy. His effort was directed towards securing independence from the never-ending investigations of science. After having extricated himself from materialistic theories in his early youth, he cherished a romantic aversion towards analysis and criticism. His polemic applies especially to the "philosophy of cause and effect" and the utilitarian ethics. In his profoundest essay, *Sartor Resartus* (1833), he develops a "*philosophy of old clothes,*" based on *Kant's* distinction between phenomenon and thing-in-itself: The world is the garment of Deity; natural science examines the garment without knowing its wearer. Nature is a mighty symbol, a revelation of ideas which no scientific method is capable of conceiving. It is the duty of philosophy ever and anon to inspire the sense of the mysterious majesty of being when men have fallen asleep through familiarity. Even our ideas of belief are garments of Deity;—but the garment of Deity must be woven anew from time to time.

Carlyle's practical view of life reveals two distinct characteristics.—Everything great takes place quietly, in silence. Great deeds are accomplished without any express consciousness of the fact. A full and clear consciousness makes everything small and mechanical. The highest truth, so far as man is concerned, can only exist in the form of a symbol: the symbol withholds and expresses, obscures and reveals at one and the same time.— The highest revelation consists of the great men, the heroes (*On Heroes and Hero-worship*, 1841). They are the guides and patterns, the founders of everything that is

good. The hero may appear as prophet, poet or statesman; but he always represents great, concentrated energy
of life, and his words and deeds reveal the hidden ideas of
the movement of life. Such heroes are especially necessary for the solution of the social problem. *Carlyle* was
one of the first authors, who—in opposition to the then
dominant school of political economy—noted the existence of this problem. He made no specific investigations.
Empirical science was too distasteful to him for that.

3. In the same year (1829) that *James Mill* published
his *Analysis*, the most important work of the associationist psychology, *William Hamilton's* profound
treatise on *The Philosophy of the Unconditioned* likewise
appeared, in which he severely criticized all philosophy
that treated the unconditioned as an object of knowledge.
Hamilton (1788–1856) spent a number of years in fruitful
professorial activity at the university of Edinburgh.—
Whatever we apprehend and conceive—by the very fact
of its apprehension and conception—is related to something else, by which it is limited and conditioned. To
think is to condition. We neither conceive an absolute
whole, nor an absolute part; each whole is a part, and
each part is a whole. We only know the conditioned
finite. We define whatever we know in terms of space,
time and degree (extensively, protensively and intensively)
and even the law of causality is likewise nothing more than
a special form of the law of relativity. *Hamilton* regards the
principle of causality as the expression of our incapacity to
conceive an absolute addition of reality. On account of
this incapacity we try to conceive the new (as effect) as a
new form of the old (as cause). If cause and effect should
fail to fully correspond to each other, we should be compelled to assume an absolute beginning of the new. Hence,

according to *Hamilton* (like *Cusanus*), philosophy ends in a *docta ignorantia*. Its value consists in its constant seeking, by means of which the energies of the mind are exercised.

Hamilton is nevertheless convinced that faith in the unconditioned is necessary in order to establish our spiritual existence. The more refined definitions of unconditioned being can only be secured by analogy with human personality.—This argument was applied to the defense of the orthodox faith by *Hamilton's* disciple, *Henry Mansel* (*Limits of Religious Thought*, 1858).

William Whewell (1795–1866), professor at Cambridge, demonstrated the principles of the critical philosophy from another point of view. He endeavored to verify *Kant's* fundamental principles as the necessary presuppositions of the inductive sciences (*History of the Inductive Sciences*, 1837; *Philosophy of the Inductive Sciences, founded on their History*, 1840). Induction signifies not only a collection of facts, but their arrangement according to some governing principle. The organization of the facts is possible only in case the investigator brings such a principle with him (as e. g. *Kepler* brought the idea of the ellipse to his studies of the planets). We must finally go back to the fundamental concepts which express the very principles of our cognitive faculty, principles which form the basis of all sense perception and all induction. Such fundamental concepts are: time, space, cause (in mechanics), end (in biology), and duty (in ethics). These cannot be analyzed into simpler concepts.

D. JOHN STUART MILL (1806–1873).

John Stuart Mill, the son of *James Mill*, was trained in the ideas of the radical enlightenment, as they had been developed by his father and *Bentham*, and he accepted

them as a veritable gospel. In his very interesting autobiography he describes how the ideas adopted during his
childhood and youth came into sharp conflict with the
ideas and moods of a later period which likewise agitated
his very soul, and how he was then compelled to struggle
through a mental crisis. This contradiction not only
appears in his life but likewise in his works, and the
inconsistencies which, despite his vigorous intellectual
effort, his theories reveal, are partly due to this fact.
There likewise exists an intimate relation between his
theoretical views and his efforts for social reform. The
fact that in philosophy he seeks to derive everything from
pure experience does not rest upon pure theoretical conviction alone, but he likewise regarded it as a weapon
against the prejudices which impede progress (similar to
the French philosophers of the eighteenth century).—
Like his father, *Mill* was an officer of the India Company;
after its dissolution he was a member of Parliament for a
short time.

a. *Stuart Mill's System of Logic* (1843) contains the
answer of the English school to *Kant's Critique of
Pure Reason* and at the same time the most radical
form of empirical epistemology. According to *Kant's*
fundamental principle, all real experience contains a rational element, which can be discovered by analysis. *Mill*
now undertakes to show not only that all knowledge
proceeds from experience, but that experience itself
involves no antecedent presuppositions. He would make
experience the standard of experience. *"We make experience its own test!"*—By *experience* (like Hume) he
means a sum of impressions, and his problem consists in
showing how universal principles can be derived from
such a sum.

Mill bases his logical investigations partly on historical and partly on psychological principles.

In matters pertaining to the history of thought, as he openly acknowledged, he was greatly benefited by *Whewell's* work on the *History of the Inductive Sciences*. *John Herschel's* book *On the Study of Natural Philosophy* (1831) was likewise one of his preparatory studies. *Mill's* problem consisted in describing the fundamental methods of inductive thought by an analysis of the methods of the empirical sciences as these had been developed during the past three centuries, and then to examine what presuppositions underlie this thought.— He discovers four methods of induction. The *method of agreement* infers, from a series of cases, in which two circumstances (A and B) always succeed each other, whilst all other circumstances vary, a causal connection between A and B. But this inference is not certain until we can at the same time apply the *method of difference* because it shows that B does not appear whenever A is excluded, and vice versa. This is the chief inductive method. To this is added the *method of residues*, in which everything previously explained is eliminated and an inference is then drawn concerning the relation of the remaining circumstances, and the *method of proportional variation*, in which we have two series of experiences which vary proportionally between each other and infer a causal relation between them. *Mill* illustrates these methods by striking examples from the history of the sciences. He attempted, by this exposition, to substitute a systematization of inductive logic for the Aristotelian systematization of deductive logic; his logic was a continuation of *Bacon's* work. He differs from *Bacon* not only in the wealth and quantity of the examples at his disposal but likewise by his clearer insight into the necessity of forming hypothesis and by the interchange of induction and deduction. The deductive method becomes necessary especially in cases where there are large numbers of contributing factors. We must then examine each factor separately by induction and then test by deduction from the results of these separate investigations whether the interplay of all the factors is explainable.

The final analysis of thought reveals the psychological basis of *Mill's* logic. According to *Mill* every deduction presupposes an induction. For—in his opinion—deduction starts from a general proposition; but whence can this proposition be derived, if not from experience? Every general proposition implies a reference to a number of experiences. We ultimately come back to the particular impressions. The beginning of the whole knowledge-process consists in the fact that two phenomena take place coincidently. Once this has happened frequently, the presence of the one phenomenon will arouse an expectation of the other. This is the fundamental form of inference. It does not however start from a general proposition, but rather proceeds from particulars to particulars. The child withdraws its hand from the burning taper, not because of its knowledge of the general proposition, that contact with fire is painful, but because the sight of fire immediately arouses the idea of pain. It is therefore an objective association (association by contact) that forms the original basis of all inference: all logical principles are eliminated. *The transition from one idea to another takes place immediately*, and, according to *Mill*, this means, *without ground*.—In the theory of causality *Mill* would likewise eliminate all presuppositions. *Mill* concedes however that the inductive methods are demonstrable only on the presupposition of the causal principle. Notwithstanding the fact that B always follows A, and B does not appear in the absence of A, nevertheless our only ground of inference to a causal relation between A and B is the presupposition that B must have a cause. What then is the source of the causal principle? Mill answers: the same as all general propositions, experience, i. e., induction.—The circumlocution which is here apparent in *Mill's* argument has been clearly exposed by *Stanley Jevons* (in a series of articles under the title, *Stuart Mill's Philosophy Tested*—(1877–1879)—reprinted in *Pure Logic and other Minor Works*). *Jevons* had already demonstrated in his *Principles of Science* (1874) that the principle of identity is presupposed as the basis of all inference, because of the fact that the proof of an induction always consists of a deduction, which carries its inference back from a hypothetical proposition to the given impressions.

Mill's attempt therefore to furnish a system of logic which is wholly inductive did not succeed. This attempt forms the counterpart to *Hegel's* attempt to invent a logic which is wholly deductive. *Mill* tried to spin the forms of thought from their content, *Hegel* the content of thought from its forms. It is in these two men that the contrast between romanticism and positivism is most sharply drawn.

b. The pyschological presuppositions at the basis of *Mill's* logic come from *James Mill's Analysis*. They were the presuppositions of the "*Associational Psychology.*" When, in his later years (1869), *Stuart Mill* published a new edition of the *Analysis*, in his appended notes he modified his psychological theory. Following *Alexander Bain* (whose chief works are *The Senses and the*

Intellect, 1856, and *The Emotions and the Will*, 1859), he here shows that the objective association (association by contact) constantly presupposes a subjective correlate (association by similarity). He had even before that, in his *Examination of Sir William Hamilton's Philosophy* (1865), indicated a still more radical change in the fundamentals of his psychology. He then saw that such phenomena as anticipation and recollection cannot be accounted for by the theory of consciousness underlying the *"Associational Psychology"*—viz., that of a mere sum of elements. The phenomena mentioned prove—so he thinks—that the bond by which the psychical elements are held together is just as real as the elements themselves, and that it cannot be derived from these elements. And the term *"Ego"* applies to this bond alone. *Mill* therefore once more revives *Hume's* *"uniting principle,"* which had been forgotten in the *"Associational Psychology,"* and as a matter of fact even accorded it a central position. Had he then been able to revise his logic, the possibilities were present of developing the principles of knowledge as idealized psychical tendencies.— The modifications and even the inconsistencies contained in *Mill's* theories bear witness to the indefatigability and candor of his investigations.

c. In ethics even as in psychology *Stuart Mill* was also originally a disciple of his father; here he was likewise a disciple of *Bentham*. The objectivity and onesideness of *Bentham's* utilitarianism had however been brought to his attention even in his early youth, especially through the influence of *Coleridge* and *Carlyle*. Nevertheless, he never surrendered the presupposition that the ultimate criterion for the evaluation of human actions must be sought in their effects on human happiness. The aim is not the greatest possible happiness for the actor himself, but the greatest possible happiness for all who are affected by the results of the action. *Stuart Mill* bases this principle, not on the self-interest of the actor properly understood as *Bentham* had done, but on the psychological nature of the moral sentiment (*Utilitarianism*, 1863). In his theory of this sentiment he adopted the doctrine of the metamorphoses of sentiments as developed by *Hartley* and *James Mill*. The origin of the moral sentiment is due to the coöperation of a large number of elements: sympathy, fear, reverence, experiences of the effects of actions, self-esteem and the desire for the esteem of others. It is in this complex nature that the cause of the mystical character attaching to the idea of moral obligation is to be found. The complex may however become so completely subjective and perfect that the sentiment itself will appear as unitary. Its development ordinarily takes place under the influence of social life by which individuals are accustomed to regard common interests and to enlist united efforts. In this way a sentiment of solidarity and unity evolves which may even (as in the case of *Comte's* religion of humanity) assume a religious character.

But *Mill* not only modified utilitarianism by the emphasis which he placed on the subjective factor, but likewise by the assumption of the qualitative differences of the sentiments. He thinks "happiness" must not be estimated according to quantity alone, but likewise according to quality. He says, like *Plato* (in the ninth book of the *Republic*), that he alone who knows the various qualities of happiness from personal experience is in position to furnish a valid estimate of their different values. A *Socrates* dissatisfied is better than a satisfied idiot.

These modifications reveal the fact that the ethical problem is far more consequential and difficult than the older utilitarians ever dreamed. *Henry Sidgwick* (1838–1900), who, in his penetrating work *The Method of Ethics* (1877), distinguishes definitely between two distinct kinds of utilitarianism, of which the one is based on self-interest, the other on altruism, saw this clearly. He likewise shows that the practical ethics (the morality of common sense) which prevails at the present time rests unconsciously upon a utilitarian presupposition.

d. *Mill* produced a number of important works in the department of social ethics, which made a profound impression upon the life of the age. Thus, e. g., in his book *On Liberty* (1859) he asserted the right of the individual to the free development of his native powers, and endeavored to establish definite limits for the interposition of legislation and of public opinion. His fundamental principle is that the impulse to everything noble and great proceeds from individual geniuses, who are the salt of the earth. In his *Subjection of Women* (1869) he makes a peculiar application of the principle of liberty to the position of woman. He likewise holds that our ideas of the "nature" of woman have been derived from the subordinate and retiring position which woman has hitherto occupied, and he anticipates splendid contributions to human culture after women are enabled to develop their faculties just as freely as man has already done for ages. In his *Considerations on Representative Government* (1861) he regards the political issue at the present time as a conflict between democracy and bureaucracy, which must be brought to an end by the former enlisting the services of the latter and only retaining a general control. He likewise recommends a proportionate franchise in order to guarantee the rights of the minority. *Mill's* future ideal however went beyond a political democracy. He is convinced that personal and political liberty cannot be secured without great social and economic changes (*Principles of Political Economy*, 1849). Here he is confronted by the profound, according to him, diametrical antithesis of individualism and socialism, and he frankly acknowledges that he is at a loss to know how to reconcile them. He holds however that neither the individualistic nor the socialistic fundamental principle has been theoretically and practically developed in its best possible form. Hence, e. g. the right of private property might readily be maintained, if the laws would take even as much pains to reduce its difficulties as they now take in order to increase them. Socialists are wrong when they make competition the ground of social evil. The cause lies in the fact that labor is subject to capital, and *Mill* expects great things from the trades unions and producers unions, especially because they encourage the virtues of independence—namely, justice and self-control.

e. *Mill's* religious views appear only by way of suggestion in the works published by himself. He holds, in opposition to *Comte* (in his book on *Comte*, 1865), that theological and metaphysical theories are not necessarily destroyed by the attainment to the positive stage of science, but they must not contradict the results of scientific investigation. There are some open questions! But he protested vigorously against the teaching of *Hamilton* and *Mansel* (especially the latter), that the concepts (particularly ethical concepts) must be treated as having an entirely different content when applied to deity than when applied to man. He would refuse to call any being good—even if that being were able to condemn him eternally for so doing—who is not what we mean when we call a man good.

He expresses himself more fully in his posthumous *Essays on Religion* (1847). He denies that he can infer an omniscient, omnipotent, and absolutely good Creator from the facts of nature. He regards it possible however on the other hand to believe in a personal God, who, in constant conflict with uncreated and persistently resistant matter, is seeking to bring about a beneficent order of nature. Man can therefore, by his own effort, be a co-laborer with God, and, according to *Mill*, the real religious attitude consists in the sentiment aroused by this fellowship. He attaches great importance to the fact that such thoughts and sentiments elevate man above the limitations of experience and the prosiness of ordinary life.

E. The Philosophy of Evolution.

About the middle of the nineteenth century the theory of evolution came into vogue and was recognized as an essential element of human thought. The romantic philosophy had indeed likewise spoken of evolution, but they simply meant by this a purely logical or systematic relation of the forms and types of being, not a real process, taking place in time. The idea of evolution had already made itself felt however in various departments of thought. Thus, e. g., in the astronomical hypothesis of *Kant* and *Laplace*, in the theory of epigenesis (i. e. the theory of the gradual evolution of the embryo from a simple rudiment) as formulated by the anatomist, *Caspar Wolff*, in the psychology of *Spinoza*, *Hartley* and *James Mill*, in the eighteenth century belief in the evolution of history, in *Comte's* theory of the three stages. *Lamarck* finally announced the theory of a continuous evolution of organic species by means of a progressive transformation of the organs brought about through the constant exercise of its powers. But the evolutionary theory only received general recognition as a fundamental principle in wider circles after the announcement of *Darwin's hypothesis of the origin of the organic species by the process of natural selection*. *Herbert Spencer* at the same time undertook to determine the fundamental forms of evolution by analysis of the phenomena in the various departments of experience, after having previously shown how characters which are unexplainable from the viewpoint of the experience of the individual may be explained from the viewpoint of race-experience.

1. The great naturalist, *Charles Darwin* (1809–1881), deserves a place in the history of philosophy, because, like *Copernicus*, *Galileo* and *Newton*, he is of profound significance in the treatment of philosophical problems, not only on account of his results, but likewise on account of his theory of science and its sphere. After a tour of the world covering three years, upon which he collected his large supply of specimens and observations, he lived in the solitude of the country as a quiet investigator.

His effort to explain the origin of the species was in complete harmony with the spirit of positivism. He referred to a fact which was actually operative in nature: namely, the necessity for every living being to possess the attributes and equipment essential to the preservation of life, or as he expressed it figuratively, the struggle for existence. If we persist in saying that the species were created, each one independently, this, in the eyes of *Darwin*, is but a pious way of expressing our ignorance. The struggle for existence however is not the whole cause. It presupposes that individual organisms reveal variations which may be either more or less favorable to their preservation or to the preservation of the species to which they belong. Those individuals which show favorable variations would naturally survive in the struggle for existence (*Origin of Species*, 1858).

Darwin found the proof of his theory in the "*intelligible thread*" by means of which a vast array of facts can be combined. He did not regard his theory as a dogma, but rather as an instrument of research. He always insisted on tracing out the significance which a given character, function or organ possessed for the struggle for existence.—He regarded the problem concerning the origin of the variations by virtue of which natural selection takes place as a weakness in his hypothesis. He assumes the fact that such variations exist, and for the time being calls them "*chance-variations*," only meaning by this however that their causes are unknown. He takes a similar attitude to the problem of life in general.

Darwin's assumption that very small variations furnish a real advantage in the struggle for existence was perhaps an error. *Hugo de Vries* has quite recently undertaken to show that very important variational "leaps" ("mutations") may take place and that a new type may thus arise at once, which must then establish itself in the struggle for existence. It has become apparent, furthermore, that these mutational types are very tough. The contrast between the types and variations consequently becomes even sharper than *Darwin*, and especially the Darwinians, who have frequently been more dogmatic than their master, ever supposed.

Darwin saw no reason for regarding man an exception from the general biological laws. In his opinion the

actual value and the actual dignity of man suffers no
diminution by regarding him as having evolved from
lower forms. For the theological and romantic conception, which regarded man as a fallen angel, he substituted
the realistic conception of man as an animal which has
evolved a spiritual nature (*The Descent of Man*, 1871).

Darwin elaborates his views on the problems of moral
philosophy in the third chapter of his book on the origin
of man. He sympathizes with the view represented by
Shaftesbury, Hutcheson and *Hume*. He starts with the
principle that a group of animals or men among which the
idea of sympathy and mutual helpfulness prevails would be
favorably situated in the struggle for existence. He thus
discovers a biological foundation for the moral sentiment.
According to *Darwin* this sentiment presupposes, besides
sociability and sympathy, the faculty of recollection and
comparison. With these conditions given we have the
basis for a more or less conscious estimate and judgment
of actions. After the faculty of language has been
evolved mutual praise and blame can likewise exert its
influence. Public opinion can then take form. Habit
and exercise in efforts for the common welfare would also
tend to give permanence and strength to the social
motives and instincts. The characters thus acquired may
perhaps likewise be transmitted by inheritance (as
Lamarck had assumed).

Touching religion *Darwin* was still a believer in revelation when he returned from his famous tour. His views
changed gradually, without any painful rupture, and he
finally (in 1876, and published in *Life and Letters of
Charles Darwin*, 1887), adopting a form of expression
introduced by *Huxley*, declared himself an agnostic, i. e.
one who knows that the solution of the problem of being

is beyond our powers. That is to say, his philosophy culminates in a *docta ignorantia*. He regarded the idea that the world is the result of chance (brute force) quite as incredible as that it should be the product of conscious design. His statement of the problem at this point reminds us of that given by *Kant* in the *Critique of Judgment*.

2. *Herbert Spencer* (1820–1903) gave up a life of practical affairs in order to devote himself to philosophical investigations. In his early youth he was an engineer, but soon acquired an interest in social problems and ideas which in turn led him to the study of psychology and biology. He was a self-made man. He never attended a university and never took an examination. He was peculiarly gifted in observing facts which might serve to illuminate general principles. His philosophy sprang from the necessity of discovering a governing principle which would serve the purpose of organizing a series of studies in natural science, psychology and social science into a system. He has described the course of his development in his *Autobiography* (1904). He remained a private citizen all his life, occupying himself with his studies and his writings.

Spencer's ideas are expressed in their purest, most original form in a series of essays, published in three volumes under the title: *Essays, Scientific, Political and Speculative*. From the literary point of view, the *Essays* form the most valuable portion of the Spencerian writings. —He had even before this, in his *Social Statics* (1850), applied the idea of evolution to social life. Following *Coleridge* he regarded the complete unfolding of life as a divine idea which is to be realized gradually. Later on he regarded this conception as too theological. He then began to search for a concept of evolution which could be applied to every sphere of experience.

According to his conception philosophy is unitary knowledge. Its task consists in the discovery of general principles under which the particular principles postulated by the special sciences can be organized. But this unitary knowledge can neither be attained by the a priori, deductive method, followed by *Hegel,* nor by the simple, encyclopedic collation of facts, as *Comte* thought. *Spencer* seeks to discover what is common in the special principles and laws by means of the comparative method. During the course of thirty-six years (1860–1896) he produced a detailed exposition of his *Synthetic Philosophy* filling ten large volumes. The first volume, containing the *First Principles* (1861), furnishes the fundamental principles of his world-theory and defines the concept of evolution both inductively and deductively as the fundamental concept of all science. The remaining volumes apply the special forms of this concept to the departments of biology, psychology, sociology and ethics. —*Otto Gaup* has published a valuable characterization and exposition of *Spencer's* philosophy (Frommann's *Klassiker, Herbert Spencer,* 1897).

a. *Spencer's* theory of knowledge shows the influence of both *Stuart Mill* and *William Hamilton* (and, through the latter, *Kant*). He challenged pure empiricism, on the ground of the fact that perceptions require elaboration before knowledge can arise and this elaboration presupposes both a faculty and a standard. The ultimate basis of all knowledge consists of the faculty of distinguishing the like from the unlike; even radical skepticism must presuppose this basal principle. The ultimate standard by which truth and error are distinguished consists of the principle that a proposition which is inherently self-contradictory cannot be true. Truth implies a perfect agreement between our ideas (representations of things) and our impressions (presentations of things). Every inference and every postulate assumes the truth of the criterion contained in the principle of contradiction. This criterion cannot therefore be derived from mere experience: it is a priori. Every individual must possess the innate faculty of comparing impressions and drawing inferences from impressions, but this faculty cannot be derived from the impressions alone. But the a priori appertains to the individual alone. If we inquire into the origin of this faculty we must appeal to the race from which the individual has sprung. Empiricism is in error only in so far as the particular individual is concerned, not as respects the whole race. The experiences acquired by the race during the course of countless generations, the incessantly recurring influence to which it was subjected, evolve dispositions which form the basis upon which single individuals begin their course of development. That is to say, the single individual possesses in his native organization the clear profit of the experiences of untold generations. That which is a priori in the case of the individual is racially a posteriori.

Even in the first edition of his psychology (1855) *Spencer*, who had early become an evolutionist, referred to the fact that the things which are inexplicable on the basis of individual experience might be explained by race experience. He imagined that this amounted to a final disposition of the controversy between empiricism and a priorism. He nevertheless perceives that in the final analysis he concedes the correctness of empiricism, and declares himself a disciple of *Locke* rather than of *Kant*. He extends the scope of the older empiricism by going back of the individual to the race. He failed to see however that the actual problem of epistemology is not the matter of the factual origin of knowledge, but its validity. In the construction of his own theory of the factual origin of knowledge he, as a matter of fact, simply assumes the criterion of truth! Furthermore, the distinction between the race and the individual is not fundamental, because the race at any given time is represented by definite single individuals. Every generation, even as every individual, must possess its own a priori faculty.

Spencer had advanced the hypothesis of the natural origin of the species, which in 1885 he applied to psychology, in an essay even as early as 1852. *Darwin* therefore regards him as one of his precursors. At that time however he stood closer to *Lamarck* than to *Darwin*, because he was not yet acquainted with the idea of the struggle for existence in its bearing on the theory of evolution. It was impossible for him therefore to construe knowledge as an instrument in the struggle for existence.

b. According to *Spencer* the sphere of knowledge is determined by the fundamental function of thought, which, as a matter of fact, consists in distinguishing like from unlike. We can only know such things as can be compared with other things, i. e. related to other things. Here *Spencer* adheres closely to *William Hamilton*, except that he dropped the latter's theological viewpoints. The things which we presume to know must necessarily be relative, i. e. they must bear definite relations and they must therefore be limited. The absolute and uncondi-

tioned cannot be related to anything else, neither can it
be defined in terms of likeness or unlikeness.

The absolute, according to *Spencer*, is nevertheless a
positive concept. We are always under the necessity of
assuming something which can be defined, marked out,
compared—something which is independent of the definite
form ascribed to it by our thought. We represent it to
ourselves, after the analogy of our own energy, as a
universal energy which underlies all objective and subjective changes and forms the content of our knowledge—but which cannot itself be expressed by any
concept.

Spencer moreover regards this as offering a possible
solution of the controversy between religion and science.
It is the common aim of all religions to furnish knowledge
of the universal energy. But it is still only in its most
primitive stages that religion pretends to furnish complete knowledge of the absolute. The higher the development of religion, the more readily it concedes the existence of an inexplicable mystery. When the evolution of
religion has once been perfected religion and science will
join hands in the common acknowledgment that the real
nature of things is unknowable, and religion will cease to
oppose the scientific explanation of phenomena.—*Spencer*
is well aware of the fact that men are loath to surrender
the well-defined intuitive ideas of the various religions.
He nevertheless anticipates a progressive development in
this direction. He fondly hopes that the emotional side of
religion, its musical temper, may be able to survive, even
though its dogmas must perish.

Spencer failed to overcome the discrepancy between the
so-called absolute and relative. Even though, e. g., he
assumes the applicability of the concept of evolution to

every sphere of phenomena, he nevertheless denies that this concept applies to "the Absolute" itself.

c. Philosophy, as unitary knowledge, is in search of a common principle or a general type of all phenomena. *Spencer* discovers such a principle by the method of induction and analysis, which he afterwards seeks to deduce from a general principle.

The principle which philosophy has been seeking is the principle of evolution. Every phenomenon has come into being, so far as we are concerned, by a process of evolution, and we understand a phenomenon whenever we know its evolution. But what is evolution? There are, according to *Spencer*, three characteristics by which it can be described.

In its simplest forms evolution consists of concentration, a transition from a more attenuated to a more permanent state of coherence. The formation of a pile of sand on the ocean beach is a simple example. The evolution of the solar system (in its primitive phase, as the formation of the primeval nebula) and the earth (by its assuming the spherical form within the original nebula), the growth of an organism by means of assimilating nourishment, the origin of a people from its stems and groups, etc., furnish examples on a larger scale.—*Differentiation goes hand in hand with integration,* especially on the higher levels. *There follows then a transition from a state of greater homogeneity to one of greater heterogeneity.* It is not the whole, as such, that differentiates itself; different parts within the whole differentiate themselves from one another and assume definite forms. Thus the various heavenly bodies of the solar system have taken form, and each of the heavenly bodies in turn develop differences between the respective parts of their surfaces and their internal structure as well as between the parts of the surfaces themselves.

The various organs are developed by the process of specialization during the course of the evolution of the organism. Organic life on the earth divides into various species. And in the sphere of social life we have an example in the division of labor.—Whenever differentiation proceeds one-sidedly, dissolution quickly follows. A third characteristic of evolution must therefore be added, namely, that it consists of a determination which presupposes a definite harmony between integration and differentiation.

The concept of evolution just described applies to every particular phenomenon, and to every phenomenal sphere (but not, as some have misunderstood *Spencer*, to "the universe" as a whole). It has been discovered by induction, but it must also be verified by deduction. Here *Spencer* falls back on a principle which he regards the foundation of all real science: *the principle of the persistence of energy*. With *Spencer* this principle (as with *Hamilton* and even *Descartes* and *Spinoza*) is really identical with the principle of causality. Every experiment rests upon the assumption of this principle: for if energy could originate or be lost during the course of an experiment it would be impossible to draw any inference. It follows therefore that similar elements must be similarly affected by similar energies, which establishes the principle of integration. It follows further that similar elements must be differently affected by different energies; which establishes the principle of differentiation. Proof of the necessity of the third characteristic determination is lacking. It is not a mere accident that *Spencer* was unable to establish this principle. From the viewpoint of experience it is impossible to furnish any guarantee for the harmony of integration and differentiation, whilst the hypothetical conditions demand the presence of both processes. Notwithstanding his sublime optimism, *Spencer* was therefore unable to furnish a proof of harmonious evolution. With *Hegel* "*the higher unity*" was a logical necessity; but a final deduction is impossible in the case of *Spencer's* systematic positivism, even though the problem which here arises did not clearly occur to him.

d. The series of works which furnish a detailed development of the theories advanced in the *First Principles* contain a gap, due to the fact that *Spencer* failed to furnish a specific treatise on evolution in the sphere of inorganic phenomena. On the other hand he demonstrates the general forms of evolution in the realms of biology, psychology, sociology and ethics in detail.

Life, according to *Spencer, consists of an adjustment of internal relations to external relations.* Organisms are not only directly determined by external factors, but there are indirect factors likewise developed from within by means of which they are enabled to adjust themselves more advantageously to future conditions than in the past. That is to say these influences lead to a transposition of the organic elements; the structure changes under the influence of function. This gives rise to variations which then endeavor to survive in the struggle for existence. *Spencer* attaches greater importance to the adaptation resulting from the exercise of the functions than to that resulting from the loss and death of such forms as are ill-adapted by "natural selection" (which *Spencer* prefers to call "*the survival of the fittest*").

Consciousness is likewise a form of adaptation. As soon as the number of objective impressions increases, the corresponding subjective states can only adjust themselves advantageously by arranging them in serial order, and such arrangement is the characteristic function of consciousness.

Psychology is a division of biology. We must nevertheless make a distinction between subjective and objective psychology. Objective psychology consists of the natural science of the material processes with which the phenomena of consciousness are ordinarily associated. Subjective psychology rests upon introspection and forms the correlate of all the other sciences; with the single difference, that it treats of the knowledge process as such, whilst all others treat of the objects of knowledge.

In the sphere of consciousness we again discover the general characteristics of evolution: concentration, differentiation and determination. We rise by gradual transitions from reflex movement through instinct and memory to reason in a constantly increasing concentration, and likewise from the simplest sensory discriminations to the most refined distinctions of the intellect. And we find that each stage is modified by the necessary correspondence with the conditions of life and its relations.

Spencer seems to be somewhat vacillating on the problem of the relation existing between consciousness and matter. He at first conceives this relation as a case of metamorphosis of natural forces according to which consciousness bears a relation to the brain process analogous to that of heat to motion. Later on however he regarded mind and matter as two irreducible empirical forms of universal energy. This theory however has not been consistently carried out in his works. The task which *Spencer* had set for himself was to discover the fundamental principles of the evolutionary theory in every department of science, and for this purpose it was really immaterial what psychological theory was subsumed. He says however—in harmony with his attitude towards subjective psychology as compared with all other sciences—that if he were to choose between the two alternatives of referring psychical phenomena to material processes or vice versa, he would regard the latter solution as the most acceptable.

In sociology *Spencer* lays the chief stress upon its direct bearing upon the actual problems of life. The struggle for existence is intended to develop human character, and hence no social ordinance and no state institution dare be interposed between the individual and real life. Because of the fact that the whole matter turns on the development of character, evolution progresses slowly and *Spencer* is far less sanguine at this point than *Comte* and *Mill.*—His pedagogical theory is governed by the same line of argument. The child is to acquire independent experiences as early as possible and be under the guidance of authority and tradition as little as possible. Otherwise twofold adjustment would be required, namely, first to the authority and then to the actual conditions of life (*Education*, 1861).

Concentration prevails during the earlier stages of social evolution, i. e. the individual is subordinate to the whole. It is conditioned by the necessities of common protection. It is here that militarism enjoys its classic period. Later on—as the individual forges to the front— a differentiation takes place. Individuals are then able to realize their own ends according to their pleasure, and they can advance their mutual interests by the free organization of individual energies. The struggle between militarism and industrialism is still in full sway. But *Spencer* anticipates a third stage in which labor for the

sheer necessities of life will no longer occupy the central
place, but in which devotion to occupations which are
valuable per se will be far more general than now.

It is the duty of ethics to develop the content of the
highest stages of social life. The method of ethics is
essentially constructive: from the highest principles of
evolutionary theory it constructs the idea of the perfect
life as a harmony of concentration and differentiation, a
complete determination. In the perfect organic type the
development of the one suffers no limitation save the
recognition of the corresponding right of the other to
development, and the individual is not coerced to undertake occupations which offer no immediate satisfaction.
Altruism on the contrary furnishes the individual opportunity to develop faculties and dispositions which would
otherwise remain fallow. The contrast between altruism
and egoism is thus reconciled.—For the present we are
still far removed from such an ideal state. For this
reason we can only have a relative ethics, not an absolute
system; but the absolute ethics can nevertheless be formulated and serve as a guide to relative ethics.

Spencer regards the utilitarianism of *Bentham* and *Mill*
as too empirical. The highest ethical ideas can be discovered only by the theory of evolution. But in his ethics
as in his theory of knowledge, he still differs from his precursors only in the matter of having extended the horizon.

F. POSITIVISM IN GERMANY AND ITALY.

As we have already observed, positivism is by no means
to be conceived merely as a movement which is opposed to
romanticism. It is the result of well-defined intellectual
motives which are peculiar to it alone. Within the positive school (in its broader sense) we have seen men like

Stuart Mill and *Spencer*, each taking their own course. We have likewise found investigators outside of France and England, who have become positivists independently. Among these we wish to describe *Eugen Dühring* of Germany and *Roberto Ardigo*, the Italian.

1. *Eugen Dühring* (born 1883), despite the fact that he became blind early in life, has shown a remarkable activity as a teacher and author. His external misfortunes were due to his severe opposition to and distrust of academic authorities, on account of which he was dismissed from his position as a Privatdocent at the University of Berlin. He has published a characteristic autobiography under the title, *Sache, Leben und Feinde Als Hauptwerk und Schlüssel zu seinen sammtlichen Werken* (1882).

His first work of any consequence was *Natural Dialectic* (1865). Here he is still in close touch with the critical philosophy, and he distinguishes sharply between formal and real science. The intellect is constantly striving to discover continuous transitions and to form infinite series (i. e. capable of continuation according to the same principle). In mathematics, e. g. we have the concept of infinity and in logic the principle of sufficient reason. But we must not transfer this tendency to continuity to the sphere of real being. Here the principle of definite number prevails, as experience shows. Astronomy, physics and chemistry show how completely the character of natural processes and natural elements are governed by the law of definite proportions. Each separate series of causes which nature reveals consists of a finite number of members.

Dühring's theory of the vital relation between the laws of thought and being presents a singular contrast to the above distinction. Thought is a continuation of being.

The uniformity revealed in nature as well as in the interplay of nature's forces corresponds to the combinations and deductions of the intellect; the identical nature of particular elements under varied conditions corresponds to the logical principle of identity; the real relation of cause and effect corresponds to the logical relation of premise and conclusion, etc. The fact that man is capable of knowing nature rests upon the fact that the laws of human consciousness are likewise nature's laws.

This latter view is decidedly in the ascendent in *Dühring's* later writings, where he indulges in vigorous polemic against the critical philosophy, which makes a distinction between our knowledge of things and the things-in-themselves. *Dühring* here regards this distinction as an attempt to enlist the services of philosophy in the defense of transcendental fancies. His positivism vanquishes his criticism (*Cursus der Philosophie*, 1875—rewritten under the title *Wirklichkeitsphilosophie*, 1895; *Logik und Wissenchaftslehre*, 1878).

The problem of the philosophy of reality consists in formulating a "world-scheme," a problem which must be solved by the systematization of experience. It is evident that the forces of nature constantly act in a definite way, and in a way moreover that the results of their coöperation invariably show definite totals. This provides for the origin of beings which not only exist and act, but which are likewise conscious of their existence and action and the enjoyment which it produces. The possibility of such an evolution is due to the combination of different forces. The idea of an everlasting conflict of forces would be an absurdity, and a universe wholly unconscious would represent the anomaly of a half-done performance. But nature contains a logic of its own which precludes absurdity. True, the antagonism of forces likewise plays an important part; but this antagonism is the very condition of the potential discharges of motion and experience. The value of life and the attainment of its higher planes depend wholly upon the differences and rhythms of nature. The profound satisfaction which life furnishes would be impossible without the cruel, the bitter and the painful (*Das Werth des Lebens*, 1865).

Dühring, like *Comte*, finds the germinal principle of the moral life in the instinct of sympathy. The sufferings of others have a direct effect upon individual feelings, and its influence increases with civilization. Moral progress however consists both in individualization and socialization. Crude force is still the governing principle in existing states, but in the free organizations of the future the interest of the individual will be devoted directly to his work, not merely to the products of his work. The ideal of the future does not consist in socialistic concentration, but in the growth of free industrial communities. *Dühring* anchors his hope to a progressive evolution by the progressive unfolding and survival of the good, and he strongly opposes *Darwin's* struggle for existence and *Marx's* catastrophe theory.—The contemplation of the majestic order of the universe, which has made such an evolution possible, begets a universal affection,—the equivalent of the religious sentiment of the past (*Ersatz der Religion durch Vollkommneres*, 1883).

2. In Italy a period of depression and lassitude followed the promising mental activity of the period of the Renaissance, and the general history of philosophy has

but few names to record that are of any consequence in the general trend of the evolution of thought. The nineteenth century 'produced a new Renaissance, which at first assumed a romantic speculative form. During the first half of the century *Rosmini* and *Gioberti* developed a kind of *Platonism* by which they hoped to harmonize religion and science. These philosophical efforts were intimately associated with political issues, because it was generally believed that the head of the church would lead the movement for political rehabilitation. But the hopes of Italy were to be realized by an entirely different method. The harmony of religion and science was broken—in the first place because the head of the Catholic church sanctioned the scholastic philosophy of the Middle Ages as the only one permissible, and, secondly, because philosophy assumed a more critical and positive character. We shall here treat of *Roberto Ardigo* (born 1828), a representative of the latter tendency.

Ardigo became a positivist by a process of gradual development. His studies in natural science and philosophy carried him step by step, without being aware of it at the time, away from the scholasticism which he had practiced as a Catholic ecclesiastic. The growth of his ideas proceeded so smoothly, that, when all of a sudden the veil was withdrawn, he thought he had always been a positivist. The evolution experienced in his own intellectual life became the theme of his philosophizing when he accepted the chair of philosophy at Pavia after quitting the church. He regarded his own course of development as a type which reveals the general characteristics of all development, no matter in what department it occurs. Whilst *Spencer* really started from the analogy of organic evolution, *Ardigo* starts from the analogy of intellectual evolution,—"*this most remarkable of all natural formations.*" He did not become acquainted with the French-English positivism until later. He calls himself a positivist, but at the same time emphasizes that the essential element of positivism consists in its empirical starting-point, rather than its systematic conclusion. He says: *the positivist proceeds step by step, with a constantly widening horizon.*

He elaborated his theory of evolution in connection with an analysis of the *Kant-Laplace* theory which he regarded a typical example of the scientific method of explanation (*La formazione naturale nel fatto del sistema solare,* 1877). The present state of the solar system came into being by a process of separation (*distinzione*), in which smaller bodies (*distinti*) were formed within larger undifferentiated bodies (*indistinto*). The larger body is not destroyed by this process. It persists and forms the basis of the interaction of the smaller body. There exists therefore an inherent continuity between the larger body and the smaller bodies which constitute its parts. The possibilities potentially contained within each of these *indistinto* (as "*forze latente or virtuale*") can only be developed by interaction with other objects! Each *indistinto* is therefore in turn a part of a more comprehensive whole, so that the distinction between *indistinto* and *distinti* is merely relative. Science is here confronted by an infinite series of processes; but its only task consists in explaining the fundamental relation of *indistinto* and *distinti* in each particular case, because it assumes that all differences, no matter where they occur, proceed from one whole and are forever comprehended within it.

The theory of knowledge is but a special case of the general theory of evolution. Every explanation consists

of a differentiation, an analysis; there is nothing understood which is not differentiated (*indistinto*). The theory
has a certain tendency to stop with finite elements
(*distinti finiti*); but the principle that every particular is
part of a whole imposes the necessity of an infinite
continuum. Hence, since even thought is simply a special
case of the natural process, it is impossible to deduce
the whole process of nature from thought. We never
attain a final term.—There is a problem at this point
which *Ardigo* failed to estimate correctly, in that knowledge is nevertheless the natural process through which
alone we acquire our knowledge of all other processes of
nature. On the other hand he (especially in *La Ragione*,
1894) describes the cognitive functions in detail, especially
emphasizing the intimate relationship of recollection and
judgment, and finding once more the relation of *indistinto*
and *distinti* in the rhythm of synthesis and of analysis.
He likewise extols the services of *Kant* to the morphol-
ogy of knowledge in this work. And he afterwards
emphasized *Kant's* theory of the synthetic unity of
consciousness in his chief work *L'unita della coscienza*
(1898) in still stronger terms. Psychic life consists of
a continuous synthetic process. There is a profound
tendency in things to combine all elements and functions
in a single stream. This confluence (*confluenza mentale*)
is the only explanation of the association of ideas. It
is impossible to explain this unity of consciousness as
a product of separate elements, because the only way we
can discover the elements is by an analytic process of
thought which already presupposes a given whole.
Ardigo's admiration for *Kant*, whom he called *il secondo
Galilei della filosofia nei tempi moderni*, does not prevent him from severely criticizing the theory of the

thing-in-itself (*L' idealismo nella vecchia speculazione*, 1903).

Ardigo likewise applies the theory of the *indistinto* and of the *distinti* to the problem of soul and body. The facts given in experience consist of the psychophysical reality in its undifferentiated form. But our investigations must in this case be divided into psychology and physiology, each of which is obliged to deal with abstractions. The psychical and the physical never exist in reality apart from each other; one and the same reality (*reale indistinto*) underlies both (*La psicologia come scienza positiva*).—As a psychologist *Ardigo* reveals a remarkable faculty of describing both the continuity as well as the more refined nuances of psychical phenomena.

Ardigo's fundamental viewpoint likewise has a striking application to ethics. Each individual is a *distinto* whose real existence is in an *indistinto*, i. e. in a society. Each individual is evolved within a social body (family, state, etc.), and thus learns to judge human actions from the viewpoint of the whole, which provides for the evolution of an anti-egoistic tendency. It is in this that what *Ardigo* calls "*the social ideality*" consists. This tendency assumes the form of a holy affection at its culminating points, which impels to sacrifice and begets a faith in The Eternal despite the tragedy of human life.

EIGHTH BOOK.

New Solutions of the Problem of Being on the Basis of Realism.

The romantic philosophy believed it could reform natural science. And this notwithstanding the fact that at the very time of the origin of this philosophy, the closing decades of the eighteenth century, natural science was making astounding progress. The traditional conviction of the persistence of matter throughout all changes was experimentally demonstrated by *Lavoisier*, by means of the quantitative method,—by weighing,—and the fundamental laws governing the material changes involved in the constitution of plant and animal life were discovered by a number of investigators (*Priestley, Saussure*, etc.), and organic life was thus incorporated within the majestic cycle of material processes.

Natural science received a new impetus during the forties of the nineteenth century, due especially to *Robert Mayer's* discovery of the principle of the conservation of energy (1842). Ideas which had already been suggested by *Descartes, Huyghens* and *Leibnitz* now received their empirical authentication, because the demonstration that there is no dissipation of force, already established in pure mechanics, could likewise be demonstrated in the interaction of the particular forces of nature, because it could be shown that a definite quantitative relation exists between the potential value (e. g. motion) which vanishes and the new potential value (e. g. heat) which arises.

In addition to this we note *Darwin's* hypothesis of the origin of the species announced during the fifties. Natural science thus demonstrated the existence of a profound vital relationship, where man had previously seen nothing more than gaps and fragments, in a brilliant manner. The only question was as to what would be the bearing of these discoveries on the treatment of philosophic problems. The appropriation of the new views came most natural to positivism, and we have already seen how *Herbert Spencer* endeavored to incorporate them in his evolutional system.

The new impulse of natural science furnished the occasion for a large German literature of a materialistic trend, which had the effect of disseminating the ideas and discoveries of natural science very widely. About the middle of the nineteenth century the German materialists were supported in their opposition to dogmatics and spiritualistic speculation—as had been the case with their French precursors of the eighteenth century—by an idealistic movement based upon the interests of humanity and progress. It is to be observed that idealism is not incongruous with theoretical materialism: the materialist can consistently recognize the value of mental phenomena and efficiency, even though he does regard them as due to mere molecular changes.

The most noted writer in this movement is the physiologist, *Jacob Moleschott* (1822–1893), who was born in Holland, was Docent at Heidelberg in his youth, and, after being dismissed there on account of his views, went to Zürich and later to Italy, where he enjoyed a long and successful career as professor of physiology. In his book, *Kreislauf des Lebens* (1852), he extols chemistry as the highest science because it shows how matter—and together with matter, how life, and with life in turn, how thought—accomplishes its sublime cycle. He expounds the history of his ideas in his autobiography (*An meine Freunde, Reminiscences*, 1895) and says that as a matter of fact his only contention was against dualism, and that his theory—on account of the inherent relation of force, mind and matter—might quite as well be called idealism as materialism!

The physician, *Louis Büchner* (1824–1899), whose *Kraft und Stoff* (1855) was for a long time one of the most widely read books of the age, similarly goes beyond the specific views of materialism, only less clearly, and this is likewise the case with *Heinrich Czolbe* (1819–1873), who, like *Büchner* and *Moleschott*, was also a physician. *Czolbe* directly inverts the proposition that sensation is motion, and consequently attains an idealistic theory (*Die Entstehung des Selbstbewusstseins*, 1856). In his later works he undertook to establish a new world theory by the use of more speculative methods. It is a matter of peculiar interest in the case of *Czolbe* that he is fully aware of assuming certain axiomatic principles, namely, the theoretical requirement of the perspicuous and intuitive nature of thought, and the ethical requirement of life and its relations in the present world-order, with complete exclusion of everything transcendent.

A little later the famous zoologist, *Ernst Haeckel* (born 1834), undertook to organize the latest results and hypotheses of natural science into a system of *Monism*. The first work specifically devoted to this purpose was his *Generalle Morphologie* (1862–1866), which was followed by his more vigorous and more dogmatic *Welträtzel* (1899). He regards everything as animated; atoms and cells have souls as well as the brain. These souls may interpose in material processes on the one hand just as material processes may be the causes of psychical phenomena on the other. The *Monism* of *Haeckel* therefore combines spiritualistic and materialistic ideas in a way that is not altogether clear. But *Haeckel's* significance, who in this respect shows an affinity to the thinkers of the Renaissance, does not consist in his logical consistency, but in the tremendous enthusiasm aroused by his ideas, and in the fanciful vividness of his expositions.

It appears therefore that dogmatic materialism, according to the testimony of the materialistic author himself, is no longer possible. The results of criticism have therefore not been in vain.

Another group of thinkers who still adhered to the fundamental principles of romanticism, even though they clearly saw the necessity of a reconstruction of the foundation and a restatement of definitions, elaborated the results of modern science in an entirely different way from the investigators just mentioned.

A. THE NEW IDEALISM IN GERMANY.

1. *Hermann Lotze* (1817-1881) began his scholastic career as a scientist and as a philosopher contemporaneously, but eventually devoted himself wholly to philosophy, in which capacity he served the University of Göttingen for a number of years. As a scientist he aimed to treat medicine and physiology as pure natural sciences, without reference to any appeal to a specific "vital force" such as was then still in vogue. He construes the phenomena which characterize organisms as the results of the coöperation of material elements according to the laws of physics and chemistry (*Allgemeine Pathologie*

und Therapie als mechanische Naturwissenschaften, 1842;
Allgemeine Physiologie, 1851). He had even previous
to this given expression to his philosophical ideas (*Metaphysik*, 1840) which were more fully elaborated later on
(*Medicinische Psychologie*, 1852, and *Mikrokosmus*, 1864–
1868), and brought to their conclusion in the *Drei Bücher
der Logik* (1874) and the *Drei Bücher der Metaphysik*
(1879).

Lotze's reflections have a twofold starting-point, the
mechanical view of modern science, the application of
which to organic life he insisted on, and the fundamental
principles of romantic idealism. The resulting problem
for him therefore was to show how to reconcile these
two points of view. He was firmly convinced that being
cannot consist of a mere mechanism, and just as firmly
that the highest ideas cannot be realized except by the
method of causal, mechanical processes. He then seeks
to show, by the analysis of the conception of mechanism
developed by the modern sciences, how we are led to
presuppositions which may readily be reconciled with
idealistic principles.

The mechanical theory of nature regards all phenomena
as determined by the interaction of atoms. This conception follows as the inevitable presupposition of the
scientific explanation of natural phenomena. But it
does not follow from this that mechanism should be the
last word of reflective thought. There are two points at
which it transcends itself.

The atoms of natural science are extended, even though
their extension may be regarded as infinitely small.
But whatever is extended must consist of parts and cannot
therefore be regarded as absolutely simple. And extension is an attribute, a quality, which, like all other quali-

ties, demands its explanation, an explanation which—according to the principles of science and after the analogy of the explanation of colors and tones—can be found only in the reciprocity of elements. These elements must therefore be still more simple than the atoms of natural science. They cannot be extended, but must be centers of force by the interactions of which the phenomenon which we call extension arises.

But this interaction would be inconceivable if the ultimate elements in themselves were absolutely independent. The only way in which the element A can affect the element B requires that A and B are not absolutely different entities; their respective states must really be the states of one and the same principle which comprehends them both: this is the only way of explaining the possibility of an inner (immanent) transition from a status A to a status B. We are thus driven to the ultimate concept of an original substance (as above to the ultimate concept of centers of force). Beyond this the analysis of the concept of mechanism cannot go.

But there is likewise another source of information on this point. Where analysis fails we must resort to analogy. *Lotze* saw that analogy is the only recourse for the authentication of metaphysical idealism with a clearness nowhere to be found before him except in *Leibnitz, Fries* and *Beneke*. Is being in its ultimate nature spiritual or material? *Lotze* answers this question by saying, that if we wish to explain the unknown by reference to the known, *we must inevitably construe everything material as the eternal manifestation of spiritual reality*. Matter (or better materiality) is only known to us as objective, whilst we know the spiritual from our own subjectivity, as immediately identical with "our self."

The only way of obtaining a comprehensible world-theory therefore is by construing the material universe after the analogy of the spiritual. In which case we construe both the elements (centers of force) and the primary substance as spiritual realities, the former representing an infinite variety of stages of development, the latter as an infinite personality.

Lotze's psychology is likewise affected by his metaphysics. According to him the relation of soul and body is but a single example of interaction in general. Just as atoms can transmit impulses from one to another, so can the soul and an atom of the nervous system likewise transmit impulses from one to the other. *Lotze* sees no ground therefore in the principle of the conservation of energy for surrendering the common (Cartesian) conception of the interaction of soul and body. He makes a thorough study of the difficult problem of distinguishing between such mental phenomena as find their causes within the soul itself, and such as have their causes in the influences of the nervous system. Among the former are memory, reflection, the æsthetic and moral feelings, etc.; among the latter, sensations, which merely furnish the materials of thought.—Of *Lotze's* more specifically psychological theories we must first of all mention his ingenious doctrine of *"local signs"* (i. e. the specific sensations which furnish the basis of the construction of the theory of space), and then also his fine description and analysis of the relation of feeling and idea.

Although *Lotze* means to defend the common (Cartesian) theory of the interaction of soul and body, in his metaphysics, based on analogy, he has nevertheless made some important modifications. The interaction of soul and body is no longer (as in *Descartes*) an interaction of *different* essences, but an interaction of elements which are all of a psychical nature. And now, after finding that it is easier to conceive the interaction of soul and body, he actually grants that a causal relation is really comprehensible only between like elements.

Lotze's theory therefore culminates in a spiritualistic *Monism*. He likewise places increasing emphasis on the immanence of the elements in primary substance. On this latter point he stands much closer to the Spinozistic view than he is aware.

2. *Edward von Hartmann* (1842–1906) gave his chief work (*Die Philosophie des Unbewussten*, 1868) the subtitle, *Speculative Resultate nach induktio-wissenschaftlicher Methode*. After his military career was cut short by a fall from a horse in which he sustained a crippled knee, he finally decided, after some mental struggle, to devote himself to philosophy. He then conceived the plan of a further development of the ideas of *Hegel* and *Schopenhauer* in mutual harmony, and then to construe these romantic theories on the basis of empirical science. His program reminds us of *Lotze*. But whilst *Lotze* accepts the mechanical conception of nature with frank consistency, and inquires only concerning its presuppositions, *Hartmann* seeks to prove inductively that this conception of nature is inadequate, and that it requires the supplement of a spiritual principle which he calls "*The Unconscious*," to prevent its being construed anthropomorphically. *The forces ascribed to atoms must be conceived as wills or efforts: they must have an unconscious idea of their destiny in order to be able to realize it. Matter therefore consists of idea and will.* The only explanation of the organism is the guidance of its growth by an unconscious will. Between growth and instinct there is only a

difference of degree. The association of ideas likewise presupposes that the unconscious within us selects the ideas which are most closely related or possess an affinity for the stock of ideas on hand. In the process of history the unconscious operates in such a way that individuals, whilst seeming to themselves to be striving for their own conscious ends, serve the higher purposes of the universe as a whole.—The activity of the unconscious is thus everywhere manifest—from atom to world-process. This principle is not personal, but rather super-personal. *Hartmann* nevertheless regards himself in agreement, barring several modifications, with the speculative theism of *Schelling, Weisse* and *Lotze*.

Hartmann's philosophy did not originate from pure induction. It rests on the subsumption of a psychologico-historical aperçu: namely, the observation on the one hand of the prejudicial view of mere reflection and analysis, the onesided attitude of criticism, and the tremendous importance of the immediate, the instinctive and ingenious on the other. Consciousness, according to *Hartmann*, is predominantly analytical, critical and negative; it is only the unconscious that furnishes the grand total and provides for the new insertions. Starting from this theoretical motive, suggesting the influence of *Rousseau*, and *Romanticism*, *Hartmann* finally ascribes a mystic-metaphysical character to the unconscious which is active everywhere in nature and in history—and which, in *Hartmann's* view, explains everything.

Replying to his opponents, in an anonymous self-criticism (*Das Unbewusste vom Standpunkte der Physiologie und der Descendenzlehre*, 1872), he demonstrates his mastery of the methods and results of the natural sciences. He had the satisfaction of seeing this work regarded as the refutation of his views.—But it is the more remarkable therefore that he could still adhere to his romantic method of explanation.

How then is the universe, in which the unconscious operates, constituted? According to *Hartmann*, the "inductive method" shows that there is more misery than happiness in the world. The recognition of the world's wretchedness is of course not yet fully developed, but it is growing. Men at first expected to find happiness in this present earthly life; then they hoped to be able to attain it in a future, immortal life; and when this faith likewise finally vanished, hope was centered on the happiness of future generations here upon earth. The illusion of happiness is untenable in all three of these forms. But if this is the case, the unconscious, which is everywhere active, cannot be a purely rational principle. The explanation of evil and misery can only be found in the fact that the volitional element of the unconscious has, as blind impulse, severed all relation with the ideational element and instituted the world process as the sheer "*will to live*."—*Hartmann* is here using the ideas of *Böhme, Schelling* and *Schopenhauer*. The world-process consists in a constant strife between these two elements. Here man can enter the lists as a rival. It is his business to attack the illusions, not only directly, but likewise indirectly in his efforts towards civilization. The greater the advancement in civilization, the more evident the illusory character of happiness becomes, for civilization and happiness are absolute opposites. The highest aim is the redemption of the suffering of deity by the consummation of pessimism. As soon as the will-to-live is annulled, the world-process introduced by the Fall within the unconscious, referred to above, will be at an end.

But this lies in the distant future. For the present therefore pessimism can feel quite at ease and at home in the world!

Besides his masterpiece, *Hartmann* has written a number of important works in the departments of ethics, the philosophy of religion and æsthetics, as he was, generally speaking, a rather voluminous author. *Arthur Drews* has published a detailed and quite sympathetic exposition of his whole activity (*Hartmann's Philosophical System in Outlines*, 2d ed., 1906).

3. *Gustav Theodore Fechner* (1801–1887) was originally a physicist. But along with his scientific investigations his mind dwelt on a world of speculation and poetic imagination in which the ideas of romanticism are peculiarly prominent,—this was especially the case after the objective world was closed to him through failure of eyesight. By the method of the most daring analogies, he construed the universe (in the highly fanciful book *Zendavesta*, 1851, and later in the *Seelenfrage*, 1861) as an animated whole within which every possible degree of psychic life is manifest,—in the form of plant and animal souls, human souls, the souls of the heavenly bodies, etc. When *Fechner* began to reflect on the problem of the relation of the psychical side of the universe to its physical side he came upon the fundamental idea of his masterpiece, *Elemente der Psychophysik* (1860). Like *Kepler*, with whom he shows a striking mental sympathy, he took fantastic speculations for his starting-point, but by diligent reflection he finally discovered principles which could be verified in experience. He was convinced from the beginning that the relation of spirit and matter could not be objective, as if they were different entities. Later on he defends this view (in the fifth chapter of the *Ele-*

mente der Psychophysik) by appealing to the principle of the conservation of physical energy, and he is the first to have applied this principle to the relation of soul and body. He thinks that the brain and nervous system, like all matter, must come under this principle, and that the ordinary assumption of a real interaction of spirit and matter cannot therefore be correct, because in that case physical energy would begin and cease. The relation is rather one of identity, and the distinction depends on the viewpoint of the observer. Just as the observer standing on the external surface of a sphere sees nothing but convexity, and one standing on the internal surface sees only concavity, so the materialist sees nothing but matter and the idealist only spirit—and both are right, each from his own viewpoint.—The resulting problem then is, what quantitative relations do the psychical phenomena sustain to their corresponding material phenomena? *Fechner* thinks that this relation cannot be one of direct proportion, but that it must be logarithmic, i. e. the psychical changes correspond quantitatively to the relation of the increase of its corresponding material process and the process already present. *Fechner* thus assumes that the relation between the external stimulus and the brain process to which it gives rise is directly proportional, because both are material events, but the relation between the psychical process of sensation and the brain process on the other hand must be logarithmic. He regarded Weber's Law (so called in honor of his precursor, the physiologist *E. H. Weber*), which he assumed and verified experimentally, as an expression of the relation of spirit and matter in general. Upon the basis of experiments of his own as well as of others, on the relation of sensation and stimulus, he found that his law applied within certain limits. This problem gave rise to a long controversy. *Fechner* founded experimental psychology by means of this hypothesis. He participated in this controversy with a number of articles even into his old age, but always in a serious and chivalrous spirit. But it has become more and more apparent that *Fechner's* law, so far as it applies at all, expresses the relation of the psychical process (sensation) and the external stimulus, but not the relation of the psychical process and the brain process, which is apparently much more directly proportional. This conception would also agree better with *Fechner's* hypothesis of identity (and with his excellent illustrations).

In addition to his famous masterpiece *Fechner* produced two more scientific works of importance: *Über die physikalische und philosophische Atomenlehre* (1855), in which he assumes a position similar to that of *Lotze* with respect to the atom-concept, and *Vorschule der Æsthetik* (1876), in which he treats a number of æsthetic problems empirically.

W. Wundt has written an excellent essay on the inherent consistency of *Fechner's* intellectual labors (*Gustav Theodor Fechner, Rede zur Feier seines hundertjährigen Geburtsstages*, 1901).

4. *William Wundt* (born 1832, professor of physiology at Heidelberg, afterwards professor of philosophy at Zürich and since then, 1874, at Leipzig) passed to philosophy from physiology, induced partly by psychological and partly by epistemological motives. After he had made the change, new motives impressed him, especially the effort to elaborate a theory of the universe and of life at once satisfying to the affections and the intellect. *Wundt's* final theory, according to his own

conception, is closely related to the philosophy of romanticism. But *Wundt's* idealism has been attained by the method of scientific investigation even to a greater extent than in the case of *Lotze, Hartmann* and *Fechner*.

The psychological motives to philosophizing sprang from *Wundt's* investigations of the physiology of the senses. He recognized the fact that the theory of space could only arise from primary sensations by means of a creative synthesis, a synthesis whose product possesses other attributes than the elements, considered by themselves. Afterwards, while investigating the temporal progress of ideas, he came upon the problem of psychical integration (which he later called *Apperception*). This completed the foundation for the fundamental theories of his psychology. His *Grundzüge der physiologischen Psychologie* (1874, 6th ed., 1908) treats the psychological problems which can be elucidated physiologically and experimentally with great thoroughness, and describes the methods and instruments of experimentation. *Wundt* assumes the parallelism of the physical and the psychical as a preliminary hypothesis; the difference is only a difference of viewpoint. But in its ultimate analysis he regards the psychical viewpoint as fundamental. And in his view the only necessity for assuming physiological correlates is due to the individual psychical elements which constitute the content of psychical life, not for the forms or the combinations of the elements, nor for experiences of value.

Wundt construes psychical life as pure activity. The assumption of a psychical "substance" involves the application of materialistic ideas to the sphere of spiritual reality. Psychical activity is especially evident in the form of apperception in its function of attention, association, feeling and volition. Here we have the soul as an organized whole; the whole antecedent history of consciousness expresses itself in the acts of apperception.— *Wundt* places increasing emphasis upon this activity in his later writings, and the concept of volition becomes his fundamental psychological concept so that (borrowing an expression of *Paulsen's*) he can describe his theory as *voluntarism*.

The epistemological motive which induced *Wundt* to enter the field of philosophy resulted from his recognition of the fact that all natural science rests upon certain presuppositions which condition all our knowledge (*Die physikalischen Axiome und ihre Beziehung zum Kausalprinzip*, 1866). Later on he elaborated his theory of knowledge partly in his *Logik* (1880–1883) and partly in his *System der Philosophie* (1887). Knowledge always begins with the conviction of the reality of our ideas. This naïve realism breaks down however even by the necessity of distinguishing between sense perception, memory and imagination, and still more by scientific reflection, until it gradually yields to critical realism which substitutes object concepts which remain constant for the changing content of direct perception. In the sphere of sense perception the laws of space and time are elaborated as the expression of constant forms; in the sphere of intellectual knowledge the qualities immediately given are replaced by the concept of the object in the form of quantitative distinctions alone (spatial and temporal), whilst the psychical processes are referred to a fundamental spiritual activity. But rational knowledge, which demands a completion of knowledge by the idea of totality, carries us even farther than this. Such conclusion assumes the character of materialism whenever the ideas of natural science are taken into account alone, the character of idealism whenever the psychological ideas are taken alone. It is possible however to attain a higher view by combining the two groups of ideas, in which case being is construed as a totality of striving and willing entities whose objective phenomenal form constitutes material nature. *Wundt* agrees with *Lotze* that we are obliged to choose between a material and a spiritual unity; we must either make mind the basis of matter or vice versa; there is no third alternative! But he fails to see as clearly as *Lotze* that our only recourse at this point is to the argument from analogy.

In his ethics (*Ethik, eine Untersuchung der Tatsachen und Gesetze des sittlichen Lebens*, 1886) *Wundt* shows marked sympathy with German speculation, especially with *Hegel*. He construes the individual will as an element of the total will whence both its motives and its ideals arise. The isolated individual does not exist. And the highest ends are only found in the *total will*. Even where individuals seem to be laboring for their own individual ends, they may still produce something which will extend beyond their horizon and in turn give rise to new motives. This shifting process, which *Wundt* calls the *heterogeny of ends*, is the most important evolutional process of the moral consciousness. But this likewise implies that we cannot be conscious of the ultimate ends of the whole course of historical evolution. We are co-laborers in a sublime undertaking whose absolute content we can never know. At this point ethics becomes religion. Whilst the positive religions express themselves in concrete symbols, philosophy can only express the general principle that all spiritual products possess an absolute or imperishable value.

In addition to the works mentioned *Wundt* has published a valuable *Einleitung in die Philosophie* (1901), and he is at present engaged on a comprehensively planned *Völker-psychologie*, the content of which consists of investigations concerning Language, Myth and Custom.

B. MODERN IDEALISM IN ENGLAND AND FRANCE.

1. *Francis Herbert Bradley* (born 1846, Fellow of Merton College, Oxford) is the most important English representative of the tendency which may be described as the *New Idealism*. He is particularly influenced by *Kant* and *Hegel*. *Coleridge, Carlyle* and *Hamilton* were already opposed to the classical English school as it appears in the line of thinkers from *Locke* to *Spencer* and *Sidgwick*. The critical turn which *Sidgwick* introduced into utilitarianism and the broadening of the horizon of empiricism by *Spencer* brought the old school to a point which required new instruments of thought. Of the two great English universities Oxford in particular represents the opposition to the classical English school. The ideas of *Kant* and *Hegel* have affected English thought particularly through the labors of *T. H. Green* and *Edward Caird*. Against the tendency of the older school to reduce psychical life to physical atoms and thus to apply the concept of mechanism without further qualification to the sphere of mind present-day thinkers propose the "organic" conception and the idea of totality. This conception is keenly apparent in *Bradley's Ethical Studies* (1876). The unity of consciousness is the condition without which we could not even perceive ourselves. *Bradley* thus takes for his starting-point (without noting the fact) the view with which *Stuart Mill* concluded in the later editions of his *Examination of Hamilton's Philosophy*.

Bradley makes the ethical standard consist of the degree to which we have developed the unity which is so deeply imbedded in our nature so as to combine a rich content with inner harmony. And the metaphysical principle forms an analogy with the psychological and ethical principles: *being must be conceived as a coherent and consistent whole.*

Bradley's chief work bears the title *Appearance and Reality* (1893). It consists of an investigation of the criterion by which we are enabled to distinguish true reality from mere appearance. Although *Bradley* himself (along with many of his critics) thinks that his position is closely identical with *Hegel*, and notwithstanding the fact that "the Absolute" in the Spinozistic and Hegelian sense, as of an objective final statement, appears in the background of his thought, his reflections are nevertheless more epistemological than metaphysical. Like *Kant*, he makes the concept of experience fundamental. True reality can only exist where complete and perfect experience—i. e. all-inclusive perception—and an absolutely mutual relation of the contents of perception—is present. This is an ideal which finite beings can approach only approximately. Neither the natural nor the mental sciences satisfy this ideal. Such concepts as matter, space, time, and energy are applicable whenever it is necessary to express the relation of finite appearances; they are working ideas,—but they can never describe the absolute nature of being. And the same is true of the psychological concepts. As a matter of course we find a more vital relationship between unity and multiplicity in the sphere of mind than in physical nature, and psychological experience therefore constitutes our highest experience. But antitheses and disharmonies take place within the psychical processes; the soul is subject to changes as a whole; and the concept of the soul—like its correlative concept, the body—is formed only by abstraction. Psychological concepts can therefore no more express absolute reality than the concepts of natural science.

When *Bradley* insists on the idea of the absolute, even though there is no concept that can give it adequate expression, he appears at once as a mystic and a sceptic. The unifying bond of these two sides of his nature lies in the idea of a constant striving which is the lot of all finite beings. Our thought, says *Bradley*, is always striving for something which is more than thought,— our personality for something which is more than personality,—our morality for something which is more than morality! The only thing which philosophy can do for us is to furnish us a criterion to serve as a guide whenever we distinguish between higher and lower degrees of reality. Religion can do no more at this point than philosophy. It too must express the highest by means of ideas which have their source in the sphere of the finite. The advantage of religion consists in the fact that it is capable of allowing the recognition of a highest reality to permeate our entire being.

Bradley has no points of contact with the special sciences, as is the case with *Fechner, Lotze* and *Wundt.* He has no interest in purely empirical considerations. He is completely absorbed in the idea of his ideal criterion. This gives energy and depth to his mode of thought, but it likewise frequently makes him unjust towards other viewpoints, even such as he could really appropriate with advantage. When, e. g., he calls the viewpoints and hypotheses of the special sciences *"useless fictions"* and "*mere practical compromises*," he is inconsistent with the importance which he ascribes to them as "*working ideas.*" As a matter of fact according to his conception every finite experience, i. e. every experience which it is possible for us to have, is a working idea. And, according to *Bradley's* own principles, that which he calls "*the Absolute*" must be present in all our working ideas, like *Spinoza's* Substance in all the Attributes and in all the Modes.

2. In France *Alfred Fouillée* (born 1838, professor at Bordeaux, afterwards in Paris, now (1906) living in southern France) assumes a position which may justly be described as idealism on a realistic basis. Greek philosophy, especially *Plato*, forms the subject-matter of his earliest studies; later on he regarded it his peculiar task "*to bring back the ideas of Plato from heaven to earth and thus reconcile idealism and naturalism.*" His fundamental principle is the original and natural relation of thought and motion (*idée-force*). His precursor in this view is *Taine*, whose *De l'intelligence* (1870) attaches great importance to the motive tendencies primarily combined with all ideas which only assume the purely theoretical character of ideas through increasing mental development. *Fouillée* constructs his concept of *idée-force* from a physiologico-psychological fact, which he then in turn discovers by the method of analogy in the lower stages of nature. His chief work, *La psychologie des idées-forces* (1893), is a classic in voluntaristic psychology. Psychical phenomena always consist of the manifestations of an impulse or desire (appetition) which is attended by pleasure or pain according as it is fostered or inhibited. Discernment and preference are primarily one and the same thing, as e. g. the discernment of an animal between

the edible and the non-edible. Sensation is originally
limited to such things as are of practical importance in
the struggle for existence; it is the will (in the broadest
sense of the term) that impels the sensations to new
differentiations. And just as in the case of sensation
so it is with knowledge in general. Every thought, every
idea describes a more or less conscious and definite
tendency of life.

Fouillée regards the application of the analogy of mental
life, the most immediate experience which we possess,
as furnishing the possibility of a metaphysics. Our
knowledge of mental life however does not rest upon
psychology alone, but likewise upon sociology; the
individual and the social, liberty and solidarity are
inseparable. This theory which *Fouillée* applied to the
sphere of sociology and ethics (*La science sociale contemporaine*, 1880; *Critique des systemes de morale contemporaine*, 1883) likewise acquires cosmological significance
for him. The universe must be conceived as a grand
total, a community of striving energies. But in this
sphere we cannot attain anything more than a hypothetical scheme, for the synthesis which forms the completion of our knowledge cannot be carried out positively—
as in the cases of the finite synthesis of the special departments of phenomena. But this nevertheless furnishes
us a criterion by which to judge the various metaphysical
systems: such a system is complete in proportion as both
multiplicity as well as unity, analysis as well as synthesis, receive due recognition (*L'avenir de la Metaphysique*,
1889).

NINTH BOOK.

New Theories of the Problems of Knowledge and of Value.

A. The Problem of Knowledge.

1. German Neo-Kantianism.

With the declining influence of the speculative philosophy and the growing demand for a scientific world theory following it again making itself felt, partly in positivism, partly in materialism, partly in the new idealism, it was but natural that the problem of knowledge—as was the case in the period of *Hume* and *Kant*—should again assume a position of prominence. It raised the inevitable question of the ability of the human intellect, from its inherent nature, to construct such a world-theory, and of the limitations to which it is subject. It was evident that the reaction against *Kant*, in both its positivistic and its romantic aspects, had overreached itself, an. ` the study of *Kant* was again resumed for the purpose of orientation. As we have observed, there was a critical undercurrent constantly making itself felt during the first half of the century (cf. *Fries* and *Beneke*, as well as *Herbart, Schleiermacher* and *Schopenhauer*). This now becomes the dominant current for a time, supported by the revival of a thorough study of the master both philologically and historically.

In his *Geschichte des Materialismus* (1865) *Friederich Albert Lange* (1828–1875), who was professor of philosophy at Zürich and later at Marburg, opposes the epistemolog-

ical method to both the romantic speculation and the
materialistic conception of nature. Like *Fechner*, he
conceives the whole of material nature—including the
brains of men and of animals—as explainable by means of
continuously active material energies. So far as method
is concerned, materialism is right. But the phenomena
of consciousness are not to be construed as members of
the material series; they are subjective experiences whose
objective correlates constitute the brain processes.—
That is to say, *Lange*, like *Fechner* and *Wundt*, accepts the
Spinozistic hypothesis. He furthermore combines with
this the Kantian point of view. For even if we should
assume that our sensations and ideas are products of
material processes, these material processes themselves
would still be nothing more than objects of consciousness,
ideas formed by us according to the laws of our mind.
As a matter of fact, it may readily be that even the Kantian distinction between phenomenon and thing-in-itself
is a product of our mental organization (*Lange* offers
this suggestion in a letter published in *Ellisen's Biographie
Lange's*, see p. 258 ff., published letters.)

In addition to natural science and epistemology, *Lange*
likewise finds room for speculative and religious ideas.
But he does not regard such ideas as having any theoretical
and objective significance. They are subjective supple-
ments of empirical reality, proceeding from the needs of
the spirit. They must be understood from the viewpoint of their value to human life, and not from the viewpoint of their foundation and their origin. *Lange* here
combines a liberal practical idealism with theoretical
idealism. But it can only be expressed in figurative or
symbolical form. *Lange* insists that criticism should
place more stress on the ideal and psychologically valuable

elements of positive faith, instead of directly attacking the dogmas of popular religion. In this way the general public would not dissipate its energy in useless dogmatic controversies.

Lange elaborated his ideal and critical theory of the social problem in his essay on *Die Arbeiterfrage* (1865). The central thought of this essay is this, namely, that the chief duty of human society consists in seeking to put an end to the struggle for existence.

Lange is the most influential of the German Neo-Kantians. His masterly work affects wide circles both by the excellence of its form as by the richness of its content and its profound statement of the problem. He was however the herald of a new school which, with various nuances, strove to renew the Kantian theory of knowledge. *Hermann Cohen's* works are specifically devoted to an elaboration of the rationalistic elements in *Kant's* philosophy, whilst *Alois Riehl* inclines more towards positivism. *Frederick Paulsen,* whose general views are closely related to those of *Fechner* and *Wundt,* in his exposition of *Kant,* has directed special attention to *Kant's* metaphysical assumptions which are unaffected by the *Critique of Reason.* *Windelband* and *Rickert* conceive genuine criticism as the theory of eternal values, in which the standard of the true, the good and the beautiful is found, and they lay great stress on the distinction between the method of concept-formation practiced by the natural sciences as compared with that of the historical sciences, which are related to each other as generalization and individualization.

Criticism has become a vital factor both in the statement and in the treatment of the problems in German thought through the labors of this group of scholars.

2. FRENCH CRITICISM AND THE PHILOSOPHY OF DISCONTINUITY.

In France, after the middle of the nineteenth century, the critical school is represented by the vigorous thinker *Charles Renouvier* (1815–1903), who in the name of logic and ethics attacks all idealistic and realistic attempts to construe being as a continuous totality. He directed his polemics with particular force against the concept of actual infinity, which he regarded as a logical contradiction and an empirical falsehood. For an infinite which is at the same time regarded as a determinate whole is a contradiction, and experience teaches us that the principle of definite number applies to everything. With actual infinity continuity is likewise destroyed,—for continuity must indeed presuppose infinitely many gradations,— and with continuity necessity. In opposition to *Kant's* attempt to prove the principle of causality, *Renouvier* returns to *Hume's* position and thus attains a radical philosophy of discontinuity. He regards every distinction as a discontinuity. And as a matter of fact it is not only in our knowledge of nature that we are constantly compelled to recognize leaps. The first principles of our knowledge are postulated by a leap, i. e. by an act of choice. *Renouvier* was profoundly influenced by *Kant's* antinomies; it is his opinion however that, if we wish to retain the principles of logic, we are obliged to accept the theses and reject the antitheses.

Renouvier has published a sketch of his philosophical development in an exceedingly interesting essay found in *Equisse d'une classification des systemes philosophiques* (1885) (*Comment je suis arrive a cette conclusion*, ibid., II, pp. 355–405).—For the various phases of *Renouvier's* philosophy I must refer the reader to *Gabriel Seailles: La philosophie de Charles Renouvier,* 1905.

The choice of first principles determines the world-theory, and in this connection *Renouvier* in his latter years (*Les dilemmes de la metaphysique,* 1901) emphasized more and more the antithesis of thing and personality. If we remember that things always exist only as objects for personalities, our world-view must necessarily assume the character of monadology or of personalism. (See particularly *Renouvier's* last essay, *L'Personalisme,* 1903.) In this way he passes from criticism and the theory of discontinuity to spiritualistic metaphysics. As a critical philosopher he seeks to show that the universe must have a beginning—because of the principle of definite number—as a personalist he explains this beginning as the act of a god who (on account of the existence of evil) is not however to be regarded as absolute or almighty. *Renouvier* constantly insists on the epistemological principle of relativity (*la loi de relation*): our knowledge aims to discover the relations which things bear to each other; each object represents to us a system of relations; our knowledge itself consists of a relation of things to us and hence all objects are only phenomena. Religious postulates alone can transcend phenomena—but even these postulates, as acts of thought, are governed by the principle, or, more correctly, the method of relativity (*la methode des relations*).

This vigorous and profound thinker remained busily occupied with his philosophy even on his death-bed. He experienced a sense of incompleteness, and he did not wish to die until he had given his ideas a definite form. A close friend has preserved his last words and exposi-

tions (*Ch. Renouvier: Les derniers entretiens. Recueil-
lis par L. Prat*).

The philosophy of *Emile Boutroux* (born 1845, erst-
while professor at the Sorbonne, now *directeur de la
fondation Thiers*) belongs to a tendency originating from
Maine de Biran. In his criticism of the principle of
causality he approaches *Renouvier;* but it is not so much
the theory of continuity that he opposes, as the attempts
to conceive everything as identical or homogeneous and
to reduce the individual to the universal (*De la contingence des lois de la nature,* 1875; *De l'idée de la loi naturelle
dans la science et la philosophie contemporaine,* 1895).
Like *Comte* he insists that every new field of experience
requires new principles which cannot be deduced from the
principles which apply to other fields. The more concrete principles cannot be reduced to abstract principles.
The more we enter into the concrete, so much the more
does the dynamic gain transcendence over the mechanical,
the qualitative over the quantitative. It is possible
furthermore for new beginnings to take place in nature
which cannot be derived from their antecedents. As a
matter of fact the whole uniform system of nature
revealed to us by science is nothing more than the river
bed which is formed by an inherent spontaneous evolution, and which may be changed by variations of this
evolution. The spontaneous variations (*les variations
contingentes*) bear witness to the freedom which constitutes the inner nature of things.—Epistemologically
considered the so-called laws of nature are nothing more
than a summary of the methods applied in the effort to
understand things (*assimiler les choses à notre intelligence*).

Henri Bergson (born 1859, professor at the College de
France) carries forward the movement begun by *Renou-*

vier and *Boutroux* in a manner which is quite unique and characteristic. He regards the quantitative method of explanation as merely the technical instrument employed by us for the purpose of understanding what is actually and immediately given in experience, which is always qualitative and continuous. Even language, and the scientific method of explanation still more so, casts our experiences in atomic form, as if they sustained the same objective relations to each other as positions in space. The inner stream of spiritual phenomena are thus transformed into a mechanically arranged mass. This is how it happens that the inner, dynamic, free and continuous activity is denied. The indeterminists are here guilty of the same error as the determinists, because they likewise isolate the individual moments of psychical evolution. The whole problem of freedom has arisen through a misunderstanding. Spontaneous evolution has its origin in the soul as a whole and there is no analysis that can do it justice (*Les données immédiates de la conscience*, 1888).

Bergson criticizes the fundamental presupposition of science. It is only by a process of analytic and distinguishing definition that we are enabled to discover the elements between which the laws prevail. It is a matter of profound importance that the difference between the given continuity and the scientific distinctions be insisted on. This is the only way that thought can conform to life. *Bergson* hopes however to realize a higher science, a metaphysics, by means of the fact that he reverts from differentiation to integration, from analysis to intuition—and thus to true empiricism (*Introduction a la Metaphysique, Revue de la Metaphysique et Morale*, 1903). At this point *Bergson* reminds us of *Bradley*. The real problem would be whether "metaphysics," or even any intelligent comprehension of the world whatever, is possible without a dissolution of the intuitions. Analysis is therefore an indispensable instrument of thought, even though, as *Bergson* has so effectively insisted, it must be practiced with critical precaution.

Bergson develops his concept of the soul as consisting of a memory synthesis in detail in his book *Matière et Mémoire* (1897). It is only sensation, not memory, that requires a material organ. *Bergson* thus substitutes a sort of dualism of sensation and memory for the usual distinction of soul and body, which is scarcely reconcilable with his theory of the continuity of psychical life. That is to say, he ascribes a practical significance to sensations, and hence, according to him, the whole body of natural science with its atomic theories and its similar spaces and times constitutes a great system of instruments by means of which we are enabled to assert our mastery over material nature.—

Philosophical discussion in France has in recent years been quite vigorous and significant. The *Bulletin de la société française de philosophie* furnishes the opportunity of following the progress of the refined and profound, at once personal and chivalrous, discussions of the younger French philosophers. *Adolphus Levi: L' indeterminismo nella filosofia francese contemporanea* (1905), furnishes a valuable comprehensive treatment of the whole movement in French philosophy in its relation to the concepts of causality and continuity.

3. The Economico-biological Theory of Knowledge.

The critical philosophy had already to a certain degree regarded knowledge from the economico-biological viewpoint. Viewed from the standpoint of analytical method, which *Kant* himself applied in his *Prolegomena*, the problem of *Kant's Critique of Reason* may be thus formulated: What presuppositions must I postulate in order to secure an exact empirical science?—Hence all thought is to be regarded as means to an end, at least to the intellectual end of understanding. We are confronted by similar lines of thought in recent philosophical literature from various quarters.

Noted natural scientists, reflecting upon the principles of their science, have observed that the definitions of the concepts and the presuppositions of science must seek their justification in the fact that they furnish the possibility of an intellectual elaboration and interpretation of the facts. Their necessity rests upon this fact alone, which however is not apodictic until the possibility of other concepts and presuppositions than those now in use, serving the same purpose quite as well, is excluded. *Maxwell* expressed this view in 1885, *Ernst Mach* in 1863.

Avenarius, from 1876 onward, developed his natural history of the problems from a purely psychological viewpoint: because of the fact that consciousness does not possess an infinite ideational capacity it is obliged to introduce economy into its thought, which gives rise to the problem of construing what is given in experience with the least possible subjective addition.

Pragmatism so called shows a similar tendency. This term was first introduced by the American mathematician and philosopher *Peirce* (1878), and afterwards appropriated by his fellow countryman, *William James* (1898), who combines it with a whole psychological and philosophical system. Pragmatism establishes the concepts and presuppositions by the practical consequences involved in the experiences to which they lead. If we were wholly indifferent to the consequences of our pre-suppositions we would not postulate them, we would at least draw no conclusion from them.

1. *James Clerk Maxwell* (1831–1879), the noted physicist who was a professor at Cambridge, was a student of philosophy under *William Hamilton*, of whom he reminds us by his emphasis of the dynamic character of knowledge. He regards the mind as an organ, whose use may be valuable in itself, even though its practical significance consists in the results of its functional activity. The progress of the exact sciences rests upon the fact that we are able to elaborate ideas, in which all particular facts are represented and from which exact, mathe-matical conclusions can be deduced. In this respect the formation of number series has been singularly important: we are thus enabled to conceive physical variations after the analogy of the relations in the number series, accord-ing to the laws of numbers. This analogy can likewise be carried through most readily in its application to changes of position, and the natural science of the last three centuries has therefore aimed as far as possible to construe all phenomena as processes of motion. The theory of atoms rests upon a comprehensive analogy be-tween the qualitative changes of matter and the move-ments of material points in space. As a matter of fact even geometry is really a theory of motion: a geometrical line is the path of a motion from one point to another.— The justification of the presuppositions lies in the fact that they lead to fruitful tasks and problems. Thus, e. g., the principle of the conservation of energy raises very definite questions in connection with every new phenom-enon: whence does the energy here expended originate, and into what new form is it transformed, when the

phenomenon ceases?—(*Maxwell's* epistemological treatises are found in the second volume of his *Scientific Papers.*)

Ernst Mach (born 1838, professor at Vienna) was led to the problems of epistemology by the study of the history of natural science. The following are his chief works: *Die Mechanik in ihrer Entwickelung* (4th ed., 1901), *Die Analyse der Empfindungen* (4th ed., 1903, *Erkenntniss und Irrtum* (1905).

Mach made an attempt early in life to discover a point of view which he would not be obliged to surrender when passing from the subject of physics to that of psychology. He found such a viewpoint in the priority of sensation to all concepts of atoms and souls. The concepts, formulated by scientific thought, are conditioned by the necessity of an adaptation to the given. Thought—both in its syntheses as well as in its analyses—is a case of biological adaptation. Because of the fact then that quantitative arrangements are simpler and more comprehensive than qualitative arrangements, and because they simplify the view of large groups of experiences, we apply them wherever possible, and to this end such concepts as energy, mass and atom are formulated; concepts, therefore, which have no metaphysical significance. The entire mechanical explanation of nature rests upon a sublime analogy between the movements of masses in space and the qualitative changes of things (in temperature, electrical conditions, etc.). But we have no right to construe the universe as a pure mechanism. The immediately given consists of nothing more than complexes of sensation, which physics, by the help of its fruitful analogies, interprets as movements.

2. *Richard Avenarius* (1843–1896), a professor at Zürich, was prepared for his later theories by his studies of

Spinoza (*Über die beiden ersten Phasen des Spinozistischen Pantheizmus*, 1868), for the theory of identity is a splendid example of the reduction of all ideas to a single idea. The title of a later treatise (*Philosophie als Denken der Welt nach dem Prinzip des kleinsten Kraftmasses*, 1876) gives definite expression to the economic theory, and his chief work (*Kritik der reinen Erfahrung*, 1890) consists of an investigation of the physiological and psychological conditions of the origin and the evanescence of problems. In his last essay (*Der menschliche Welthegriff*, 1891) he seeks to sift out the last vestige of animism, the reading of subjective elements into actual experience, completely.

A problem presupposes a "*vital difference,*" i. e. a state of tension between the individual and the environment. Such a state of tension arises whenever the stimuli proceeding from the objective world demand a greater or smaller expenditure of energy than the individual is capable of furnishing.

Whenever the stimulus (R) and the energy on hand (E) balance each other (so that R = E), we have a vital maximum of preservation: Recognition is possible; the individual feels at home and has confidence in his ideas and perceptions.

But if a greater effort is required than the individual is capable of putting forward (i. e. R > E), the individual discovers contradictions, deviations and exceptions in the given; it appears strange and recognition is impossible. Every extension of the circle of experience, every enlargement of the horizon, is liable to bring with it new problems. The advance of civilization increases the problems.

Conversely, if the energy is greater than the demand (so that R < E), a desire to transcend the given will arise.

The result will be a practical idealism or a romantic yearning.

Avenarius made a special study of the case of R > E. The solution involves three stages—need, effort, discharge—and the problem disappears. *Avenarius* regards these three stages of problematization and deproblematization essentially as symptoms of certain physiological processes in the brain. His theory is physiological rather than psychological—even though as a matter of fact he constantly deduces the correlative physiologica¹ processes from the psychological "symptoms."

The result of the process, the deproblematization, does not always constitute a real solution. A tentative or purely individual viewpoint may be attained, without excluding the possibility of a new state of tension, a new problematization. Deproblematization is definite and universal only whenever a perfect adaptation has taken place, from which all subjective and tentative elements have been eliminated. This is realized whenever knowledge essentially consists in a quantitative description, and a description furthermore in which the consequent is always the equivalent of the antecedent. We have then realized the viewpoint of *pure experience.*

Avenarius differs from *Maxwell* and *Mach*, especially from the fact that he failed to see the relation between economy and symbolism (analogizing), as he underestimates the significance and the necessity of analogy in general.

3. *William James* (born 1842), the Harvard professor, in an article published in 1898 (*The Pragmatic Method*, reprinted in *The Journal of Philosophy, Psychology and Scientific Methods*, 1904) laid the foundation of a theory of knowledge by which he wished at once to review and

correct the classical English philosophy. He has elaborated his theory more fully in a series of articles which
appeared in the above-mentioned periodical during the
years 1904 and 1905. He had already placed great stress
on the continuity of psychic life in his *Principles of Psychology* (1890), by insisting that what is actually given in
psychical experience consists of an incessant "*stream of
thought,*" and he has applied this conception to the special
problems of psychology with telling effect. He calls this
original flux of life "*pure experience*" (an expression which
he uses more consistently than *Avenarius*). It is only for
practical reasons that we depart from the original flux of
life: distinctions, definitions, and axioms are postulated
for the purpose of realizing certain ends. This conception
of knowledge is what constitutes *pragmatism*, whilst
rationalism, which accords the highest place to abstract
thought, regards those intellectual instruments of thought
as immediate revelations of the absolute. If we establish
the elements, which we carve out of this continuous
stream for the purposes of solving our problems concep-
tually, they may be interchanged, and operations with
these elements enable us to attain results similar to those
of actual experience. But this is not the case with all
the elements however. There is more discontinuity in
the universe than we ordinarily suppose and we cannot
always combine one part of our experience with another
or substitute it for another.

Just as pragmatism leads to empiricism, so, according to
James, does empiricism also lead to pluralism. *James*
has stated this clearly in his preface to the collection of
essays published under the title *The Will to Believe*
(1897). Pure experience really presents nothing more
than factual transitions, no "intellectual" transitions.

Our knowledge consists of combinations made by continuous transition, we know no absolute and rational unity. In addition to combinations there are as a matter of fact disparate phenomena: new facts arise in the world and there is an absolute beginning. The unity of nature is a matter which is only coming to pass gradually, i. e. in proportion as we verify our ideas.—

It is an open question whether such a radical pluralism as *James* adopts is possible. According to *James* the combination is quite as much a matter of fact as the manifold variety of phenomena, and the unity of the universe is construed as in process of realization. In addition to this *James* assumes the possibility of substitutions; but these presuppose the existence of something more than mere differences. (The author of this text-book has developed this critical suggestion more fully in an article which appeared in the *Journal of Philosophy, Psychology and Scientific Methods* (1905) under the title *A Philosophical Confession*.)

We shall have occasion to refer to *James'* philosophy of religion in the following section.

B. THE PROBLEM OF VALUES.

It is one of the signs of the times that the problem of values occupies such a prominent place in philosophical discussion at present, and that, as compared with other problems, it is coming forward with greater independence than formerly. There is a growing conviction that the final word on the value of existence cannot be established purely theoretically. Here however there will always remain at least a philosophical problem; the investigation of the psychological basis and the inherent consistency of efforts at evaluation.

This point presents three types.—*Guyau* and *Nietzsche* expect new forms of life to arise, and they base their expectation upon the fact that the overflowing fullness of vital energy in our present experience and our present conditions of life cannot find an adequate outlet. Like *Rousseau* they insist on the right of spontaneous, instinctive life as against analytic reflection. The formula R < E finds its application here.—*Rudolph Eucken* likewise makes the contradiction between the capacity and the actual status of men his starting-point. The life of every-day experience is incoherent, without any center of gravity, and suffers from the contrast between nature and value. The only possibility of a true culture is through a new concentration which lays hold of a *"spiritual substance"* beyond the confines of experience,—*"a spiritual existence"* in which what has been already acquired is preserved and from which new constructions proceed.— *William James* treats religious problems purely psychologically. He seeks to examine religion as it manifests itself at first hand in individual men,—"personal religion" (as against "institutional religion"), which is a result of the individual's life-experiences, the experiences which determine his fundamental attitude and his method of reacting towards the fact of life. This fundamental attitude or this reaction constitutes religion whenever on account of contrasts and conflicts they acquire a transcendent character.

1.   *Jean Maria Guyau* (1854–1888) exemplifies a rare combination of subjective emotion with indefatigable reflection. He feels the profound difficulty of the problems and the illusion of the majority of the solutions, but he holds that the illusions are valuable if only they are fruitful, i. e. if they excite the activity of the intellect

and the will. (See the poem, *Illusion féconde*, in *Vers d'un Philosophie*.)—*Guyau* enjoyed a home-life which was peculiarly favorable to his activity as a student and author. Early in life however he fell a victim to an incurable disease of the chest, but this did not suppress the energy of his intellect and his vital courage.

His first literary attempt was a criticism of English utilitarianism and evolutionism (*La morale Anglaise contemporaine*, 1879). Here he takes the ground that English moral philosophy must inevitably lead to the uncertainty and illusoriness of the moral feelings themselves due to their psychologico-genetic explanation of these feelings: i. e. if conscience is evolved from more elementary feelings it is really nothing more than a pure elementary feeling itself! There exists an immediate impulse however towards self-development, an impulse which may assume the character of devotion, of altruism, without the assistance of any association of ideas and evolution!—In his own theories he endeavors to avoid the difficulties which he charges against the English school (*Esquisse d' une morale sans obligation ni sanction*, 1885). The development of life is the goal which nature has set for itself, and ethics is the theory of the ways and means by which the highest and fullest development of life may be realized. It is necessary to maintain and develop both the subjective and the objective phases of life, and the sympathetic emotions and social life are of the highest importance for both phases, because isolation and egoism restrict the horizon and the efficiency of the individual. The highest virtue—the attribute of character which makes for the highest development of life—is therefore *generosity*. Reflection and analysis are thus not construed as hostile powers (as under the presuppositions of

the English school). For the expansive energy which
forms the basis of life begets hope and courage and
makes possible what would otherwise be impossible.
The only sanction which the ethics of the future will
require is that of the subjective satisfaction which corresponds to the greatness of the risk (*le plaisir de risque*).

Guyau likewise bases his philosophy of religion on the
impulse of expansion (*L' irreligion de l'avenir*, 1887). The
day of religion is past. Religion consists essentially
of man's feeling of fellowship with the personal director
of the course of the universe. It finds its characteristic
expression in the mythological explanation of nature, in a
form of worship with magic rites and in a body of dogmas
which are regarded as absolute truths. Religion is in
process of complete dissolution in every one of these
directions. What is best in religious life will be able to
survive; the impulse to transcend the bare facts of
experience and to discover a higher unity will not vanish
with religion. As a matter of fact this impulse is only now
finding room for free development, since the rigid, dogmatic forms no longer impose obstacles. Everyone will
express his sense of fellowship with existence—the ideal
sociology of existence—in his own way. The disharmonies of the universe will be felt more profoundly than
before, but the fundamental note will assume the character of sublimity, and the world will be one of hope and of
courage for life and for death.

2. *Friedrich Nietzsche* (1844–1900) builds on the same
fundamental principle as *Guyau*, only that in him the
conflict between the poet and the philosopher is even
more pronounced than in the case of the Frenchman.
Both *Guyau* and *Nietzsche* oppose an emphatic affirmative
to the negations of pessimism. But whilst *Guyau* guards

his subjective disposition and his melancholy resignation against the change and the evanescence of values, *Nietzsche* assumes an attitude of disdain and contempt for both past and present, and his hope for a glorious future constantly assumes a more untractable and spasmodic character.

As a youth *Nietzsche*, along with philosophical studies, devoted himself zealously to classical philology, and became professor in this department at Basle at the age of twenty-four. Owing to ill-health and his comprehensive literary plans he afterwards resigned his position and thereafter lived mostly in Engadine and Northern Italy, until insanity made it necessary for him to return to his German home and be cared for by his mother and sister.

Nietzsche's chief aim is to establish a new, positive estimate of life on the basis of the historical facts of civilization. The clearest statement of his purpose is found in the essay written in his youth, *The Birth of Tragedy* (1872). He contrasts the tragic-poetic view of life, symbolized in *Dionysius* and *Apollo*, with that of the intellectual optimism represented by *Socrates*. It is *Nietzsche's* purpose, as he said later on, to consider science from the viewpoint of art, and art from the viewpoint of life. *Dionysius* is consequently—i. e. the superabundant life, life absorbing and vanquishing pain and death— superior to *Apollo*, and *Apollo* is superior to *Socrates*.

This view leads to a severe criticism of *Strauss*, the optimistic free-thinker, and a glorification of *Schopenhauer* and *Richard Wagner*, given in *Unzeitgemässen Betrachtungen* (1873–1876). He soon finds however that he must go farther than both these "educators." He familiarizes himself with the latest scientific and philosophical theories, and thenceforward we find a struggle between a more realistic and a purely subjective tendency. In addition to this he was horrified at pessimism, not only as he found it in *Schopenhauer*, but likewise as he found it in *Richard Wagner*. He then assailed his own old deities. During the whole of the remaining period in which he was still able to do anything he labored towards the discovery of an adequate, decisive expression of his opposition to every form of pessimism, to every form of depreciation of life, to all levelling processes. He particularly challenges the theories of morality which have been prevalent hitherto and insisted on "*an inversion of all values.*" The most characteristic statements of this polemic are found in *Jenseits von Gut und Böse* (1886) and in the *Geneaologie der Moral* (1887). Here he develops the ideas advanced in the essays of his youth more rigidly, and the fundamental theory becomes a radical aristocratism, which leads to a social dualism. The goal of history is not in the infinitely distant future, but it is realized in the world's great men. The great mass of mankind is nothing more than an instrument, obstacle or copy. A higher, ruling caste is necessary, which exists for its own sake,—which is an end in itself, not at the same time an instrument. Corruption begins just as soon as the aristocracy no longer believe in their right to live, to rule and to treat the great masses as their laboring cyclops. Aristocracy must show the value of life by the mere fact of their existence. It is impossible to develop the highest virtues among the great masses. They are only capable of religion and civic morality. But, as history proves, the great masses have repeatedly been able to claim that their morality is the highest. The true estimate of life, as the sense of energy and might (*Nietzsche* later calls it *Der Wille zur Macht*) has frequently been overthrown by the uprising of the moral slaves—in *Buddhism*, in *Socrates*, in *Christianity*, in modern *humanism*. Even the tendency of natural science is in this direction: it even makes a democracy of nature by its principle of general uniformity!

Nietzsche frequently expresses himself as if he would abolish all morality. But he really demands nothing more than an inversion which has been necessitated by the domination of the morality of slavery. As he observes in one of his essays published posthumously (*Der Wille zur Macht*), he wishes to introduce a moral naturalism. He must however also have a standard for his "inversion." He discovers such a standard in the principle of the affirmation of life and of the increase of vital energy. From this point of view he wanted to elaborate a *"number and measurement scale of energy,"* by which all values could be systematized scientifically. There is no kind of vital energy or vital pleasure which could here be excluded. Here *Nietzsche* appears as a utilitarian of the first rank. And he finally renounces his social dualism definitively, and then proposes as the end, not the happiness of the individual but the vigorous development of *"the total life."*

This change of attitude is still more prominent in the poetic elaboration of his ideas. The real tragedy and contradiction of his life consisted in his wasting so much time and energy in the effort to set forth his antipathy and contempt for things in general, whilst he failed to describe fully and clearly the tremendous positive conception of life which constituted his central idea. The poetic-philosophic treatise, *Also sprach Zarathusthra* 1883–1891), was left unfinished. Here he elaborates his ideas on the super-man: The aim of the present struggle is to evolve a new human type, related to the man of the present as man is related to the ape. This is the common aim of the whole human race. The period of dualism and of animosity should be relegated to the past. *Zarathusthra, the seer and guide, hates his own hatred.* And *Nietzsche* paradoxically advocates the affirmation of life in the strongest terms, life of every form and on every plane. The idea that the cycle of the universe must repeat itself became a controlling idea with him. According to his view the universe consists of a finite sum of elements, and hence the number of combinations of these elements must likewise be finite. It follows therefore that when the number of combinations has been exhausted the same course of evolution must begin anew. This idea of repetition or recurrence at first horrified *Nietzsche*, and he had a severe struggle before he could reconcile himself to it. *Zarathusthra* reveals to man the blessed gospel of the coming of the super-man—but on the condition that man wishes to choose and emulate life despite its repetition. Just as all mankind yield their assent to this proposition, *Zarathusthra* dies for joy.

In this way according to *Nietzsche* the sublime expansion of the vital impulse vanquishes all disharmonies and all doubt. He is therefore admitted to a place in the history of philosophy, not because of his scientific treatment of its problems, but because of his experience of the profound antitheses of life, and because of his effort to elaborate these experiences in ideas and symbols.

3. *Rudolph Eucken* (born 1846), professor at Jena, the original seat of metaphysical idealism, following a series of preliminary treatises (*Die Einheit des Geisteslebens*, 1888;

Der Kampf um einen geistigen Lebensinhalt, 1896) has elaborated the religious problem of our age in his work on *Der Wahrheitsgehalt der Religion* (1901).

The aim of this work is to show that religion harmonizes with the innermost ground of our being. If this is true, it must follow that every attack and every criticism will serve only to bring out the eternal principle of religion with increasing clearness.

The civilization of the ancients over-estimated the form and culminated in the barrenness of plastic art; the civilization introduced by the renaissance over-estimated the energy and culminated in a restless striving without any absolute aim. The Church, as a matter of course, furnishes a total view of the useful life in its perfection, but it over-estimates the historical forms, in which the total view was once expressed, and it therefore regards all truth as imitation and repetition, whilst on the other hand it isolates the highest realities from actual, every-day life. Critical philosophy has contrasted the realm of value with the realm of reality. But there still remains the task of construing the valuable as the most truly real. A new metaphysic will avail nothing at this point. The only way to attain the goal is through living experience. *Eucken* applies the term *Noölogy* to the effort to affirm the absolute reality of the spiritual world, on the ground that it would otherwise be impossible to maintain the absolute obligations and the superiority of spiritual values. The noölogical view would direct its attention to the permanent, the free and the rational, as manifested in experience. Particularly in the case of the beginning of a new form of experience—organic, psychical and the higher spiritual life,—noölogy will discover profound motives. The noölogical view cannot justify itself by proofs; its basis consists of a spiritual impulse, which is aroused by the experience of the disharmonies of life, and which not only leads to indefinite religious ideas, to a "*universal religion,*" but at its culmination can lead to a "*characteristic religion*" with definitely formed general symbols. The great symbols formulated by the founders of the positive religions bear witness to the presence of a divine energy in spiritual evolution. *Noölogy therefore culminates in metaphysics.*

4. Whilst *Eucken* regards a purely psychological and epistemological treatment of the problem of religion inadequate, this method of treatment has nevertheless been quite prominent in recent years. A number of American investigators have made valuable individual contributions (*Stanley Hall, Leuba, Coe,* etc.). *James'* book on *Varieties of Religious Experience: A Study of Human Nature* (1902) here takes first rank.

According to *James* the study of religious phenomena reveals how scant a portion of our spiritual life can be clearly explained. Consciousness shades off through a large number of degrees into the unconscious or subconscious, and it frequently happens that the fundamental presuppositions of our conscious ideas proceed from the "subliminal" (or "submarginal") region. Conscious arguments frequently affect only the surface of our nature, and a spontaneous and immediate conviction is the deep thing in us. *James* is inclined to regard the influences which issue from that deeper region as the means by which a higher order of things works in us. Every attempt to define this order more precisely is of course an interpretation; any single experience may be the subject of various religious interpretations. The majority of people are lacking in critical insight and care, not in faith; they are too prone to base a dogmatic belief on every vivid idea.

Every emotion may, under given circumstances, acquire a religious character. This character manifests itself by the fact that man sums up his vital experiences which give rise to a total attitude, which determine his entire attitude towards life. Spiritual life thus acquires a unity and harmony which are otherwise sought for in vain. In some natures this unity of life is the result of profound spiritual struggles, and can only be realized by a crisis, a *"conversion"*; in other natures however it arises by successive growth or spontaneous unfolding. This represents the difference between religious leaders: the difference between the healthy and the sick souls, or, better still, between the once-born and the twice-born. But in both classes the goal cannot be attained without *the inflow of energy from unconscious sources*. How this fact shall be interpreted is a private matter for each individual. *James* is himself convinced of the fact that new powers and starting-points may proceed from those dark sources, and he thinks that in academic circles we dismiss this possibility all too quickly. Religion rests upon a cosmological hypothesis, which cannot however be formulated dogmatically. The religious consciousness can never accept the tragedies and shipwrecks of life as the final word concerning existence.

Our judgment of the value of religion must likewise be based on experience. We judge religious phenomena by their fruits, and as a matter of fact this has always been the case. The principle of pragmatism is likewise applicable here. Reverence for deity ceases whenever it fails to affect the heart, and whenever it conflicts, in its whole character, with something the value of which we have experienced and do not wish to deny. Mankind retains the gods which it can use, and whose commandments substantiate the requirements which they make of themselves and of others. We constantly apply human standards.

James assumes a sympathetic attitude towards religion. He is convinced that the best fruits of religious experience are the best things in history. The inner life here manifests a fervor and an energy, a subjectivity and a concentration which lifts us into a higher atmosphere.—*James* does not discuss the intimate relation which exists between "personal" and "institutional" religion. His treatise however suggests points of view which are very fruitful from which to consider the problem of religion—or, if we prefer, the problem of an equivalent of religion.

CHRONOLOGY OF THE CHIEF WORKS
IN PHILOSOPHY.

1440. Cusanus: De docta ignorantia.
1513. Machiavelli: Il principe.
1516. Pomponazzi: De immortalitate animæ.
1538. Vives: De anima et vita.
1540. Melanchthon: De anima.
1543. Copernicus: De revolutionibus orbium cœlestium.
1554. Ramus: Institutiones dialecticæ.
1565. Telesio: De rerum natura.
1577. Bodin: La république.
1580. Montaigne: Essais.
1581. Sanchez: Quod nihil scitur.
1582. Bruno: De umbris idearum.
1584.   "   Cena delle ceneri.
1584.   "   De l' infinito universo et mondi.
1584.   "   De la causa, principio, et uno.
1585.   "   De gl'heroici furori.
1591.   "   De triplici minimo.
1591.   "   De immenso.
1597. Kepler: Mysterium cosmographicum.
1603. Althusius: Politica methodice digesta.
1609. Kepler: Astronomia nova.
1612. Böhme: Aurora.
1620. Bacon: Novum Organum. (Eng. trans.)
1623.   "   De dignitate et augmentis scientiarum.
                (Eng. trans.)
1623. Galileo: Il saggiatore.
1624. Cherbury: De veritate.
1625. Grotius: De jure belli et pacis.
1632. Galileo: Dialogo sopra i due massimi systemi del mondo.
1637. Descartes: Discours de la méthode.
1638. Galileo: Discorsi.
1640. Hobbes: Elements of Law.
1641. Descartes: Meditationes. (Eng. trans.)

315

1642. Hobbes: De cive.
1644. Descartes: Principia Philosophiæ. (Eng. trans.)
1651. Hobbes: Leviathan.
1655.   "   De corpore.
1658.   "   De homine.
1658. Gassendi: Opera omnia.
1665. Geulincx: De virtute. (Vollständig 1675 unter dem Titel Ethica.)
1669. Pascal: Pensées. (Eng. trans.)
1670. Spinoza: Tractatus theologico-politicus. (Eng. trans.)
1674. Malebranche: Recherche de la vérité.
1677. Spinoza: Ethica. (Eng. trans.)
1685. Leibnitz: Petit discours métaphysique. (Eng. trans.)
1687. Newton: Principia.
1689. Locke: On Government.
1690.   "   Essay on Human Understanding.
1695.   "   Reasonableness of Christianity.
1695. Leibnitz: Système nouveau de la nature et de la communication des substance.
1695. Bayle: Dictionnaire historique et critique.
1704. Toland: Letters to Serena.
1705. Mandeville: The Fable of the Bees.
1709. Berkeley: Theory of Vision.
1710. Leibnitz: Théodicée.
1710. Berkeley: Principles of Knowledge.
1711. Shaftesbury: Characteristics (I).
1714. Leibnitz: Monadologie. (Eng. trans.)
1720. Wolff: Vernünftige Gedanken.
1725. Hutcheson: Inquiry into the Ideas of Beauty and Virtue.
1726. Butler: Sermons.
1734. Voltaire: Lettres sur les Anglais.
1739 (-1740). Hume: Treatise on Human Nature.
1745. Crusius: Entwurf der notwendigen Vernunftwahrheiten.
1748. Montesquieu: Esprit des lois. (Eng. trans.)
1748. La Mettrie: L'homme machine.
1748. Hartley: Observations on Man.
1749. Hume: Enquiry concerning the Human Understanding.
1750. Rousseau: Discours sur les sciences et les arts.
1751. Hume: Enquiry concerning the Principles of Morals.
1754. Condillac: Traité des sensations.

1754. Diderot: Interprétation de la nature.
1755. Rousseau: Discours sur l'origine de l'inégalité parmi les hommes.
1755. Mendelssohn: Briefe über die Empfindungen.
1755. Kant: Allgemeine Naturgeschichte und Theorie des Himmels.
1757. Hume: Natural History of Religion.
1758. Helvétius: De l'esprit.
1762. Rousseau: Emile. (Eng. trans.)
1762. " Contrat social.
1762. Kant: Versuch den Begriff der negativen Grössen in die Weltweisheit einzuführen.
1763. Reid: Inquiry into the Human Mind.
1764. Voltaire: Dictionnaire philosophique portatif.
1764. Lambert: Neues Organum.
1765. Leibnitz: Nouveaux essais. (Eng. trans.)
1766. Kant: Träume eines Geistersehers. (Eng. trans.)
1766. Voltaire: Le philosophe ignorant.
1770. Holbach: Système de la nature.
1770. Kant: De mundi sensibilis atque intelligibilis forma et principiis.
1776. Smith: Wealth of Nations.
1777. Tetens: Versuche über die menschliche Natur.
1778. Lessing: Duplik.
1779. Hume: Dialogues on Natural Religion.
1781. Kant: Kritik der reinen Vernunft. (Eng. trans.)
1783. " Prolegomena zu jeder künftigen Metaphysik. (Eng. trans.)
1784. " Idee zu einer allgemeinen Geschichte.
1784 (–1791). Herder: Ideen zur Philosophie der Geschichte der Menschheit.
1785. Kant: Grundlegung zur Metaphysik der Sitten. (Eng. trans.)
1786. Kant: Mutmasslicher Anfang des Menschengeschlechts.
1786. Mendelssohn: Morgenstunden.
1787. Jacobi: David Hume über den Glauben, oder Idealismus und Realismus.
1788. Kant: Kritik der praktischen Vernunft. (Eng. trans.)
1789. Reinhold: Versuch einer neuen Theorie des menschlichen Vorstellungsvermögens.
1789. Bentham: Principles of Morals and Legislation.

1790. Kant: Kritik der Urtheilskraft. (Eng. trans.)

1790. Maimon: Versuch über die Transzendental philosophie.

1793. Kant: Religion innerhalb der Grenzen der blossen Ver-
           nunft. (Eng. trans.)

1793. Schiller: Ueber Anmuth und Würde.

1794. Fichte: Grundlage der gesammten Wissenschaftslehre.
           (Eng. trans.)

1797. Schelling: Ideen zu einer Philosophie der Natur. (Eng.
           trans.)

1799. Schleiermacher: Reden über die Religion. (Eng. trans.)

1802. Cabanis: Des rapports du physique et du moral de l'homme.

1806. Fichte: Grundzüge des gegenwärtigen Zeitalters.

1806. Fries: Neue Kritik der Vernunft.

1807. Hegel: Phänomenologie des Geistes. (Eng. trans.)

1808. Herbart: Hauptpunkte der Metaphysik.

1809. de Maistre: Soirées de St. Petersbourg.

1809. Schelling: Ueber den Menschlichen Willen.

1812. Hegel: Wissenschaft der Logik. (Eng. trans.)

1813. Saint-Simon: Mémoire sur la science de l'homme.

1813. Schopenhauer: Vierfache Wurzel des Satzes vom Zureich-
           enden Grunde. (Eng. trans.)

1817. Hegel: Enzyklopädie der philosophischen Wissenschaften.

1819. Schopenhauer: Die Welt als Wille und Vorstellung. (Eng.
           trans.)

1820. Fries: Psychische Anthropologie.

1821. Hegel: Philosophie des Rechts. (Eng. trans. in part.)

1821. Schleiermacher: Der christliche Glaube.

1824. Herbart: Psychologie als Wissenschaft. (Eng. trans.)

1825 (–1827). Beneke: Psychologische Skizzen.

1829. W. Hamilton: Philosophy of the Unconditioned.

1829. James Mill: Analysis of the Human Mind.

1830 (–1842). A. Comte: Cours de philosophie positive. (Eng.
           trans.)

1833. Carlyle: Sartor Resartus.

1835. Strauss: Leben Jesu.

1840. Trendelenburg: Logische Untersuchungen.

1841. Schopenhauer: Grundprobleme der Ethik.

1841. Feuerbach: Das Wesen des Christentums.

1842. Robert Mayer: Bemerkungen über die Kräfte der unbeleb-
           ten Natur.

1843. Feuerbach: Grundsätze der Philosophie der Zukunft.

1843. Stuart Mill: System of Logic.

1843 (–1846). Kierkegaard's Hauptschriften.

1844. Schopenhauer: Welt als Wille und Vorstellung. (Eng. trans.)

1851. Lotze: Allgemeine Physiologie.

1852. Moleschott: Der Kreislauf des Lebens.

1854 (–1864). Renouvier: Essais de critique générale.

1855. Büchner: Kraft und Stoff. (Eng. trans.)

1855. Spencer: Principles of Psychology (I).

1856. Lotze: Mikrokosmus (I). (Eng. trans.)

1858. Darwin: Origin of Species.

1859. Stuart Mill: On Liberty.

1860. Fechner: Elemente der Psychophysik.

1861. Spencer: First Principles.

1864. Jevons: Pure Logic, or the Logic of Quality apart from Quantity.

1865. Dühring: Natürliche Dialektik.

1865. Lange: Geschichte des Materialismus. (Eng. trans.)

1866. Wundt: Die physikalischen Axiome.

1869. Hartmann: Die Philosophie des Unbewussten (Eng. trans.)

1871. Darwin: Descent of Man.

1871. Cohen: Kants Theorie der Erfahrung.

1872. Nietzsche: Die Geburt der Tragödie.

1874. Wundt: Grundzüge der physiologischen Psychologie.

1875. Boutroux: De la contingence des lois de la nature.

1876. Bradley: Ethical Studies.

1876. Avenarius: Philosophie als Denken der Welt.

1876. Riehl: Der philosophische Kritizismus (I). (Eng. trans.)

1877. Ardigò: La formazione naturale.

1879. Guyau: La Morale Anglaise contemporaine.

1882. Dühring: Sache, Leben und Feinde.

1883. Nietzsche: Also sprach Zarathustra (I). (Eng. trans.)

1884. Windelband: Präludien.

1885. Renouvier: Classification des systèmes philosophiques.

1885. Guyau: Esquisse d' une morale.

1886. Mach: Beiträge zur Analyse der Empfindungen. (Eng. trans.)

1886. Nietzsche: Jenseits von Gut und Böse. (Eng. trans.)

1887. Wundt: System der Philosophie.
1887. Guyau: L'irreligion de l'avenir.
1888. Avenarius: Kritik der reinen Erfahrung (I).
1888. Bergson: Les données immédiates de la conscience.
1889. Paulsen: System der Ethik. (Eng. trans.)
1890. James: Principles of Psychology.
1892. Paulsen: Einleitung in die Philosophie. (Eng. trans.)
1893. Fouillée: La psychologie des idées-forces.
1893. Bradley: Appearance and Reality.
1896. Rickert: Die Grenzen der naturwissenschaftlichen Begriffs-
                 bildung.
1897. James: The Will to Believe.
1898. Ardigò: L'unità della coscienza.
1898. James: The Pragmatic Method.
1901. Renouvier: Les dilemmes de la métaphysique pure.
1901. Eucken: Der Wahrheitsgehalt der Religion. (Eng. trans.)
1902. James: Varieties of Religious Experience.
1904. Cohen: Die Ethik des reinen Willens.
1905. Mach: Erkenntnis und Irrtum.

INDEX

321